The Power of the Unprogrammed Mind

Through the Trilogy of

Moses, Jesus, and Muhammad

Mohamed Achour

TABLE OF CONTENTS

PREFACE

Psychiatry can be defined as the science of reducing mental suffering and enhancing mental health. To date, the field has been primarily concerned with the first part of the definition. For example, in the Index to the *Standard Edition of the Complete Psychological Works of Sigmund Freud* (19), the word "neurosis" has over 400 references. In contrast, "health" is not even listed. The imbalance tends to be true of contemporary texts, as well. This situation is understandable because psychiatry originated to deal with disordered function. The question, "What is the function of a healthy person?" which require the further question "What is the purpose of human life?" is not usually asked because it is assumed to be answered by simple observation of the everyday active ties of the general population [2] (18, p. 122)

Arthur J. Deikman, M.D

We must not forget that human's soul is God's soul, and when we say God's soul that means its dimension is cosmic, eternal and it doesn't have an image by which it is recognized. If by chance it is identified by a label from this earthy world, that label might itself be the cause of its death.

Consciousness on the other hand, it was supposed to maintain the primordial state of metamorphism and fluidity of the soul and not to become embedded in emotional forces. If however the state of

I

consciousness-awake is transformed to the state of automaton, still further, if the power of self-intention is transformed to an indoctrinated consciousness followed by mechanical actions, what are left after are only depression, anxiety and so forth.

Now the way we think about politics and the system, under which we live, it is simply the result of the way we were shaped and the way we were indoctrinated in how to think about that system, and whether we are protagonists or antagonists; even when we are antagonist, our conscious revolt is itself preprogrammed.

It is likewise with religion, it was supposed to free our minds from the idolatry of the institutions, it is itself characterizing us, not from its primordial concept per se, but because of a fabricated manmade dogma.

In our current violent events, it is very hard for us to visualize the presence of these three prophets: Moses, Jesus, and Muhammad (PBUT) within our political arena and their indubitable role, it is also very hard for us to see introspectively their frequencies—personalities within ourselves.
This book serves as an embarkation on a life journey and invites the reader to discover his inner self through the personalities of these three prophets; the stages they went through during their lives, which are in reality our own stages. In a meanwhile, at the end of every chapter there is an introspective exegesis where the reader is invited to get into a deep scrutiny and analyze his inner psychic life.

INTRODUCTION

This book has been written in the form of a story while going through the stages of life that governments go through, from Moses' birth to the time when Pharaoh and his army collapsed. It shows what is taking place these days on a large scale; this happened with exactly the same mindset but on a smaller scale back then. As such, within the following story, historical names are conserved as an archetype, but in reality we are talking about current events. The story is timeless and goes back and forth between ancient times and today, although contemporaneous terminology is used for both time periods. In the meanwhile the story embarks the reader to see introspectively his own reflection and to free himself from internal psychic boundaries that he is unknowingly confronting.

What happened in history, which is considered by some to be mythology, is in reality taking place all the time not only within the siege of the government, but within an individual's psyche as well. In other words, the nation cannot help but live those events on a subconscious level; thus, individuals do the same.

The story is divided into three phases. The first phase of history is referenced to Moses and Pharaoh in ancient Egyptian civilization. His mission started at the beginning of the day of history, i.e., the age of life, and finished shortly after the meridian.

Pharaoh and his cohorts were an archetype of a hegemonic empire that did not exclude other nations from sharing the same political philosophy and the same mindset. In short, the hegemonic empire was just the visible vertex.

Pharaoh's government was composed of three personalities, as well as a group of people that served as mediators between the government and the population. We have Pharaoh who was part of the siege of the government; Haman represented the military and its derivative agencies, and Korah was the state treasurer and represented the banking system and corporations. In addition, we have the mediators—the magicians who were in charge of protecting the regime through a cover-up campaign. These are referenced to the corporate and sponsored media.

On the internal front, within an individual's psyche, Pharaoh represents grandiosity, the ideal of the ego. Haman represents the ego defense mechanisms, which are a self- protective response to a perception of psychic danger, and Korah represents addictions and desires. The magicians represent illusions within the individual.

Moses represented the wise and hidden people within the government—the last chance given to a hegemonic empire either to be useful, which will save that nation, or to be useless and ultimately cause its perdition. On the internal front, within a person's psyche, Moses represents the center of gravity—the true self, which is the "I" or the "Me."

Therefore, there is a basic reenactment of a story that correlates contemporaneous (U.S.) geopolitical climates with Pharaoh in ancient Egyptian civilization.

IV

Shortly before the downfall of Pharaoh and his army, Korah's (the state treasurer's) financial center collapsed, exactly the way this happened on and after September eleventh in New York City. The difference between the two events is that there was no terrorist attack back then; the financial center went down by itself.

The second phase of history is referred to as Jesus Christ within a nation. His mission continued from where Moses left it, just after the meridian and continuing up to the late afternoon. This time period refers to when the nation is unknowingly characterized by its own rigid institutions to such a degree that no alternative way of life is possibly envisaged. Therefore, any solution brought to the system only creates more rigidity than before. What you see is only the number of gods being created to reanimate the system, when in fact they are switching from one death to another. We see Christ's role in both the external and internal fronts—within the government and within the person's psyche.

The last phase of history is referenced to Muhammad, who represents the bootstrap journey to the metaphysical world. His mission continued from where Jesus left it and continued to the sunset. What will the person contemplate in the metaphysical world is exactly what he had prepared in his life before he left his Earthy world.

THE FIRST
PHASE OF HISTORY

CHAPTER 1

This was the beginning of the end of an empire; a person showed up at the siege of the government with a precise mission, which was to take a written statement from the emperor. This note showed the hidden weakness of that empire, and this same person later confronted the emperor with the statement that he had previously verbalized and signed.

In the middle of sunny day, he entered the solipsistic kingdom to deliver a message of mercy. Nobody paid attention to him, despite all the security systems and the cameras covering every corner and every angle. There were bodyguards, satellites protecting the whole atmosphere and the surrounding streets with the most advanced technology in the world. Still this stranger infiltrated into the kingdom of Pharaoh without being perceived. The stranger went straight to Pharaoh to talk to him. When he came closer, suddenly Pharaoh's face became an angry mask. How dare a stranger be on the red carpet close to the throne of Pharaoh without his authorization! The stranger's unauthorized presence brought to Pharaoh an unconscious realization of his actual identity of weakness. It was such a painful assault on his grandiose self-perception that conscious awareness of the true state of his being had to be diverted.

Suddenly the stranger rushed to address Pharaoh with a question. "Oh Pharaoh," the visitor politely said. "Would you please tell them what must be the punishment for someone who pretends to be God?"

"He deserves to be drowned in the sea," replied Pharaoh, who preferred to push down his budding awareness of reality into the deepest level of his subconscious and not face it anymore.

The noble stranger kept quiet for a moment and then said, "Oh Pharaoh, would you please write this hieroglyphically with your signature on it, and I shall show it to everybody who pretends to be God." When Pharaoh did so, all of a sudden the stranger disappeared...

Without a doubt, Pharaoh's nascent awareness of his true being was harshly repressed with a fabricated pretext and camouflage; yet, it threatened to come back again to the surface of Pharaoh's consciousness, although nobody knows exactly when this was.

Although hieroglyphs were called "the words of the gods," they were only used for official texts, and only a handful of people from the highest ranks could read and write. Pharaoh didn't know that the headquarters that sent this stranger understood all languages, and he didn't know that sooner or later he would be confronted and have to read the same words he had written.

It didn't take long after this dialogue for an external disaster to hit Pharaoh's nation in the form of a big flood. However, the flood was in the subjective world, his psyche, before it became externalized in the objective world.

The throne of the kingdom collapsed; Pharaoh and his army were drowned in the sea. There was only the picture of a mummy left from his existence.

His kingdom was an axis of illusory civilizations that tried to follow the same track that he tried to systematize the same pyramidal structure of political and economic exploitation and genocide with its imperial military network. His government had gained sufficient power and inspiration worldwide to be able to insert its tentacles everywhere, and it was big enough to have its impact and influence on other nations. Pharaoh's residence was called The White Solipsistic Palace and was situated in the middle of the district capital. There was also the Camp of Soliloquies where Pharaoh organized his secret, confidential meetings with his councilors. All these areas were protected with the most sophisticated security systems in the world.

Pharaoh appeared to be very smart. His nation's technology dominated almost the entire world. He had the most sophisticated armaments in the world. His espionage agency and his army were strong enough to overthrow regimes and strong enough to take all the necessary measures and precautions to protect the country from any threat.

However, no matter how cautious Pharaoh was, his nation collapsed dramatically through the hands of a baby. That baby's name was Moses, and he was unexpectedly raised in Pharaoh's own palace and nourished by Pharaoh's own food. Later on, Moses became the sole, antithetical force that caused the perdition of that regime.

It was so sad to see the innocent nation that was controlled by Pharaoh facing the consequences of Pharaoh's actions without understanding. The majority of the people were not well-informed about Pharaoh's egocentric decisions and his aggressive, hubristic foreign policies toward other nations.
No matter how extended the slack and the inducement of Pharaoh's tyranny, justice was eventually served though Moses' existence.

Introspective Exegesis

Q: Before we go any further, is this story considered a myth that concerns a specific geographic location and a particular epoch and that took place between Pharaoh and Moses between the ancient Egyptians and the Children of Israel, or is it a contemporary event that also concerns other times that is applicable to other ethnicities and other locations throughout the pages of history?

A: Although it is mythology, it is also allegory and a reenactment that has been continuously lived and seen throughout mankind's history; its archetype is reflected everywhere, in every time, and across different populations.

Q: If this myth reflects a model of an empire, do your words refer to the current geopolitical events of the United States of America?

A: Officially speaking, it refers to the United States of America, but just as an epitome of a visible hegemonic nation. However, that does not exclude other unlisted nations and other foreign populations and individuals from sharing the same objective and the same agenda as the United States, since the concept of an empire is just a vertex, which shares enigmatic support from other nations, whether the involvement of those nations is voluntarily or involuntarily.

Q: Does this story reveal what's going on externally in the political arena or what is taking place introspectively within an individual's psyche?

A: It is taking place in both the objective and the subjective worlds.

Q: Would you be more specific about the words objective and subjective

A: Man is always confronted with a tension that exists between two obvious facts. There is the existence of the external world in which he lives—the political system under which he lives, and there is the existence of his internal world—his psychic life vis-à-vis that regime.

Q: In his answer, Pharaoh said: "He deserves to be drowned in the sea," referring to the one who pretends to be God. What was behind this question and answer?

A: Actually this verbalization was a spontaneous truth expressed by Pharaoh against his own will—his sincere feeling when he was challenged by this question, It was against his own will because Pharaoh had already proclaimed to his nation that he was their supreme lord. In fact, every self-aggrandizing and domineering person who wants to monopolize people's emotions and every hegemonic nation that wants to monopolize the world's natural resources are, in reality, behaving with the same mindset—acting as though they were God.

Q: Therefore, when Pharaoh mentioned the punishment of the one who pretends to be God, he was referring to himself being God. In other words, he felt that if anybody challenged him, that person deserved to be exterminated from Earth?

A: That's correct.

CHAPTER 2

We see the symptoms of a domineering being and what causes this. We also see how feelings of oblivion and angst spur an individual to have the ambition to recoup from the outer world what was lost in his inner world, by proving himself through comparison, challenge, and hostility.

Pharaoh stood on the podium within the siege of his government; the broadcast was presented on all the TV stations without exception. He proclaimed to his nation that he was their god.

Here are the words he uttered: "My people," he said. "Is the kingdom of Egypt not mine, and are these rivers that flow at my feet not mine also? Can you not see? Am I not better than this despicable wretch, who can scarcely make his meaning plain?"

When Pharaoh said that, going so far as to claim the ownership of nature and rivers, he had a challenger in mind: Moses. When Pharaoh (as the archetype of hegemony on a governmental level or as a domineering nature within an individual personality) reached this level, it was not easy for him to accept the logic that the adversary was inside his own psyche.

As a result, he experienced feelings of torment that led to defy another existence. In other words, as a domineering Authoritarian Mentality, he felt the need to prove his place by continuously claiming victory, and in order to do so, he had to combat a personal enemy, which Pharaoh projected onto the external world, even though the real enemy consisted of his own underlying feelings.

The time of identifying this enemy was posterior, but the time when the enemy was created unconsciously in Pharaoh's mind was anterior. However, these were facts that he completely ignored.

This idea of fear of an existing enemy was developed without understanding, and it was the accumulation of many factors. Pharaoh felt this angst, but he did not show it externally. A part of the reason had to do with eternity; human beings crave eternity. There is a constant manifestation of the feeling of angst in a human being; he is in the obscure world of nothingness, and then he is brought into existence. Furthermore, there is another disappearance that is expected and felt, which is his sudden death. Thus, he is caught in a vise between two painful absences that for him are unrealities. He is constantly in unconscious combat with this feeling, which is the repressed panic of disappearing at any moment and of going back to the void. In some rare cases, this unconscious fight remains internal within the self, but most of the time this combat takes an external form and is directed outwardly against otherness. In other words, the person is dragged from an internal implosion and mistakenly seeks an external expansion.

This painful feeling usually spurs the domineering person or tyrant to impose on others, and on a governmental level it spurs a hegemonic nation to monopolize the material world unfairly. Supposedly this is in an attempt to extend its eternity through its perpetual, imperial supremacy. In turn, this hubristic monopoly creates a territory of isolation and polarization in the state of consciousness of the tyrant's mentality and also on the hegemonic nation's political philosophy. What is beyond its reach, such as the existence of different beliefs and different regimes, is fear, uncertainty, and a perceived threat to its power. The only option left for such a person and such a nation is the use of force, leading initially to abuse of confidence and then to outright delusions of grandiosity. A person caught up in this process then becomes subject to a type of self- hypnotism, in which he is unaware and unconscious of his mistakes—mistakes that are the result of his ego defense mechanisms allowing him to transgress all bounds.

Another source has to do with the instinctual, symptomatic thrust of the Divine Oneness in this existence. This thrust demonstrates that there is a secret phenomenon infiltrated intuitively into a human being, which provokes every individual to have the ambition to be unique. This ambition is not his in the first place, but is instead a counter-phobic reaction against his own dependency and against his undeniable return to the Singularity—monism. If this ambition to be unique, which is the source of a person's self-pride, is not converted into renunciation and humility through worship, it becomes extremely harmful.

Now if no person is completely devoid of pride, then what is the authentic identity of a human being through that Oneness? The following two conclusions have the same source, but they have different results, according to the passivity and the predisposed nature of each one.

The first outcome is reflected by the person who is authentic when recognizing his inadequacy and his fragility— his dependency.

As for the second outcome, it results from the egocentric, emotional individuality of a person who is denying his dependency and who is consequently being inspired by his illusory self-aggrandizement, a self-aggrandizement that provokes in him the pain of being isolated, the pain of being pushed off, the pain of being left off, the pain of being neglected, and the pain of being oblivious. Of course, this fragility is largely camouflaged from the self and others, and it is seldom clearly

8

demonstrated. Ironically, such a person doesn't even know by who this pain is being inflicted.

Introspective Exegesis

Q: Even though you already addressed this issue, would you explain again how this feeling of angst develops in man? Please elaborate.

A: Being oblivious is being forgotten; it is an emptiness and a painful solitude in the consciousness that can occur seldom or often. It happens to everybody without exception. But what spurs the person to the severe stage of having a chronic feeling of angst is the lack of something vis-à-vis his psyche. In return, he starts mistakenly trying to prove his life in the arena of existence, defying and challenging with a gladiatorial attitude vis-à-vis his fellow creatures. After a long struggle, chances are he will achieve a mood of self-aggrandizement, which is a desirable feeling sought by everybody. Yet, there is hidden vertigo— insecurity. Such a person is regarded as two concentric circles; his flamboyance, vanity, and preoccupation with perceived social status form the outer circle, and the fear of being emotionally dethroned forms the inner circle. Whether from the diminution of the constituents of the so-called "ideal of the ego" or from the disappearance of admirers that serve as an energizer to his ego, this can cause a feeling of oblivion leading to angst in the long run.

Q: Being oblivious necessitates the presence of the subject. Correct me if I'm wrong. In other words, there is the one who actively forgets another, and this other, being passively forgotten, feels oblivious? Now who is the subject, and who is the object?

A: The subject is the observer in a person's state of consciousness that the human is himself responsible for

9

generating. Both the subject and the object are in this person's psyche.

Q: Any concrete example?

A: Visualize a laser coming from a certain direction above you. At the same time, visualize that when someone presses a button the laser is pointed at you and that when someone releases the button the laser stops? Can you possibly imagine that?

Q: Yes.

A: Now, I said "someone," but in reality there is no "someone" here. Instead, it's you. The activation of this laser does not depend on anybody outside you, but it is entirely your responsibility.

Q: How's that?

A: We are talking about consciousness and the observer observing you. You generate any observer you want, which is the laser I mentioned above. The laser is not detonated by itself, but it is ignited by your consciousness. If you are conscious, the laser is on; if you are unconscious, the laser is off.

Q: To what type of observer or audience are you referring?

A: You are subject mainly to one of three audiences: people; the self, i.e., the ego; or the Absolute, which you may call God, Deity, or whatever.

Q: What is the difference among these three audiences in terms of time and space?

A: When it comes to an audience concerning people or your ego, this laser has a time and has a space from where it is

10

generated. When it comes to the Absolute, this laser does not have a time, and it does not have a space. It is timeless; it is eternal; it is boundless; it is universal.

Q: What is the difference among these three audiences in terms of emotions?

A: During this process, or I should say during your conscious awareness, you are either in a state of formation by inflowing something from outer to inner, or you are in a state of conformity in which you are ready to burst and develop something that was inside you already—an inner spark, or self- animation. When it comes to an audience consisting of creatures or other people, you form an emotion that becomes the epicenter, an epicenter that is outside the nucleus or extraneous parts and that is precarious with regard to your center of gravity. This is a neural net that is inside you. When it comes to the Absolute, you are in a state of conformity with someone who creates an emotion that potentially, yet intrinsically, exists inside you already. This emotion harmonizes with your passivity and becomes a part of your behavior. This is from where true spontaneity is spawned. Of note, the truth of the matter is that we don't have the right to express an intrinsic emotion when it comes to the Absolute because it becomes a part of our behavior; in other words, it need not be stored.

Q: What is the role as a concerned person in all of this?

A: Sometimes encoded emotions become superfluous, and other emotions become intrinsic; they become a part of your behavior and a part of your impetuous dynamism. This is what makes one person feel oblivious and makes another one feel harmonious. Extraneous emotions are the cause of oblivion, and intrinsic emotions are the cause of harmony and of serenity with nature in general.

Q: Does a person have a choice of avoiding or rejecting all these audiences?

A: No matter what, you are subject to feeling that someone is watching you to approve or to confirm your act. You are always subject to substantiation and validation from someone. You escape the audiences only when you are asleep or unconscious by some kind of intoxicant; here we are far from the word "consciousness."

Q: You cannot observe and be observed at the same time, but I noticed all you have been talking about is being observed.

A: You cannot help but be either an observer or an observed person, and you cannot process the two states at the same time. That is absolutely true. Of note, at the time when you are an observer, you are a transmitter; at the time when you are observed, you are a receptor. In the first stage you are transmitting waves and signals; in the second stage you are conceiving waves and signals.

Q: How do you define that?

A: At the time when you are an observer your emotions are actively reaching out. When you are an observed person, your emotions are passively submitting to a viewer. Now when you are an observer of creatures, your observation eventually gets to a dead end, a point of standstill or stagnation. In contrast, when you are an observer of the Absolute, your emotions are also actively reaching out, but this time with wonder and ambivalence, and then your observation eventually rebounds and shifts to your inner psyche with a scrutiny that does not have a limit. You experience a dead end with a powerless stage, and a state of renunciation of your forces occurs. In fact, your sincere recognition of this incapability is itself an unusual type of vehicle of navigation; it is another type of force. Then the state of observing rebounds and becomes the state of being observed, but this time your emotions burst and become a constant expansion and amelioration. What will surprise you is the discovery of the unknown, the discovery of your real self, and the pleasure of mystery that you did not plan initially.

Q: What is the length of time between observing and having those emotions encoded or developed, whether observing creatures or the Creator?

A: There is absolutely no time. At the moment we lift an object, there is also the contraction of some muscles. You don't say that the lifting of the object is before the contraction of the muscles, and you don't say the contraction of the muscles is before the lifting of the object; there is no before and after.

Q: Would you elaborate on what you mean when you refer to conformity to something already existing inside you?

A: The Absolute is inside you already. All you have to do is confess and acknowledge while being transparent; we call that faith. Now do you see this urge that you have? You want to have something that nobody has. You want to reach a level that nobody has ever reached. You want to beat every record ever previously made. You want to dominate. You want to control others. You have the ambition to be unique in your art, to be unique in your talents, to be exceptional. Some people want to control the world; other people want to save the world. You want to be noticed, to be a celebrity, etc. All of this autonomous uniqueness is intuitively a part of your ambition and of everybody's ambition. However, your true feeling of harmony regarding this identity is not in seeking it or in claiming this credit or this prideful identity. Instead, it is your renunciation of that; it is your divestiture of self-attributes.

Q: I don't see my position as being the acknowledgment of someone while renouncing myself at the same time; I mean, where is my position?

A: Do you remember when it was said that the human is caught in a vise between two absences? Do you remember that for him these are unrealities? One is before he was born, and the other is his sudden death.

Q: Yes, I do.

A: When you are performing any action in this life, you are subject to an inescapable observer. The first reality that precedes you is your choice of the observer, and your existence is in the second position while being observed and while physically and independently performing those actions. Then your renunciation of the force is in the third position. I know it's a little complicated and confusing. However, the first absence that seems unreal to you is, in fact, reality by generating the presence of the Observer in your psyche. The second is your presence that seems real to you; it is, in fact, not real unless you both choose your absence and submission to the Observer that precedes you and renounce self-attributes. Our analysis is that it is not you, and then it is you, and then it is not you.

Q: Can you summarize it and make it a little easier?

A: Your independent existence is centered between your dependent consciousness being focused on the Absolute and on your voluntary renunciation. In one micro-unit of time, everything fuses: spirit, mind, and body. It suspends the "before" and suspends the "after" and makes it a micro-unit. This is the stream

14

of universal consciousness; it is the flow of creative energy that reaches from the past into the future and that is sparked within you at that moment, which is your own segment from eternity.

Q: Concerning concentration on the Absolute—either observing or being observed—don't you think it is almost impossible to have this kind of concentration in the midst of this hectic life?

A: I totally agree with you. The reason there is punctuality of worship is in accordance with time and space. It is a way to entangle the past with the future. Both form an inter-current burst within the person's psyche—a cosmic consciousness.

Q: In other words?

A: One remembrance of the Absolute results in your conscious awareness compensating for and recuperating from a lengthy time of unconsciousness. This depends upon two factors, one is humble effacement and the second is sincerity.

CHAPTER 3

We have Pharaoh (the prototype of hegemony), and we have Moses (Pharaoh's targeted adversary that Pharaoh unconsciously created) whose existence was initially a potential presence in Pharaoh's subconscious before being epitomized in an actual physical existence.

Why had this person, who was the targeted Moses, not yet existed, and why was he already considered to be a danger?

Before we go any further, it should be pointed out that Pharaoh initially issued a decree that all male babies from the Children of Israel had to be slaughtered as soon as they were born. This was done because Pharaoh feared the threat posed by one particular baby who was yet to be born. In Pharaoh's view, this unidentified person was a threat, and this potential threat had so constantly preoccupied his mind that he had even dreamed about it. His dream revealed that his kingdom would perish through the hands of this unknown baby from the Children of Israel, a baby who would be born that year.

The main reason behind this was that there was a motive of revenge that had developed in Pharaoh's mind, and he didn't even understand against whom it was directed. He didn't realize that, in the final analysis, this revenge could only be directed against the self-aggrandizement of his inner psyche. He deluded himself in attempting to aim his revenge at an external other. Since he had already reached a narcissistic stage of egomania, he was no longer able to observe this reality. Therefore, he decided to direct his revenge against an external being. Finally, Pharaoh began to tremble and to be tyrannically obsessed and terrorized to such an extent by the possible appearance of the unknown Moses that Pharaoh decided to issue an urgent decree. This decree was a barbaric one that was covered, as was usually the case, with a fabricated pretext.

Introspective Exegesis

Q: Why is it that the only person who felt the presence of Moses in his mind was Pharaoh?

A: When a grandiose delusion is developed in a person, there is initially a state of relaxation corresponding to the person being dominant. This feeling is followed by abuse of confidence because he is alone with his domination. Then shortly thereafter, it is followed by a feeling of isolation. This is the beginning of fearing some existing challenger. Where is he, the one who wants to challenge my uniqueness and dethrone me? What if he is hiding somewhere I don't know? Is it better for me to take my precautions and fight this terror before it reaches me? All this speech takes place in this person's inner psyche.

Q: Where was Moses' location before his birth and before he became physically epitomized?

A: He was in Pharaoh's subconscious.

Q: While being in Pharaoh's subconscious, was he identified as

17

the passive Moses, or was he identified as a primordial opponent who would collide with or contradict another force?

A: First of all, it was still too early to say that Moses was an opponent of Pharaoh. With regard to the external world, Moses was not sent as an adversary to Pharaoh or to Pharaoh's nation; with regard to the subjective world, Moses was not yet considered a conflict-provoking impulse in Pharaoh's subconscious.

Q: Do we look at Moses the physical man or at the reflection of nobleness in Moses' persona? Let me make my question more accurate; Moses was a good man; even if his frequency existed in Pharaoh, it was still good. Now how come...?

A: One aspect of Moses was a potential, energetic phenomenon that was offered to a powerful nation as a last chance, either to be useful (which would have extended the power of that nation not only in the physical world, but also in the metaphysical world) or to be useless (which caused the perdition of that nation). Now, the only one who was held accountable was Pharaoh. While it was true that Pharaoh had an instinctive compulsion to lash out against any perceived threat to his glory and grandeur, this impulse still represented only a latent behavioral tendency. Likewise, Moses represented only a potential threat. What really caused the transformation from potential to actual adversary was Pharaoh's tyranny.

Q: Why was Moses personified with the weakest image, i.e., that of a baby, and why did Pharaoh's conscious spontaneously choose babies as his adversary?

A: The unknown identity, which is a baby's identity, is a scary horizon in the eyes of the one who wants to impose his image on others; the unknown identity is a threat to the one who wants to convert people to his desires and to convert people to his political philosophy. Also, the baby's intuitive state of purity, which has not yet been conditioned, represents a blind spot for the Authoritarian Mentality. Autocracy cannot deal with the unusual and cannot stand uncertainties; uncertainties are considered a possible threat and an attack at its despotism.

Q: Why was this so-called opponent from that particular community, i.e., Israel? Why was he not from Pharaoh's own community, i.e., Egypt?

A: The adversary is manifested to the surface of the conscious according to what a person takes pride in and according to the cause of his vanity. This is because he fears a challenge. However, it is not the main source or cause of his challenge or his hatred; it is just a trigger and one aspect of the symptoms. In the case of Pharaoh, it was a racial issue; anybody who feels ethnocentrically proud of his own race is obviously challenging, comparing, and seeking to humiliate another race. This is the illusory victory sought by the barbarian's racial mentality. In the case of Pharaoh, he developed an opponent in his subconscious from the race that he humiliated and hated, which was, in reality, a displacement of his own self-hatred.

Q: You said: "The adversary is manifested to the surface of the conscious...according to the cause of his vanity." Would you comment on that?

A: You have talents, faculties, gratifications of which you feel proud...

Q: Any examples...?

A: You feel proud because of your look, your race; you feel proud because of your richness; you feel proud because of your intelligence; you feel proud because of your education; you feel proud because of your position at work, because of your property etc...

Q: And then...?

A: When you humble yourself with the state of effacement and renounce this credit and give it to God, it then becomes an intrinsic emotion that is the reality of the self, that is the reality of the "I," that is the reality of the "Me."

Q: In contrast...?

A: If you claim it and become proud of it, it then becomes an extrinsic emotion that is no longer the reality of the self; it is instead the ego. Once the ego is formed with its constituents, the manifestation of the adversary comes into being. Now the adversary is noticed by you according to the constituents of the ideal of your ego. Any faculty of which you feel overly proud, this same faculty is the means by which you will be tortured. You deeply fear losing and become panicky at the mere thought of being diminished for one or another reason.

Q: Why?

A: Because real property and deprivation have to do with the emotion inside you, not with external property. So here you already have an extrinsic emotion that is causing your own alienation from the self. Are you following me?

Q: Yes.

A: Therefore, if you develop this grandiose delusion because of your beauty, your adversary would be a beautiful person. If your grandiosity is because of wealth, your adversary would be a wealthy person.

Q: This is a weird question; I can't help but ask it. You mentioned that Moses was a potential, energetic phenomenon offered to a powerful nation as a last chance, either to be useful, which would maintain the power of that government, or to be abandoned, which would be the cause of its perdition. Does this also have application to an individual?

A: Moses' frequency exists in every single person in this existence from the beginning of this world to its end.

Q: Even before his physical appearance?

A: Yes, even before his physical appearance. Prior to his physical birth, it was only his name that was not yet known, but his frequency existed within everybody.

Q: Sorry, but I have another weird question. Did Pharaoh exist inside Moses' psyche?

A: Yes, he did, but let me clarify something. As I said before, there is a prior pride that is sought by a person who is denying his identity of humility and who becomes self- absorbed, which was Pharaoh's frequency. There is also a pride resulting from humbleness and worship for which a person does not plan and for which he is not hungry; this was the good side of Pharaoh's frequency existing in Moses.

Q: How can I recognize the good one from the bad one?

A: The first sign is that you don't monopolize any goodness you possess; instead, you wish to share it with people. Secondly, when you see someone better than you, you don't feel jealousy. Likewise, you don't feel envious, and you don't wish those gratifications would disappear from him. These are the signs of true pride.

Q: My last, perhaps bizarre, question is this. Do Pharaoh and Moses exist within every individual?

A: Yes, they do, and it's up to people to elect whomever they want, not by vote but by behavior. If they develop their grandiosity within themselves, which is the case with not only this modern society, but also with societies throughout the pages of history, they will surely see the epitome of Pharaoh on the governmental level, and that would enslave them. If they maintain a state of humility in front of the Sublimity, they will surely see nobody except the reality of their autonomous uniqueness. This is because Moses is just a transparent

apparatus within them, and this apparatus allows them to return to the self every moment of renunciation. Moses as a transparent apparatus is not looking to be seated at the siege of a government. His government is not restricted to any particularity.

CHAPTER 4

How was the conflict originated within mankind in the first place? How did it escalate to the level of violence and then to the stage of wars, genocides, the holocaust, etc.? All of the above started within the psyche of a single human being. When a person feels oblivious, when his perception regarding his existence is narrowed to no more than proving himself in challenging other creatures, and when this challenge is transformed to hostility, the birth of barbarism arrives.

From the following story we scrutinize the causes of criminality. This is how a collective nation is destroyed within an individual even before the external hostility appears as a last chance for recuperation.

Here we are not yet talking about morality; we are not talking about good and evil, nor are we talking about right and wrong. There are principles that come later on in the realm of our perception. Whether those principles of morality were engraved intuitively within us or not is another issue. Instead, we are here talking about existence and non- existence—a matter of harmony and angst.

Barbarism and civilization are innate potentials and co-exist in a mutual relationship within every person's psyche. How civilization becomes captive, a hostage of barbarism, is not from the conflict between good and evil. There was no such concept in the primitive age. What really causes the domination of barbarism over civilization is the denial of the true primordial identity of humanity that is in accordance with cosmic consciousness. If a person feels his existence, he will have a stable perception of good and evil; if a person doesn't feel his existence, good and evil become twisted and awkward in the eyes of such an individual.

I don't have the right to say that barbarism exterminated civilization; there are impending aspects in every person in the subjective world, and everyone is entitled to be civilized. Nonetheless, barbarism rises from a hermetic state of solipsism, which causes an internal tension. Therefore, barbarism monopolizes civilization within a person's psyche before it takes its external form of expansion over tribes and nations.

Good and evil are just triggers of barbarism, and often they serve as false pretexts to justify a prearranged destination—a person's egoistic agenda.

The sad part and the root-cause of the evolution of barbarism lie in a misleading concept in the eyes of the majority, namely that the idea of possessing sufficient technological interface is the true meaning of civilization.

On the front page of the newspaper, which is dated in thousands of years BC and dated also in decades AC (meaning After Creation), the headlines screamed out the story:

"For the first time on this planet, a thick liquid with a red color close to the color of burgundy was coming out of the body of one human. The name of this liquid was not yet known. The man so afflicted was not moving anymore; he was not breathing anymore. Therefore, there was no longer any life in his body. The deceased man's name was Abel. He had just been murdered by his brother Cain." However, according to the corporate media, the cause of this death was not yet disclosed. Chances are the corporate media would never determine the reason for this murder, because they dealt only with symptoms and merely scratched the surface. In contrast, the Divine Media reported the story in full: "Previously, each of the two brothers decided to give a sacrifice."

Introspective Exegesis

Q: Why did this sacrifice become necessary?

A: They both felt oblivious. The answer relates to the fact that they were both dependent on Someone, and due to some absence they both felt unreal. They both felt the inadequacy of participation in the arena of existence; they both felt insecure. These painful feelings could only be stopped through intentions and actions designed to complement that Someone upon whom they were dependent. In other words, they felt a painful solitude in their state of consciousness. Their loneliness and detachment caused their pain to grow in intensity and to spread to the point that they didn't even know its location. Their identity of self- being could only be honestly appraised through someone. It was only through this process that each of them could subjectively know his autonomous uniqueness, a uniqueness that remains indubitably and continuously visible through that Oneness. In other words, and in a primordial sense, they had only one uniquely intimate audience to please.

Q: What did each give as a sacrifice?

A: We have no idea, and it is not our concern, since the Divine Media didn't mention anything like that.

Q: To whom did they each give this sacrifice?

A: We don't know that either. The arena of existence was apparently vacant in that the Devine Media didn't speak about another possible presence. In short, the vital issue here was not the outreach of the gesture. Rather, it was the volitional nature of the gesture.

Q: For the sake of whom did they each give this sacrifice, and what is the difference between giving the sacrifice to someone and giving the sacrifice for the sake of someone?

A: Giving a sacrifice to someone is an act of freely and unconditionally handing over something of value to someone. Further, this something of value is embodied and incarnated, usually in an animal that has to be slaughtered and die, not in the sense of being necessarily exterminated, but in the sense of no longer being the concern or the preoccupation of the giver. In other words, the object of value has to be given over without expecting any return for it, no matter who the someone was who would receive that value. The behavioral act of giving the sacrifice for the sake of some other emphasizes the importance and glory of the spectator, eyewitness, and observer to the sacrificial event. With regard to this spectator, there are three mutually exclusive possibilities: the Oneness of the Absolute, other people, and one's own ego.

Q: Why is the sacrifice always an act of giving?

A: Realistically, receiving is not an effortful act; instead, it is an act of acceptance and passivity. However, the act of giving is an act of struggle against the ego. A human always has the urge or the tendency to hold back, keeping something within himself. He wants to monopolize, mistakenly thinking that this will extend his survival. When it comes to his substantial existence, he wants to externalize that onto which he initially was holding tightly, but this time it is to gain approval from an audience, in order to validate himself and to demonstrate how much he can do. That does not indicate that he is a real giver, for what was done so far is just a show that has to be put under scrutiny.

Q: What is next?

A: The Divine Media said, "It was accepted from one of them"—I mean the sacrifice, "and it was not accepted from the other."

Q: Why was this statement put in the passive voice instead of in the active voice?

A: The passive voice is used in the terrestrial world when the subject behind the action, I mean the doer, is unknown, and the passive voice is used in the celestial world when there is an impossible association with the singularity of the doer. Mentioning the subject would put doubt in the uniqueness of that subject. However, in our present situation, both cases apply. If the Creator had said, "I accepted from one of them, and I did not accept from the other," with an active voice, it would be sort of unfair in that the responsibility for rejection would have been partially or entirely on the Creator. However, God said it in a passive voice because each of the two brothers was entirely responsible for his own sacrificial offering and for its eventual acceptance or rejection.

Q: With regard to the non-acceptance of the one sacrifice, what could be the reason?

A: There are two reasons. The first one is the observer, and the second one is the expectation. Do you remember what we said about observing the Absolute, about how the reversibility of emotions rebounds at that precise time and the person becomes observed? Here, we find the reversibility of the intention.
When the intention, followed by the gesture, was directed to the Creator, in other words, for His sake it would reach Him—the Creator inside you. The Absolute is inside you already. If it was directed to another, rather than to the Creator, it would create detached and extraneous emotions in which the person starts to feel the separation while being oblivious to it.

Q: How did you imagine the possibility of another observer, I mean another audience?

A: After going through a deep criminological investigation, it was reported by the Divine Media that one brother's soul told him to kill his brother. Why did the other's soul not tell him to do the same thing?

Q: I can see the hostility, but its source is still obscure. I still don't see the link between the non-acceptance and the murder.

A: When an audience is created in the mind, the only one responsible for this creation is the individual himself. Further, the reason he wants to create an observer in his state of consciousness is to validate his own self. The stages of this labyrinth are as follows. Before he demonstrates his action to an observer, there is initially the creation of an audience according to the popularity and the prestige of that particular entourage, which is at this point only a preliminary concept. Secondly, there is an expansion of this audience according to the individual's desires. Thirdly, there is the issue of the person unknowingly being in control of this audience. Finally, the fourth stage is fear of disappointing the constructed audience and of doing anything to displease it. Are you there?

Q: I'm listening.

A: Let's analyze this event from a volitional standpoint. When Abel gave his sacrifice, there was of course an intention; the internal intention was transmitted before the external gesture. Taking into consideration the process of reversibility from observing to being observed, Abel became observed—a receptor by the fact of directing his intention to the Absolute. The second reason was that he had the intention of giving the sacrifice freely and unconditionally. He gave it to the Unique Audience, the Observer already being present in his conscience, without expecting anything in return. All of a sudden and at that precise moment, the feeling of existence was felt. There was no transition period; there was no length of time that transpired between the intention and its reversibility, which generated the feeling of existence. It was immediate—an event that could transpire and burst, since the presence of the Absolute was inside both of them already.

Q: How about Cain?

A: In contrast, Cain's intentional decision was to give his sacrifice to himself or to his ego. In other words, his ego was the only eyewitness and spectator when this gesture was done. He gave it with the expectation of reinforcing his self-aggrandizement, and the only spectator that admired his gesture was himself. All of a sudden and at the same precise moment, there was an internal implosion and tension that were spawned from an extraneous emotion, and the feeling of inexistence was felt. In both cases, the feeling was internal. If Cain had given his sacrifice to God or for the sake of God, God would have welcomed his offering even if it was cheap. However, Cain gave his sacrifice as an expression of his self-importance. In other words, he gave it with the feeling that he was the only reality, and the gesture wasn't distanced from his own self. There was no dimension in Cain's heart except tightness. As such, the repercussion of himself came right back to him. Abel felt the internal pleasure of existence, and his heart expanded, which was a sign of, "It was accepted from one of them," and Cain felt the internal implosion that is always followed by seeking an external expansion, the pain of inexistence that is a sign of, "It was not accepted from the other." What really happened was just a repercussion of intention. God didn't mean to hurt either one of them. For Abel, the activity was a sacrifice vis-à-vis his Creator. For Cain, the activity was a gladiatorial challenge to an external opponent, who was his brother. As a result, Cain killed his brother.

Q: Why was killing his brother the first thing that crossed Cain's mind?

A: This was the birth of duality, stemming from perceived self-importance or self-aggrandizement. The image of an opponent developed in Cain's subconscious; he was staring with grandeur at his ego. Abel was staring at the Absolute through humble effacement of the self. Any person who feels what Cain felt starts looking for a challenger or an opponent. Death was already inside Cain's mind, and that feeling of death was spreading like a cancer all through his existence. He felt such pain of angst and rage that, in his imagination, he thought that by taking the life of his brother he would recuperate his life. Unfortunately, he was deceived into believing that by spreading his rage on others in epidemic-like proportions he would feel better. Assuming that there was a gathering mass next to Cain that seemed to contradict his political opinion, he would invade their country and exterminate them as well.

Q: What are the manifest signs that show the presence of the second audience, which was, as you stated, his own self-grandiosity?

A: After the death of Abel, God sent a crow to Cain for two different reasons. The main reason was so that Cain would repent to God and recognize his mistake. The second reason was to show Cain how to bury his brother, which Cain learned to do by observing the crow digging in the earth. (Note that vanity is always a character trait of the Authoritarian Mentality.) When the crow started digging in the earth, instead of being preoccupied with his own remorse over his heinous deed, Cain's thoughts turned once again to preserving and protecting his own pride.

This can be seen in his saying: "How come I was so inadequate as not to know how to bury my brother's body, when even this crow knew enough to dig in the dirt?"

He whispered these words within himself; if there had been an audience present, he wouldn't have verbalized them or shown his incapacity. The challenge was shifted from a human to an animal. The Authoritarian Mentality doesn't deal with the facts; it deals with self-aggrandizement, it never admits its former mistakes either, and even if it does, its repentance is not directed to seeking forgiveness from an external other. Instead, it is a repentance that is directed to protecting the pride of one's own self.

Q: What does Cane represent, and what does Abel represent?

A: Cane represents barbarism, and Abel represents civilization. This is not to say that civilization was killed; instead, it was buried alive and became a part of the circle of the inner life—the esoteric. You can understand what kind of effort you have to provide in order to resurrect it; you have to pinpoint introspectively your eyes into the inner circle of life in order to develop civilization. This was how the struggle between civilization and barbarism began.

Q: How about advanced technology?

A: What do you mean by advanced technology?

Q: Don't you think that technology is a part of civilization?

A: Everything is based on what a person's mind is carrying; everything is a refection of spontaneous impulses that pop up to the surface of a person's state of consciousness. If the anterior impulses within a person's mind that are sparked from emotions are impulses of compassion, love, mercy, generosity, honesty, etc., then what follows in terms of the use of technology in the posterior

31

world will only promote what the nature of those impulses was. In other words, technology will be flowing with compassion, love, mercy, and generosity. Here, you can speak about civilization, and you can speak about animism.

In contrast, if the anterior impulses are reflections of hatred, greed, hypocrisy, intolerance, hostility, and so forth, what follows in the posterior world in terms of the use of technology will only be what the nature of those impulses was. Therefore, in this case, technology will be flowing with hatred, greed, hypocrisy, intolerance, and hostility, and what you will see is barbarism with anomie, despite the fact that there will be modernism and technology. In the first case, technology was a tool to promote civilization; in the later case, technology was a tool to promote barbarism. Thus, technology is an independent, extrinsic component with regard to humans.

CHAPTER 5

Throughout the pages of history, the hegemonic nation has always fabricated pretexts to justify its force against a challenger that doesn't even exist. Let's assume that he does exist. Here is the flagrance of the conqueror—hegemony with its carnage (Pharaoh), and here is the archetype of innocence—a little baby (Moses).

In the eyes of Pharaoh's administration, the ultimate decision with regard to any threatening event was always death. The congress didn't hesitate to give its approval to Pharaoh's decision

At this point, it should be pointed out that this death did not just target babies, but anyone who still carried the intuitive state of purity and who did not surrender to Pharaoh's regime and gloomy doctrine. They were considered to be like a baby was, and they were, therefore, considered to be threats to Pharaoh. Since the Authoritarian Mentality was in a very sensitive state of insecurity with regard to dealing with or accepting diversities and other ideologies, it tried to convert everybody to its own doctrine or regime, even by force if that was deemed necessary. As for the ones who were domestically within Pharaoh's territory, those people had already been slaughtered in a different manner, i.e., by being victimized and conditioned with a specific doctrine. This doctrine was instilled by the mainstream media and by the various boards of education that controlled the schools. Through the mind control exerted by the media and the schools, the people weren't even allowed to envision any alternative to the present system or even allowed to think beyond their bondage. This

33

system of propaganda and educational conditioning was known to produce a docile automaton, a person who behaved mechanically without emotion, true understanding, or functional autonomy.

It was so strange. There was no objection to Pharaoh's command from the majority of his congressmen; most of them actively agreed with the congressional resolution authorizing Pharaoh to issue his barbaric decree that ordered that all the boys from the Children of Israel were to be killed as soon as they were born. Included among those who supported Pharaoh's decision was the wealthy State Treasurer Korah, a multibillionaire who was originally from the Children of Israel. He had joined Pharaoh a while before and didn't object to the barbaric resolution, even though a lot of subjugated people among the Children of Israel thought that he would lobby for them in that government. They failed to appreciate that narcissism can easily blind one to his duties of loyalty and to any type of higher calling. As such, Korah didn't object to the so-called resolution, and this was because he owned most of the banking system with its usury. His primary goal was to protect his interests under Pharaoh's regime.

The beginning of Moses' biography and his birth occurred in quite a fearful context, which extended throughout the whole of Pharaoh's country and its tentacles. It penetrated every house and traumatized every family. Women hid their pregnancies. A lot of them had miscarriages, and others prematurely delivered their babies due to fear. Others ran from one corner to another as tons of bombs were dropped on their houses and as a massive bombardments fell on their villages, destroying schools, hospitals, and randomly selected buildings. The whole nation was without a power supply; children were screaming and running while their skin melted off from all the chemical weapons Pharaoh experimentally used upon that population. Some survivors escaped to isolated, wild, and deserted areas where they couldn't find one drop of clean water to drink. They were forced to drink from the sewage with their babies in their arms, both finally dying from the sanitary catastrophe that befell them. Some families temporarily escaped by fleeing from one house to another, but in the final analysis there was no place to hide. Pharaoh's secret, undercover agents had infiltrated everywhere. They were ready, willing, and well- trained to slaughter any baby who uttered the slightest cry.

Domestically, Pharaoh was smart enough to instill fear and safety simultaneously in his nation by showing them television images of tragedies happening to others, while at the same time promising them safety. This media-induced fear appeared to accomplish its aims, even though watching the televised tragedies being inflicted upon the oppressed put each person in Pharaoh's realm on a common platform of shared responsibility when it came to the continuation of those crimes against humanity. This might have led to a revolt against Pharaoh's regime, if it hadn't been for the fact that Pharaoh repressed this stirring of conscience by having his magicians expose the populace to a variety of televised, materialistic pleasures. These materialistic images tended to keep the populace in a labyrinth of entertainment.

However, one of Pharaoh's biggest mistakes was that he thought the battlefield could be confined to the community in which Moses resided. Thus, he tried to take all necessary measures to keep the war far away from his own country.

The Authoritarian Mentality always seemed to be very smart in taking all necessary precautions and by having an extreme vigilance with regard to any feeble point that might be a surprise from an external source. However, Pharaoh didn't understand that before the war took place on the battlefield, it was already being fought in his subconscious, in the subconscious of his supporters, and in the Camp of Soliloquies where his meetings took place.

All the newborn boys from the Children of Israel were slaughtered that year, just because in Pharaoh's view they carried the future identity of one innocent person whose name was Moses.

Pharaoh once again appeared on television because some noble and wise people had organized demonstrations against his policy. These demonstrators took to the streets and even paraded close to his White Solipsistic Palace. As such, he again appeared on television, spoke to his nation, and convinced his people that this baby constituted a threat to his nation. In order for his country to be safe, the execution of these newborn boys was necessary. Surely by taking the lives of all these innocent babies, they would strike Moses, the one about whom they were concerned.

Pharaoh spoke about respect for the law, but only while he himself was attempting to stand above that law. He could issue his decrees because he had the power to make those decrees applicable on other, poorer nations. However, he never respected the same decree if someone tried to make it applicable to him. Such was the case when it came to following the Geneva Conventions etc.

Historically speaking, there were an uncountable number of treaties made by Pharaoh or with his participation, whether with his indigenous people or concerning international affairs. Were they respected? How could a baby be a threat to Pharaoh? Could a loyal mentality imagine such a scenario?

If only Pharaoh had tried to be authentic and just respected the charters that he and the previous Pharaohs had framed in participation with other nations... Back then, humanity was living in an age of innocence; yet, Pharaoh was overthrowing regimes, infiltrating his spies, engineering wars, etc. Those charters exposed the contradictions within Pharaoh. Eventually, as had to be the case, his own hidden secrets, secrecies that he had kept hidden throughout all this recent history, would be disclosed.

The Nuremberg Trials affirmed that there were four major crimes in international affairs. These include crimes against humanity, war crimes, crimes against peace, and conspiracy to commit these crimes. These crimes probably escaped Pharaoh's notice; he needed to be reminded of them, even though it was he and his experts who were behind the wars in most of parts of the world. Often, Pharaoh's regime was involved in these wars in a clandestine manner. They have supplied many other countries with sophisticated armaments. Obviously, once these weapons were obtained, they had to be used and not merely stockpiled for inventory. Further, it was Pharaoh's secret intelligence agency that had overthrown many regimes and placed Pharaoh's puppet rulers in positions of power in those nations. It had destabilized many countries and plunged them into decades of bloodshed, which resulted in poverty, prostitution, and the spread of epidemics. As such, it followed that he was just as much a threat and just as guilty of these crimes as any other terrorist who may have once existed on this planet throughout the course of human history.

The Nuremberg Trials also stated that it was a crime to belong to a criminal organization. However, Pharaoh had conveniently forgotten that he was the one who established many terrorist training camps, both in his own backyard and abroad. He had also infiltrated his tentacles into many so-called military schools, where he sponsored and trained terrorists. As such, it should be known that Pharaoh's nation was the only country condemned for international terrorism by the World Court.

Afterwards, all the authorities made sure that there was no surviving baby left, and all the country was for Pharaoh and his congressmen. It finally felt safe to them, and they celebrated their victory with an aperitif. It was such a very big victory. Meanwhile Pharaoh's smiling image appeared once again on television and said to the grieving families: "I'll promise you freedom, peace, and democracy, and we will start sending humanitarian food and relief."

Introspective Exegesis

Q: Since you said already that sometimes this story or phenomena is an objective one that takes place in the external world, and sometimes it is a subjective one that takes place in a person's psyche, what is the role of Pharaoh, his congressmen, Korah, the resolution itself, etc.? I don't know if I am making myself understandable, but what is the phenomenon of this puzzle in man's psyche?

A: As previously stated, Pharaoh represents self-aggrandizement within a person's psyche, and Moses represents humility, renunciation, and divestiture of self- attributes—a chance given to the person to develop the self. The congressmen represent the ideas of the self-opinionated person—a monomaniac when he is soliloquizing and obsessed by his ideas and by his prearranged agenda. All he can consult and listen to is his inner speech.

Q: How about Korah?

A: Korah's frequency represents the constituents of the ego, i.e., the desires. Sometimes they are chemical addictions, and sometimes they are psychological addictions. In either case, they are the desires by which a person becomes driven; you can call them compulsions.

Q: You said that Korah worked for Pharaoh or with Pharaoh. You also said that he was one of the subjugated people who previously happened to join the government. What is the reflection of this phenomenon in man's psyche?

A: Its reflection is when a fuzzy perception from a person vacillates between his obsessive interests and the potential nobleness already existing within him, a nobleness that is mirrored by Moses. This Mosaic quality in men is the underestimated impulse that the extrovert ignores; its negligence causes his gradual deterioration, which was the case with Korah. He was from Moses' community, but still his obsession about money blinded him.

Q: Getting back to the puzzle of the whole, Pharaoh had issued a resolution that all the newborn boys from the Children of Israel had to be slaughtered as soon as they were born. He consulted his congressmen, who in return gave him a green light. Included among them was Korah, the State Treasurer. Can you elaborate and decode this enigma?

A: All these states of affairs take part in every single person's psyche during his life. Either he gains an eternal government, or he loses his government and is drowned in the sea of perdition and subjected to eternal anxiety.

Q: Are you saying every single person?

A: Yes, without exception. The only thing we should emphasize is that not everybody is subject to the killing, but everyone is subject to the potential of developing one aspect or another.

Q: Getting back to the puzzle…

A: There is already the presence of Pharaoh in a person's psyche. As such, there is an inner speech, proclaiming: "I am, and I am, and of course I am, and without me they are not." This being who is enthroned with the flamboyance of "I am" must not be sporadic in the mind of the domineering person, because the gaps of uncertainties between segmental moments create fear. Instead, it has to be permanent, so he (Pharaoh's frequency) has to convert his surroundings to his ideology, so that he cannot be surprised by any challenged diversity. However, Moses' frequency of intuition inside the domineering person's conscience is showing an individual his fragility and is blocking his hostility with an inner speech: "Be careful; that's not who you are. The camouflage is taking you nowhere except towards denying your authentic identity." In other words, if by chance Pharaoh becomes an introvert, he will be surprised by this reality. However, the Authoritarian Mentality doesn't want to accept that. Moses' frequency keeps popping up to the surface of the Authoritarian Mentality (Pharaoh), and at the same time he (Pharaoh) is obsessed by his domination, i.e., his agenda. Therefore, he belligerently tries to exploit and subjugate. At the same time, Moses' frequency, which was previously a potential power, is transformed and becomes a weakness and a threat in the domineering person's mentality, which is Pharaoh's.

Now the Authoritarian Mentality is disturbed; he is worried about the possible appearance of a challenger who will dethrone him and share in or take his monopoly. Now it's time to exterminate this impulse, i.e., to issue a resolution to exterminate Moses' frequency within himself.

All the Authoritarian Mentality can hear at this moment is his own inner speech, which is a monomaniacal soliloquizing, although he does consult his own hypnotic thoughts, which are represented by the congressmen, and they, of course, agree with him, since they are his manufactured products. If by chance, or I should say by miracle, there is an objection from a wise one among them who has good intentions, Pharaoh won't be able to hear it/him at all.

Q: The resolution…

A: Before exterminating Moses' frequency, the resolution has to be triggered by a pretext, not because the Authoritarian Mentality is loyal and agrees with common sense, but because the truth is constantly popping up to the surface of the conscious, creating internal implosion in the mind of such a person, and also creating political conflicts within the echoed population of the administration. Thus, the existence of a resolution that is triggered with a pretext serves as a buffer within the thread of ambivalence that vacillates between the obsessed agenda and common sense.

CHAPTER 6

This is the precise moment at which the hegemonic nation is giving birth to an exponentially unknown antithetical force that is located within the siege of the government and will ultimately drain its forces.

The more concentrated a system becomes globally, ultimately forming one single vertex, i.e., a pyramidal structure of domination, the more it becomes vulnerable at a single point. Such a system creates retaliation against itself.
Pharaoh took all his precautions with extreme vigilance by supposedly eliminating the antithetical force externally. He made sure that no exception whatsoever was left. However, when he came back to the siege of his government, he was surprised by an unknown force that he thought he had eliminated. Instead, it was under his own throne of autocracy.

When he was born, the unique, surviving baby was put in a basket that looked like a coffin. The basket was then dropped into the river of life that had been formerly known as the river of complacency. At the time of this event, the river was controlled by nobody.

His blessed mother was caught between two mutually exclusive decisions. One was to keep her baby in her house where he would be visible and exposed to the authorities. This course of action necessitated inevitable death. Without doubt, the authorities would have found the infant and killed him. The alternative decision was to drop him into the river and to keep hope and faith. Her decision was made when she was told by inspiration to nurse her baby, and if she feared anything she was to put him in the basket and drop him into the river. Surely, he would be returned to her. Seen from an external perspective, the situation seemed to be a picture of death. After all, there was what appeared to be a coffin that was being driven along by the waves of the river of life. This was the image obtained by Pharaoh through his National Security Agency cameras, cameras that were mounted on the most sophisticated satellites in the world. There was merely a basket that was deprived of any visible force. The external perspective also revealed a picture of fear that was captured in the seemingly frantic motions of the mother running with her baby in her hands before she placed him in the basket. However, the esoteric perspective revealed a basket of life, not a coffin of death. Thus, there was confidence and holy comfort in the mother's heart when she put her baby into the hands of the Most Trustworthy.

Despite the attempted obstructions of others, and unknown to mortal observers, the waves of the river were driving the baby to a precise and previously selected destination. The pre- selected site was a very dangerous destination. Yet, somehow this most dangerous of places became the safest and the most comfortable place for the baby and his family, just as it became a very dangerous place for the enemies of this baby.

The mother's position in having to decide on a fateful course of action foreshadowed the future position of Pharaoh as he stood with his councilors of state and hesitated between two monumental decisions. He could either cross the sea or turn back and return home. Crossing the sea represented a chance to reinvigorate his fallen pride, a pride that had been tarnished when he and his troops were following Moses and the believers. Turning back symbolized a complete loss of pride. By changing

43

his mind, turning back, and bringing his troops back home, he would also have lost his ability to intimidate the world in the future. For Pharaoh, the latter was a fear too big to face. Pharaoh and his congressmen simply couldn't accept such a loss. It would have undermined their national pride and the rationale for their suspension of civil liberties under the guise of their Patriot Act. They would no longer have been able to continue invading one country after another and dispersing their troops everywhere around the world, right up until the time they had at last to face eternal death, which would have been the epitome of the last act and the collapse of their kingdom. It was a dramatic contrast to the previous image, the one with Moses in the coffin. This time it was Pharaoh, not the mother of Moses, who had to make a fateful decision. Despite all of Pharaoh's pride in his sophisticated armaments, and despite all those decisions made in the Camp of Soliloquies, Pharaoh and his congressmen were carrying their own deaths with them, as were all of Pharaoh's soldiers, with the exception of some baby soldiers who had been given some fake promises to ensure their participation.

"Pharaoh's household picked him (Moses) up, so that he might become their adversary and their scourge."

The lost baby was found on the surface of the river of life near the House of Solipsism. He was rescued by the First Lady Asiya, a woman who had never given birth. Asiya pleaded with and suggested to Pharaoh that they keep the beautiful baby as their adopted son. Pharaoh trembled with rage that anyone would dare to disagree with him. However, the First Lady's strong arguments finally convinced him when she said: "This child may bring joy to us both. Do not slay him. He may show promise, and we may adopt him as our son." (However, they knew little about what they were doing.)

44

Asiya didn't lie; she meant something good for the baby and for Pharaoh. But the mystery of life is in nobody's hands. Pharaoh tried several times to kill Moses, but the First Lady noticed a shining light of prophecy from the baby's face and always intervened to save him.

The Authoritarian Mentality always seeks the safety of distance, even when it comes to militarizing space. It always tries to prevent outside forces from reaching it and tries to condition the far-distant people to accept its policy. However, the mystery is this: the feeble points of Pharaoh's nation were developed from inside. Such feeble points are always the underestimated mistakes that the autocracy commits. The final collapse of a nation is always caused by what that nation is underestimating and by that nation relying on that which is less than it appears to be.

Introspective Exegesis

Q: The reflection of the outer world and its primary cause in the inner world...

A: When a domineering person, the symbol of grandiosity (Pharaoh's frequency), takes a decision to eliminate the impulse, denying the true self (Moses' frequency) from within himself, this is the moment when he creates an opponent who works against his development; in other words, he develops his own weaknesses.

Q: Can you give a concrete example?

A: Your immune system was meant to work for you to defend you from any foreign virus and to secure your health. There are times when this immune system will work against you.

Q: The unique, surviving baby, what is its reflection in the psyche, allegorically speaking?

A: An Authoritarian Mentality is always an extrovert and is always characterized by his agenda. That agenda is one that he thinks he will achieve no matter what. But in reality, what he will achieve is his own obsession, which he carries with him along his journey from the time he took the decision until the time he sees his reflective and reflected obsession. In other words, the reflection becomes a sort of holographic image without an origin in the mind of the flight simulator. His ambition doesn't let him touch reality.

Q: What about the basket in which Moses was placed, the one that looked like a coffin?

A: The answer is the same as before, i.e., the authentic impulse. It seems covered with death in the domineering person's perception. It is underestimated and veiled in his eyes. Nonetheless, this truth carries an antithetical life.

Q: What about the waves of the river carrying the coffin...the basket...sorry, I mean the baby?

A: This is the flow of emotions. No matter how carefully a person resists in order to avoid conscious awareness of his guilt, he will be surprised by the remorse of his conscience.

Q: How does the position of the mother and her existence pertain to the topic?

A: This shows the involuntary transit or movement of the basket, which is the impulse (Mosaic frequency). It was not Moses' voluntary action; instead, it was his mother's intuitiveness. In other words, the mother symbolized intuitiveness.

Q: What about the hesitation of the mother in choosing between two mutual decisions?

A: The intuitiveness within every person creates a state of ambivalence without the person's knowledge. This state of ambivalence represents a healthy effort to bring a merciful message to everyone without exception, even to the authoritarian one.

Q: What did Pharaoh's wife Asiya represent?

A: Asiya represented receptiveness. In this case, she represented a chance offered to a person with grandiosity, despite the fact that he, the self-aggrandizing being, took all the necessary measures and all his precautions to kill Moses. This was the impulse of reality, a remaining chance for this person (Pharaoh) to observe the reality that would confront him if he didn't kill the receptiveness within himself, as will be seen later. This killing of his receptiveness was his act of uxoricide, i.e., the murdering his own wife.

Q: When you said the mother's position in having to decide on a fateful course of action foreshadowed the future position of Pharaoh, what did you mean by that?

A: Everybody believes in karma. Here we are not only talking about karma, but also the identical manner of karma. This is the same way in which a person obligates people to do something against their desires or provokes them or squeezes them with some trauma. Why? It's because everything is taking place in his own psyche. Pharaoh created fear in Moses' mother before she dropped her baby in the water of life. The same fear occurred during Pharaoh's situation in the water of anxiety shortly before

47

his death.

CHAPTER 7

In the previous chapter, we discussed the creation of an antithetical force; in this chapter, we see how one visible force is disintegrated and one invisible force is reinforced. We have Moses representing humility and effacement (deconditioning), and we have Asiya representing receptiveness.

How could there be two contradictory tendencies, which supposedly oppose each other, if one of them is nourished from the other, and if one is disintegrated by the other?

Was Pharaoh capable of stopping the baby Moses from eating and being nourished? Perhaps he was, but he could not stop his instinctive impulses, which in reality were his feeble points, from being developed and fed by his exaggerated way of ruling, both in his administration and in his own state of consciousness.

However, Moses represented a hidden, internal innocence that Pharaoh did not give a chance to develop within himself. It was an innocence that was energized by the imbalance and the overflow of Pharaoh's forces, which were internally located in his subconscious. This external innocence that was the baby was to be nourished by Pharaoh's internal surplus.

All the women who recently gave birth in the White Solipsistic Palace and in its surroundings competed and tried to nurse the rescued baby. This was done to gain prestige, since it was in response to a request from the First Lady. (In reality, there were numerous first ladies, but Asiya was unique in her dignity and virtuosity.) Later on, Asiya was officially listed among the believers and followers of Moses, but with regard to her dutiful

49

service to Moses, she was already a follower long before she was so listed.

It is so sad to remember that she was tortured to death by Pharaoh's secret agents, just because she chose to believe in One God and to follow the prophetic guidance given by Moses. She died by being hung with nails to a palm tree. Her death was ironic in that Pharaoh so often mouthed words about freedom and the protection of human rights; yet, he didn't hesitate to kill his own wife, a wife who represented the pathway to prosperity, both for his kingdom and his heart.

All of a sudden, they realized that the baby didn't want to be nursed by any woman who belonged to the White Solipsistic Palace, and he might, therefore, face death from hunger. This state of affairs was obviously to Pharaoh's satisfaction, but death from starvation was not to be. The majority were still not aware that the baby was rescued from the river of life to save people from the ocean of death. The same mercy that rescued him from the river would later train him to dive back into the ocean. So hunger was not an issue or an obstacle for the continuity of his life.

It was reported by the media of the kingdom that nobody knew the reason why Moses refused to nurse from the ladies of the palace. Although Moses did not have a known identity when he was found, one girl among the employees in the region recognized him. Nobody knows for sure who this girl was, although it might have been Moses' sister. After all, Moses' mother had asked his sister to follow him from a distance when she dropped her baby into the river. In any case, the virtuous girl suggested to the officials of the White Solipsistic Palace that there was a woman who had a good chance of successfully nursing the baby. This unidentified woman was actually Moses' mother, and the girl was his sister.

Moses' mother was now nursing her baby, not with fear, but under the security afforded by a universal witness protection program. Moses and his family were safe and were protected by their own enemy, and nobody was aware of this state of affairs. For sure, Pharaoh was not aware that he was internally feeding his own feeble points in his own state of consciousness.

Introspective Exegesis

Q: I just want to see my role regarding Moses and Asiya from this particular event.

A: Moses represents humility—a truth existing within everybody. Asiya represents the receptiveness that allows that truth to enter you. That truth that is incarnated by Moses' frequency within you is something you don't make an effort to achieve; instead, it comes to you like the waves of the river drove the baby to the kingdom, which is also your kingdom and everybody's kingdom. All you have to do is to let it be, to be submissive. When you allow the truth to penetrate you, you are giving a chance to both the Mosaic (Moses) and Asiyanic (Asiya) frequencies to burst within you.

Q: When it comes to conflict, I can understand the Moses-Asiya side and Pharaoh's side and that each of the two poles is different in the objective world, but how about the subjective world? In other words, what about what is within a person's psyche?

A: When the truth is offered to you, and you let it be, then you surrender to it. The truth of the matter is that truth is not coming from outside, as it seemed to be with regard to the baby Moses being driven by the waves of the river. Instead, it is inside you already; you cannot say it is a centripetal force while ignoring a

51

centrifugal one, and you cannot say it is centrifugal force while ignoring the other. Therefore, it is just conformity of the two forces that you allow to unite by being receptive.

Q: Yes, I understand, but why is there conflict?

A: As noted previously, truth was sent to Pharaoh as a force either to be useful, or to be useless, which causes the deterioration of the person and perdition on the national level. Once you accept this truth, you form a center of gravity of your own existence and of what comes or flows and rotates around you. You absorb it and benefit from it, and it becomes a part of your power. Now, here comes unity—the two forces become one. If you don't accept the truth, you become an epicenter, and you become eccentric. In other words, even if goodness is coming to you, it forms conflict; the two forces remain separate, and then comes the process of counterpoise—the weak force starts disintegrating the big force and is simultaneously reinforced against you.

Q: Did Pharaoh really kill his wife Asiya?

A: Yes, he did, but he didn't kill her then. He killed her when he saw that she followed the divine message with Moses.

Q: Therefore…

A: Therefore, anybody who was not receptive and submissive to the truth was likewise killing his own Asiyanic frequency within himself, and that was the main cause of the perdition of that nation.

Q: Why did the baby Moses refuse the milk? I mean why did he refuse to be nursed by those women?

A: The milk from the White Solipsistic Palace was just a symbol for an Authoritarian Mentality and its gloomy doctrine, as

52

opposed to representing the unconditioned purity and morality with which Moses was born. Since the chemical system of that nation had taken over and spirituality was no longer effective, the milk was also a symbol for the lack of spirituality in the pedagogy of the board of education, a philosophy of instruction that had traumatized society.

Q: Now within myself…

A: When the system is corrupt, it seems there is no escape but to embrace the gloomy doctrine of that system. If you oppose it, you think you are not going to survive. When you choose rejection, it doesn't mean you embrace another gloomy doctrine; your role is just to disagree. Your true logic of intuition is inside you, just like the mother was told to nurse the baby before dropping him into the river. That milk was in reality a sort of vaccination of purity against future impurity. In addition to that, you are the microcosm; there is the macrocosm outside you with which you synchronize. You don't synchronize with it with a physical effort. You don't synchronize with it with an intellectual effort. However, just being a baby with intuition, all the love of the universe comes to you.

Q: What does the sister represent?

A: The sister was the instrument that facilitated the return of the baby to the intuitive state of purity, which was his mother. It was a return to the same milk of intuitivism that was present when the mother was told by the divine inspiration to nurse Moses just after his birth.

Q: No, no. I meant what does she represent in the psyche?

A: She represents 'The How' when it is not planned. She represents 'The When' when it is not predetermined, and she represents 'The Where' when it is not prearranged.

Q: Would you comment on that?

A: If someone is relying on physical issues or causes without absorbing a glimpse from the One (God) who made those causes, he is completely detached from the soul of this existence, because these causes and effects have a protocol. They have a time, and they have a manner. These causes then become an obstacle that paralyze him and prevent him from completing his journey. If someone claims to be in contact with the One (God) Who made those causes and yet ignores them, he is really deviating from the continuous enrichment of that particular cause. In contrast, the one who deals with the causes without expectations, without an agenda, and without a particular preset manner, while keeping his eyes focused on the One Who made those causes, is the noble and clever person of wisdom who can successfully move and navigate throughout his journey.

CHAPTER 8

There is a time within a nation when the subjugated and oppressed people go into a revolt, sometimes with violence and even vandalism. This is not to say that these people are right or wrong, but it is to say that this insurgency is usually the result of peremptory seeds. In this chapter, we see Moses making a distinction between the source of terror and the symptoms of terror.

We have the terrorism of the rich, and we have the terrorism of the poor. The terrorism of the rich is clandestine and continuous, while the terrorism of the poor is flagrant and momentary.

The terrorism of the rich is part of the broad political philosophy of a nation and part of its agenda, except for the few brave citizens of that nation who stand in opposition. The agenda regarding the terrorism of the poor is from a very narrow base; that base has to do with expressing the anger of the poor.

The terrorism of the rich is brought about by a meticulous plan, which is calmly and purposefully laid out around tables of greed and narcissism. The terrorism of the poor results from the poor being dominated by continuous stress and extreme frustration. Their decision to resort to terrorism is taken in fear and hiding in the bushes of poverty.

The terrorism of the rich has a global view and a strategy that works for the long run. If plan (A) doesn't work, there is plan

(B); if plan (B) doesn't work, there is plan (C). Everything about the terrorism of the rich is engineered in meticulous detail. In contrast, the terrorism of the poor does not have a farsighted strategy, being based on the momentary opportunities encountered by violent people. Such violent people don't have much choice in choosing their target. The only ones they have are those to which they have possible access.

The terrorism of the rich is not limited to visible acts of violence or sabotage; their terrorism spreads and infiltrates every domain and every aspect of life. However, despite this spread and infiltration, there are few or no visible recordings of the implantation of these seeds of terror. Further, there is no terminology for this type of terror in the dictionary of loyalty. There is no terminology for economic terrorism, which is the terrorism of usury. There is no terminology for the medical terrorism of hijacking people's immune systems with antigens by the big pharmaceutical companies. There is no terminology for the terrorism of converting corn into fuel, which robs the world of food and causes hunger and death all over the world.

The front page of that morning's newspaper screamed out a headline: "Moses, the Israelite, is wanted by Pharaoh's authorities for a murder he committed."

The reported story from the Divine Media stated that there was an argument and fight between a uniformed man from Pharaoh's community and a man from the Children of Israel, a subjugated community that was inhumanely exploited and enslaved by the regime to which Moses belonged. The Egyptian was indirectly given carte blanche; it was common under Pharaoh's regime for an Egyptian to have the right to humiliate anyone who didn't share the Pharaonic mentality of Pharaoh and his puppet rulers.

As the two men were fighting, the Israelite felt helpless and called out to Moses for help, who by coincidence was near him. Moses initially tried to stop the Egyptian by pushing him. Eventually, the Egyptian's resistance caused Moses to hit him. The Egyptian then fell to the ground and died on the spot. It happened during a very quiet time when nobody else was around.

Moses was terrified when he saw the man dying at his feet. He poured forth his remorse of conscience, saying, "This is the work of Satan, for he is an enemy who manifestly misleads!" He didn't hesitate to repent, saying: "Oh, my Lord! I have indeed wronged my soul! Do Thou then forgive me?" Immediately the response of forgiveness came back to him.

Pharaoh came on TV speaking on behalf of the high-tech north and said: "Terrorism is immoral."

The day before, he had slaughtered an uncountable number of babies; then that day, he was talking about morality. The day before, he had overthrown a number of regimes and had plunged their people into chaos; then that day, he had the nerve to preach about morality.

The next morning, Moses cautiously and fearfully went into town. All of a sudden, he was surprised to see the same Israelite man whom he had saved the day before, fighting with another man. The Israelite again cried out to Moses for help. Moses then immediately realized that his fellow Israelite was a quarrelsome and confrontational person. As such, he approached the Israelite with the intention of correcting him and teaching him a lesson. When he was about to lay his hand on him, the man began shouting: "Oh Moses, are you going to kill me as you killed that man yesterday? You are surely seeking to be a tyrant in this land, not an upright man!"

If there were any loyalty or righteousness in the Israelite who sought the help of Moses, he would have felt the way Moses felt and shared with him a deep remorse of conscience. He would have recognized that he was the main source of this confrontation to begin with. However, this man was dealing with his own selfish interests and wasn't taking anyone else into consideration. He didn't even hesitate to provoke another conflict the following day, and he didn't even apologize for or regret his actions. He preferred to put all the blame for the death of the Egyptian upon Moses.

During the first confrontation between the Israelite and the Egyptian, Moses approached the situation independently of any particular polarity and excluded loyalty and justice from being the private possession of any pole or division. In other words, he directly approached the oppressive regime, the source of terrorism. He wasn't so much approaching either one of the two fighters, the Egyptian and the Israelite, as he was confronting the origin and source of terror. This was a terror that was spawned by Pharaoh and practiced by those Egyptians who followed Pharaoh's ethnic and racial bigotry and hatred, which had resulted in the exploitation and enslavement of the Israelite people and in the slaughtering of Israelite children. During the second confrontation, Moses dealt with the symptoms caused by the longstanding terrorizing of the Israelite people. Thus, he confronted the exaggeration of the Israelite, even though he was from the same ethnic community as Moses.

A stranger came from the other side of the town. He rushed forward to let Moses know that Pharaoh and his officials were in the court and plotting against him. "They are going to kill you. I'm one of those who wish you well. Therefore, flee for your life!"

Who was this man? He probably wasn't from the Children of

Israel. With the exception of Korah, these people did not have access to Pharaoh's House of Solipsism or the Camp of Soliloquies where Pharaoh organized his secret meetings with his advisers. As such, he was probably an Egyptian, because an Egyptian would have had access to the court where Pharaoh and his officials were making their decisions.

Why had Pharaoh decided to kill Moses? Why did the arbitrary accusation against Moses dominate the White Solipsistic Palace, even though Pharaoh didn't have the slightest idea of what had actually happened during the confrontation involving the Israelite, the Egyptian, and Moses? Why did the decision that Moses was guilty come spontaneously to Pharaoh and his colleagues, even though Moses had been raised within Pharaoh's administration and had given every indication of gentleness, nobility, loyalty, etc.? Why did the arbitrary accusation against Moses override and vanquish the leniency that should have been given to him? The answer was very obvious, i.e., the invasion of nations, the killing of their people, and the seizing of their natural resources is part of the political and economic agenda of the Authoritarian System and the Pharaonic mentalities of this world. Such ideas were in Pharaoh's mind long before the appearance of any cause that might have served as a pretext to legitimize the future violence of Pharaoh's administration. In other words, it was not the last drop that caused the overflow of the vase. Even if Moses had not touched the Egyptian and if nothing had happened between them, another accusation would have sooner or later been made against Moses, since these additional accusations already existed in Pharaoh's subconscious. These accusations had been in Pharaoh's mind even before the birth of Moses. In reality, Pharaoh was after something that he initially didn't even know or recognize.

Introspective Exegesis

Q: With regard to my psyche?

A: You are living under this system whether you like it or not. In other words, you are occupying one sector or another, and you become a part of that machinery. Now, here arrives the source of the coming terror, spawned and engineered by Pharaoh and clandestinely touching every sector, and you have people being subjected to that terror, not in the sense of being hit by the terror, but in the sense of being unconsciously complicit with that terror.

Q: That's a little foggy.

A: When Moses approached the two fighters, one of them was an Egyptian, and the other one was from the Children of Israel, the community to which Moses belonged. In other words, one represented the source of terror, and the other one was the symptom of terror. In reality, Moses approached neither the Egyptian nor the Israelite; instead, he approached the source of terror.

Q: What do both of the two fighters represent within my psyche?

A: Sometimes you get confused between them, between the source and the symptom. At that time, you have one glance externally to the system and one glance introspectively toward your inner psyche. When your vision focuses externally and perceives terror in any field or any domain, you simultaneously look to your interests and find yourself leaning to them because you think they are in danger. The Mosaic frequency within you is not the one that objects to the source of terror because of an egoistic platform; the Mosaic frequency is the one that looks neither to the system nor to personal interests. Instead, it is the one that stands for loyalty. Now, do you know who the two fighters are?

Q: Yes, you can keep going with the commentary?

A: These are the ambivalent decisions that vacillate between an externality that represents oppression and your internal, misplaced sympathy. As such, you find yourself either with the regime or with your misplaced sympathy. (As Pharaoh once said in a speech, "Either you are with the terrorists, or you are with us." In other words, he unconsciously verbalized an expression that says: "You are with the terrorists anyway, whether you are with us or with them. However, we are more civilized with our terrorism than are others.") So here the Mosaic frequency is neither-nor.

Q: Now in terms of the emotions…

A: When you come to the decision to object to oppression on the basis of your emotions, do not object to it with the idea of killing it. Object to it with the idea of disagreeing. If your emotions resist, you resist with them until the oppression is killed by itself and no longer has any power to pop up to the surface of your conscious. Thereby, you gain the strength of your character. When it comes to your sympathy for your interests, correct that feeling by not objecting to the oppression based upon the seeds of your personal interests. The true migration from the problem is not the migration of the physical body, but the primary migration from the oppressed regime is a loyalty that is not leaning toward any polarity.

Q: In terms of the position of the emotions…

A: You need to be in your center of gravity; you don't want to be an epicenter. When your sympathy towards a polarity drags you from your center of gravity, it causes satisfaction at that moment, but it is then followed by disequilibrium—in other words, tumultuous emotions.

Q: Who was the stranger who came to warn Moses about Pharaoh's decision against Moses?

A: Externally, he was among Pharaoh's community, but he was not a part of Pharaoh's team of dictatorship. Internally, it was a healthy emotion that vacillated between an abnormality and the intuitiveness of the person. It is like the white cells in the physical body protecting the immune system against any foreign virus. Therefore, Moses is the intuitiveness, and the virus is Pharaoh, and the white cell is this noble stranger who brought the message of protection to Moses.

CHAPTER 9

Moses and Pharaoh were initially in one place. Now, however, we focus on the time of the breakaway of the two forces. It was a time when the nation was transferring its power to an opponent without realizing it. Also, we see the three fundamental pillars in that nation, what Pharaoh's external government was destroying, and what Moses' internal government was building.

Pharaoh's blind spot not only involved space or geographic location; it also included time and the manner of an action's occurrence. In short the blind spot refers to what will happen in a particular space at a particular time and the manner in which it will happen. All of these considerations are unknown to everyone.

There was one man who represented a subjective government and was migrating toward that blind spot. During his transit, he was converting and adapting himself to any unexpected situation with receptiveness, love, and mercy. In his deeply held faith, he recognized and accepted that the time, location, and manner of actions belong to the Creator. This man was the wise Moses. This person was physically moving with composed emotions. There was another man who represented an objective government. He feared the blind spot and wanted to convert that unknown time, place, and manner of occurrence according to his political agenda. His reach extended all over the world. This was Pharaoh in his White Solipsistic Palace. This man was not moving, but his emotions were in turmoil.

During his migration following the death of the Egyptian, Moses was unknowingly establishing the foundations of the internal government inside his own world of consciousness, while simultaneously carrying all the feeble points from the White Solipsistic Palace. He was not, however, carrying them in the sense of having them be a part of his behavior. Rather, he was becoming intellectually aware of their chaotic nature and was learning to contradict them with his own leniency.

Some snapshots and characteristics of the development of different sectors of the utopian government of Moses follow.

Resting in the shade of a rock, Moses noticed a community of people drawing water for their animals from a fountain. Meanwhile, two young women stood nearby, holding back their thirsty flock. Moses asked the two women about the reason for their presence in such a place. They said, "We can't approach the source of the water until the other people are distant, and our father is an old man."

Moses voluntarily rose to give the women a helping hand. When he took their sheep to the source of the water, he suddenly noticed that the other people had already left and that a giant rock was on the top of the well or cistern. It was impossible for one man to remove the rock by himself. In order for people to access the water, they had to come as a group and had to work together to remove the rock. They then had to put the rock back in place in order to avoid the earth sliding down into and clogging the well. It appeared to be impossible for a person to access the water by himself.

Moses removed the giant rock by himself. After he finished this task for the women, he went back, sat under the shade, and sought a reward from the Unique Audience that constantly occupied his mind. The ladies were amazed by his strength and were equally surprised by the unusually thoughtful and considerate behavior of this wise knight and noble man. After doing all that he had for them, he didn't even stare at their faces or ask them for any kind of reward, even though he was exhausted, hungry, and alone. Shortly thereafter, one of the women returned to Moses. She walked shyly and modestly to him and said, "Our father is asking you to come. He wishes to reward you for watering our flock."

The external government refers credit to the self, and the internal government refers credit to the Creator. When an individual feels vanity because of any faculty and thus refers credit to himself, this faculty is then externalized materially for substantiation, but internally it becomes a characterization and a deprivation, we may ask why? The answer to that, it's because this person becomes captive of that audience. If the individual refers credit to the Creator, the faculty is also externalized with a materialistic force. However, in this case, and despite it being externalized, the faculty still remains internal and in the possession of the concerned person.

When the Creator describes a uniqueness or supremacy in terms of beauty, wealth, knowledge, or something else, He always describes its reflection or its echo. In the case of Moses, He didn't say that Moses was the strongest man on earth, but He described an action done by Moses, i.e., Moses moved a giant rock by himself. However, Moses didn't claim to have the biggest biceps, pectorals, and deltoids on earth. He didn't show off or make boastful claims. After what he did for the women, he merely said, "Oh Lord, I surely stand in need of the blessing, which You have sent me." He was still showing his humbleness and poverty.

The doctrine under Pharaoh's regime is built on substantiation; every person is eagerly in need of exhibition, also people are connected to the consumer- producer system.

Hospitals, for instance, were part of the consumer-producer

65

system, and patients were merely customers. Medical students too often thought about, or I should say obsessed about, how much money they would make, instead of thinking about how many patients they would try to cure.

Religious institutions were also a part of the consumer- producer system, as they mainly promoted the vehicle, while failing to promote the destination. They waited for specific religious holidays to celebrate and in which to collect money.

The next criterion has to do with the protection of social life and the dignity of families, which are the nucleus and the core of any nation. If the cell of a nation is jeopardized, then the whole nation is compromised and under threat.

When Moses met the women at the well for the first time, the Divine Media did not record the women's behavior, except for noting that they avoided the crowd around the well. After Moses befriended and helped them and one of them came back to him, the Divine Media recorded that the woman walked with appropriate shyness and modesty toward Moses. How come? Moses' attitude was the main source of the woman's beauty. He beautified her with prestige and modesty through his gallantry, and in return that honor came back to him.

Imagine a woman who is sitting with crossed legs in an office. A man enters the office, and the woman remains in the same position. Another man enters the office, and the woman immediately changes her position. If you ask her why, she might not even have an answer.

There is a man with whom the woman feels secure; he conserves his masculinity first and protects her femininity second; she shrunk to the center of herself out of shyness and provokes a state of wonder in the man, she leaves a room for imagination. Unlike the case of the seductive, there is no room left for imagination, everything is there, there is stagnation.

That man represents the Mosaic frequency. She changes her position when she sees him, not because he beats her, not because he yells at her, but because she feels safe in her primordial refuge, which is his presence.

The position of women within a given society provides an accurate barometer of the shelter that society provides. If women are honored with gallant behavior and actions, everybody in that society is honored. If women are exploited and treated like mere entertainment and distraction, everybody is exploited without even being aware of the leash of their slavery. This is the case today with the systems throughout the world.

There is telepathy between a man and a woman that expresses how much he cares about her. There is also telepathy between a man and a woman that conveys how much he wants to use and exploit her. Unlike the situation of women under Pharaoh's regime, modern women are respected so long as they satisfy either the production end of the consumer-producer system or the people behind that production. The concept of sexual harassment has not gained recognition because of any respect for women in the work environment or because of any intrinsic care for and concern about women. The taboo against sexual harassment developed out of a fear of disrupting the consumer-producer process.

The next criterion has to do with keeping a promise. After having first heard her indirectly propose the marriage, the old man offered Moses his daughter as a wife on the condition that he stays with the family for a certain period of time. Moses was pleasantly surprised, agreed to the proposed marriage, and stayed with them the full period. There was no written agreement and no police state to enforce the marriage contract, for words have their effect and importance to a civilized person and in a civilized individual government.

Introspective Exegesis

Q: Rupture of the two forces..............?

A: We spoke about the potential existence of two forces in conflict internally within the person's psyche (the "I" and the ego) and externally within the siege of a government (Moses and Pharaoh)? Now, this is the time when these two forces become physically separated.

Q: I meant to ask you this question before. What is the position of the external government with regard to this existence?

A: From an astrophysical standpoint, the position of the external government is an epicenter, meaning outside the center of Earth, outside the universal tree, and outside the ecosystem. From a psychological standpoint, the emotions of individuals who are influenced by such a government are extrinsic with regard to the nucleus; their emotions are superfluous with regard to the core, the neural net. Their emotions are precarious with regard to their center of gravity. Summarizing our analysis: the accumulation of all these extrinsic emotions forms an ego, which is the precarious position of such an individual; this corresponds to the external government.

Q: Would you comment on that in terms of interaction?

A: When emotions are intrinsic (a part of the nucleus or a part of the core), it follows that the neural net of Mr. (A) and the neural net of Mr. (B) do not form two neural nets. Instead, they are one, despite the fact that the two men have different opinions, different perspectives, different ideas, and different approaches. Also, the neural net of people from a particular area and the neural net of people from another geographic location do not form two or many neural nets. Instead, they are all a part of the universal tree. Within such a nature and within such a framework, the energy of these people's emotions flows freely and unobstructed, with the same laws as the universe and with the same laws as the galaxies and the planets. Transactions of any kind are from people to people; feelings are likewise from people to people. When someone is hurt, for instance, there is a bad feeling in the other, even if he is far away. If one group is oppressed, the others don't feel they are free. It is in this sort of situation that free trade originated.

Q: In contrast to the former one...

A: When emotions are extrinsic, in other words, in the epicenter, people stare at the vertex and devote themselves to it. That vertex is the external government with its institutions, organizations, rules, policies, and bureaucracies. It has such rigidity that even the trees in nature feel suffocated. You find certain expressions constantly circulating, such as: effective such and such date, we will no longer do that; and effective such and such date, we will no longer accept that. Time and space are reduced, and all of this is created unconsciously by people who feel precarious and who want to stabilize instability. Within such a framework, the disintegration and the suspension of people's emotions flow through institutions. Their emotions flow through various organizations etc. People are next to each other; yet, they are far from each other. A person can die next to them; yet, they don't have any feelings for him. Husbands and wives live in the same house, but they are only friends who happen to share a roof and share some organs. This is what you call the hostages of the monocracy.

Q: Getting back to the psyche...

69

A: Here you are far from Pharaoh. In other words, you want the Mosaic frequency to be developed within you, and not Pharaoh's frequency, which is vanity. Now, it's the time for migration.

Q: Migration from where to where?

A: Migration from the ego that has a clandestine link to Pharaoh's to the "I" with humility that has a direct contact with the Sublimity.

Q: In terms of the emotions?

A: You are hopefully in your center, your center of gravity. You are not an epicenter. Now, your emotions are intrinsic and not extraneous, which means they are part of your behavior.

Q: And then what?

A: You are going to establish and form your own cabinet within the siege of your internal government. Initially, you have actions being done that are mainly based on and for the sake of an invisibility. In other words, your choice of audience is beyond time and space; therefore, your actions are beyond time and space and manner. They are not connected to any institution with its rules, which apply at a particular place and during business hours, holidays, and special events?

Q: Forming a government…do you call this a government?

A: The majority of people throughout the pages of history focused on the external government and how it formed its cabinet. Meanwhile, they sat and waited helplessly and hopelessly while staring at that vertex. Introspectively, they never paid attention to their own individual government and how they should have formed their own cabinet.

The regime deals with the external world, the objective world, while its citizens have absolutely no clue about the doctrine derived from that regime and have no idea about that doctrine's repercussions on the individual.

Here, in this dialogue, I'm talking about your own government; I'm directing you introspectively to your internal and eternal government, your subjective world—your psyche; this government is based on a harmonious qualitative agenda.

Q: Primary roles.............?

A: First is the invisibility of the audience. Any action must be performed just for the sake of it. The second is gender, and the third is your extension. What Moses did for the women? He did it because of the duty of conscience that is linked to the Sublimity beyond time and space, not because of the company's policy and not to conserve his prestige among an audience. He did it alone, free from any supervision. When he finished, he kept showing his humbleness to the Sublimity.

There is a beginning, a center, and an end of an action. When actions are done spontaneously and without preset conditions, this is the beginning. Now, you are accomplishing an action with your transparency. This is your center of gravity. Have you seen him—the physical Moses and what he did after he finished his action? He sought reward from the Sublimity. This is the end of an action—renunciation of self-attributes.

Q: What do you mean by transparency?

A: When you are performing an action, try to eliminate the monologue of: "How good I am!" Instead, try to establish the monologue of: "How much I am not, and how God is good!"

71

Q: Could you in some way summarize the whole idea?

A: Eliminate the "when." Eliminate the "where," and eliminate the "how." From the resulting emotions, you will be the master of your time; you will be the owner of space. You will be the owner of a composed and balanced metamorphosis, and you will not be subject to a tumultuous metamorphosis. The waft of the wind will be with you, instead of you being hit by it. The flow of water will follow you, instead of you being hit by its tide, and the night and the day of the Milky Way will follow you, instead of you being sad about its past and wondering about its future. If you characterize yourself within these three metaphors, you will be owned by time; you will be owned by space; you will be owned by the manner. This is the primary cause of psychological trauma, which doctors under the modern regimes unfortunately haven't realized yet. What they rush to do is to transfer people to the chemo-system with its OTC (over-the-counter) remedies.

Q: You mentioned something about when an individual feels vanity, it is then externalized materially for substantiation, but internally it becomes a characterization and a deprivation; why is that?

A: The position of the ego as we know it is an epicenter and is precarious, as are the person's emotions with regard to the center—the core, which is the "I," which is the "Me." When a person develops the constituents of his ego, he only reinforces the severity of his feelings of being oblivious. In other words, any faculty he possesses becomes subservient and a platform upon which he relies. Now because of his insecurity, he impatiently wants to show off by externalizing that faculty with a proof, which could be either a material or an abstract substantiation, but most importantly it has to be visualized by a spectator, an audience that validates him. Once he has accomplishments,

72

which are only assumptions in his imagination, those brief accomplishments may exist, or they may not exist. He then feels happy, but, in reality, he creates a state of stagnation, and he creates a state of insecurity. This is because the audience has a time, a space, and a specific manner of acceptance. The other reason is, as stated previously in the astrophysical, subatomic metaphor, he is flowing with an orbit, and he is not in his center of gravity.

Q: Contrast that case with the 'I'.

A: The position of the "I" is in the center, here the emotions are not forming an externality in the first place. Therefore, there is no image in the subconscious upon which the person is relying. Taking into consideration the state of renunciation, Moses did not monopolize the credit. Instead, he let it go with his divestiture.

If by chance there was visibility of that faculty, talent, or quality to an audience, it was not intentionally sought by Moses; instead, it became epitomized by spontaneity, just as his physical power was seen by those girls.

Q: You said there is no image in the subconscious. How about a memory? It is always there, and if there is a memory, then there is an image; don't you think so?

A: When you speak about a memory and about emotion, it seems they are almost the same, but there is a difference. One process shows that you have captured, collected, and stored an event in your subconscious, which is the case with memory. The other process demonstrates the whole involvement of your psychological state and inner feelings. When you speak about a memory, you are speaking about a trace, a sketch like some holographic image that brings and reminds you of an event. When you speak about an emotion, you are speaking about the core of the image itself—something that would influence your behavior.

Q: You mentioned gender. Is that in the secondary position?

A: Yes, the gender. You can be masculine, just as you can be feminine—it is your role towards the opposite sex. What really stabilizes the nation is the family, and I don't necessarily mean a family as husband, wife, and children. I mean one person alone is already a family when he respects the principles that will be mentioned shortly. Now what really stabilizes the family is the preservation of masculinity by being masculine and the protection of femininity by being feminine. What really stabilizes both genders is shyness. Of note, shyness is not primarily the responsibility of women, as most religious people think and fanaticize in their enthusiasm about this issue. Shyness is a healthy intuition in both sexes; that's for sure. Nevertheless, its prime responsibility relies on men; women are subject to being beautified by shyness, but men are the main essence in providing this beauty by their abstention.

Q: Providing a beauty with an abstention…I don't get it?

A: Let's get back to something that facilitates our understanding. We spoke a lot about humility and sublimity; if a human being trespasses the sector of worship to the sector of lordship, then that is his vanity. He suffers, and at a certain point his force flips over and become weakness. Richness, for instance, rebounds and becomes poverty; satiety, for example, rebounds and becomes hunger. So here is what we meant by abstention: even if those limits appear to the individual's false perception of freedom to be traversable, permissible, and accessible, the real forces that you gain and that become a part of your character, a part of your spiritual harmony, do not lie in the slack of crossing those limits. Instead, those forces are infiltrated into your force that is obtained from refraining from crossing those limits.

Getting back to the gender issue, when masculinity goes to the sector of femininity by acting feminine (I'm not talking about

such things as cooking, washing, ironing, etc.; these gestures have nothing to do with femininity; it's even a noble man who helps his woman), it not only suffers, but it destroys the opposite sex as well. Reciprocity is indeed evident. When femininity goes to the sector of masculinity by acting masculine, it suffers and destroys the ambiance of tranquility.

Q: Can you give an example regarding this phenomenon?

A: Water is composed of hydrogen and oxygen; we have two atoms of hydrogen, and we have one atom of oxygen. Both elements form water; the equation is (H_2O). We don't say that hydrogen is superior and oxygen is inferior; there is no superiority, and there is no inferiority. Instead, there is complementarity. Water is a symbol of life, a symbol of harmony. If you ask hydrogen what is water, chances are that it doesn't know. If you ask oxygen what is water, chances are that it doesn't know either. But their togetherness forms water— harmony. The reason why there is water is because every particle is conserving its own nature: hydrogen doesn't jump vicariously to the nature of oxygen by diminishing its number of atoms from two to one, and the oxygen doesn't jump vicariously to the nature of hydrogen by increasing the number of its atoms from one to two. It's all a matter of being satisfied and surrendering to the intuition; each one enjoys the other by preserving its own virginity. The joy is not necessarily in looking for external pleasure outside the self; the pleasure is in just maintaining nature with a balance of testosterone and estrogen in the two sexes.

Q: You mentioned the counterbalance of testosterone and estrogen in the two sexes.

A: Generally speaking, hormones in humans are vital chemical substances. They are referred to as "chemical messengers." They carry information and instructions from one group of cells to another. What we need is to understand how they regulate the two opposite sexes in a state of equilibrium.

We have testosterone, which is the principal male sex hormone, and we have estrogen, which is the principal female sex hormone. Now, when we say sex hormones, we don't restrict them to promoting only the sexual drive. Instead, these hormones affect the brain, bones, liver, heart, and other tissues. In other words, they affect behavior; they affect thoughts; they affect gestures; they affect voice. As such, there are masculine thoughts, and there are feminine thoughts; there are masculine gestures, and there are feminine gestures; there are masculine tones of voice, and there are feminine tones of voice. In addition, testosterone is not exclusively a male hormone, and estrogen is not exclusively a female hormone. In fact, males and females produce them both, but in a healthy counterbalance.

Q: What do you mean by counterbalance?

A: Testosterone is greater in males than in females, and estrogen is greater in females than in males; this is the healthy counterbalance. However, the most important thing hasn't been said. What really maintains this counterbalance of hormones in men and women is behavior that conserves masculinity and protects femininity in terms of thoughts, gestures, and general behavior. As you can see, modern life completely destroys the nature of women by telling them that they are equal to men, that they can compete with men in the workforce, and that there is equal opportunity.

A poor woman works 10 to 12 hours a day and sometimes more.

She works in harsh situations. She is encouraged to lift heavy weights in a gym, to work very late hours, etc. This is not to say that women are intentionally responsible for this situation, because it's a type of self-defense on her part. However, once she feels neglect from both the system and her entourage, she feels exploited. She feels the abuse. She knows they respect her just during a narrow interval of age, and she doesn't know how to define it. She doesn't even want to face it. All she feels is the need for revenge, which is expressed in nudism. By attracting spectators and then showing them her self-sufficiency and prideful independence, she feels a brief and transitory happiness, which will eventually be followed by an unexpected discomfort.

Q: In terms of interaction...

A: When men are looking for their tranquility, which is femininity in women, they don't find femininity. Instead, they find masculinity. Likewise, when women are looking for their sheltered refuge, which is masculinity in men, they don't find masculinity. Instead, they find femininity. Now, conflict arises because what is left is the physiognomy of the genders and the sex organs. Thoughts are now in conflict, and gestures are in conflict. Voices are in conflict, and the whole vibration of signals that are supposed to magnetize is in conflict. That physical encounter between male and female becomes more of spectacle than reality of love, because what really participate in that sexual contact are only organs. Sex becomes more exploitation than compassion, because each one of them feels the lack of something in the other. Yet, he or she is involuntarily submissive to the sex drive and not to the love and harmony that is supposed to unite them.

Romanticism and love, in reality, never need to disappear between a husband and wife, but when limits are crossed, there is a destination without a journey.

Q: Destination without journey! Would you be more specific?

A: Take pregnancy, for instance. Why do you think there is this "coupling" between husband and wife? Why is it an inner and not an outer coupling? Is it simply to have sexual pleasure and a baby? The mystery doesn't lie there.

Q: Well, there is also love.

A: That is true, but something more important is still missing; it is the dimension.

Q: What is the dimension, and what did you mean by inner and outer coupling?

A: We have the physical encounter, and we have actions within this physical encounter. These actions are not meant for the climax (orgasm); instead, they are meant for what results in the subconscious and in the heart during that process. There is an external coupling with some animals, like with fish, where the female drops her uncountable number of eggs, and the male does the same thing with his sperm, and that is their external coupling. Those animals' missions are simply reproduction, because there is no contact between male and female; the coupling is outside the two animals. One of the reasons behind internal coupling as it occurs in humans is intimacy, feeling each other, interlacing with each other, melting in each other as male and female become one. This is just like the interaction of hydrogen and oxygen in forming water (H_2O).

Q: And what results in the subconscious and the heart?

A: Affection, compassion, love, etc. Now, there is an encoded memory that results from every gesture during that process, and once stored that memory forms an emotion. That emotion is a dimension according to the intention; it differs from one person to another. That emotion creates a feeling in the heart. So the whole process was meant to create and to enjoy both the journey and the destination. As such, the person who enjoys the climax without a journey is enjoying a holographic image without an origin. In other words, originally there was a point of departure and a destination point, but in this case both the destination and the departure point overlap and become one without dimension.

Q: You used the word "shelter" somewhere when discussing woman. Why do you consider the male to be her shelter?

A: Chromosomally speaking, men and women each carry 46 chromosomes. In the sex-linked chromosome, the male has a Y that represents masculinity and an X that represents femininity. In contrast, the sex-linked chromosome in females consists of an X and another X; there is no Y. Therefore, we can understand that men include women, and women inhabit men.

As the proverb says, "Timidity hides a treasure," and I assume everybody loves to explore a treasure. The real meaning of treasure is not the gold bullion you have found, which is overexposure, but the infinite remaining ones that you haven't yet found, but which keep you wondering and searching. This is the joy of the journey. Consider another example; a table of food. The table was not meant to be eaten by that food; instead, it was meant for its preparation or presentation. When dialogue between a couple takes place, then when a couple is gently teasing each other and the man goes to do the shopping, he is not only shopping for food, he is shopping for the development of his concern, love, and compassion for the table of togetherness. When the woman is cooking, she is not, in reality, cooking the food; she is, instead, preparing her compassion, her affection, her sympathy, and her love for that family. So in reality, the food on the table is just the climax. This family was eating before the table was ready. The true meaning of food is not that which is on the table, but is the preparation of the dimension leading to that table.

Q: You mentioned something about the extension.........?

A: The extension here is the children, and again I don't necessarily mean boys and girls; I mean emotions. Bear in mind that kids exist by accepting their extension, even if the man and woman are barren and sterile.

Q: I don't get it.

A: You just gave birth; once you have delivered the baby, you have milk in your breast, right?

Q: Yes.

A: Did you make any effort in terms of providing this milk?

Q: No.

A: Now consider that milk is not in your breast, but in a different part of your body; let's say it is in your toes. In other words, you nurse your baby while you are sitting and watching a TV, and you put your toe in the month of your baby to feed him. What do you think about the difference?

Q: Gosh, it's inhuman.

A: Why is that?

Q: I don't know how to put it into words, but it's not

appropriate.

A: Touching something with your toes is reflecting an action of neglect, something you no longer need, something you don't care about and something that is not a part of your existence.

Q: Right.

A: Now the action of holding your baby to your chest, to your heart by nursing him, is showing an action of care, an action of compassion, an action of sympathy, an action of generosity, an action of love, and an action of something you don't want to lose.

Q: Correct.

A: Now, who really creates that milk, you or the baby? Who is the cause of that milk?

Q: I guess that my baby is.

A: Now, who is controlling your hugging gestures, gestures that reflect compassion, affection, generosity, sympathy, and love?

Q: I control them.

A: No, you don't control them; your baby controls them, and he controls you.

Q: I'll accept that.

A: He was the main source of producing milk in your breast. That milk, in reality, is his possession. That milk, in reality, is not only milk, but it's a symbol of affection, as well. It's a symbol of compassion; it's a symbol of generosity; it's a symbol of love. Therefore, he, the baby, owns all of the above. Now, let's get to something a little bit deeper. You have a heavy package on the floor that you want to pick up or that you want to move by providing an effort. My question to you is this, which is first, the contraction of your muscles, which includes biceps, deltoids, muscles in your abdomen, quadriceps in your legs, etc. or the lifting of the package?

Q: I assume it's the contraction of the muscles that is first

A: In reality, it's neither the contraction of the muscles nor the lifting of the package. The actions happen simultaneously. The lifting of the package is in need of the muscles, and the muscles are in need of the package. The moment of the lifting is the same moment as the muscular contraction; there is no before, and there is no after. Therefore, the muscles are developed because of the existence of the package. In our hypothetical example, your baby is the main cause of that milk in your breast. By bending yourself to your baby, holding him tightly against your chest, and nursing him, you are simultaneously developing affection, compassion, generosity, sympathy, and love that did not exist previously. This is similar to the previous example with the package; the muscles do not contract before the lifting of the package. We are not talking about the development of the muscles; we are talking about the development of the sentimental emotions. As we said previously about the milk, it is the baby's property. It is likewise with the sentiments; they are his property also. In the final analysis, you did not create the baby, he created you.

CHAPTER 10

There is an age of puberty in an individual when he starts breaking away from the identity of his parents. There is an age of puberty when a person starts breaking away from his tribe, his culture, his nationalism, or any other sectarianism. There is an age of the collectivity when it starts a revolution. This phenomenon is potentially manifest in every human. It's up to the person to be receptive to this call or not.

There are a lot of factors that separate people's identities from each other in terms of reasoning. Take cultures for instance; the common definition of the word 'culture' consists of four insuperable components, which include people's customs, traditions, languages, and religion. For some reason, religion is sometimes placed outside the main structure.
In other words, it's like a brick left in the backyard. Don't worry; it doesn't affect the main structure of the house.

When we say customs, we mean that to which people have been accustomed. In other words, we're talking about their habits. Once those habits become second nature or devotional, they become sacred traditions. The next stage concerns language. Language serves as a thread and a vehicle to facilitate contact among those individuals who belong to that particular culture.

Culture creates personality, and at the same time personality creates culture. On the other hand, on a larger scale, we have politics. The definition of the word "politics," officially speaking, is a party and a system that involve the government. This is the state that is engaged in the civil administration of its citizens.

Politics encompasses a polarized doctrine that is infiltrated into every sector of industry and every aspect of life, which include the board of education, the broadcast news companies and the manner of broadcasting, the banking system, agriculture, and other sectors that don't even cross the average person's mind. All these domains enable the government to control its citizens in a smooth manner. It synchronizes both a group at the top of the government and its other citizens in terms of reasoning. If polarization vis-à-vis other countries takes effect on the governmental level, it has repercussions on individual mentalities. When conflicts become apparent within nations in the political arenas, the repercussions of these conflicts are reflected in people's psyches. This creates racism and regionalism, but the recapitulation of all this is xenophobia, even if people are ashamed to verbalize such a word. You can see these triplets of racism, regionalism, and xenophobia when people only socialize through an organization, an institution, a non-profit organization through activism, even a religious institution, etc. Individually, the person fears otherness, so he has to be institutionalized within his own group in order to express himself.

When culture and nationalism become a part of people's identities, people can hear only one speech from a specific source. Science becomes an axis; the source of a solution becomes an axis; love among mankind becomes an axis; trade between individuals and nations becomes an axis. In other words, people cannot hear alternative speech from a different source. The speech can even be reduced and narrowed down to no more than a phrase or a word, and that word or expression is, in reality, in conformance to what people have been conditioned to hear.

What is really bizarre is that most people in this modern society speak about and claim democracy and freedom. Yet, they live in a hermitage of their own culture, and they live in the solipsism of their own nationalism. They totally ignore that they are just a product of a previous indoctrination, a product of their culture, and a product of their nationalism.

On the front page of the newspaper, I mean the Divine Media, the news was as follows: Moses heard a voiceless message coming from a burning bush on the right side of the mountain. It was the same message he had heard in the pre- existence before he was brought forth into existence from a nothingness that was beyond time and space. They were the same words he had heard when he was in his mother's womb before he was born. They were the same words he had heard when he was dropped into the river to escape death. When Moses approached the bush, he realized that it was a fire, but not an ordinary fire. It was an illuminating bush, a sign of glory. He was surprised by a higher and holier comfort.

Then the voice without words came out: "Blessed be He Who is in this fire and all around it! Glory to God, the Lord of the Universes! O Moses, verily I am your Lord, the Mighty, and the Wise One."

It was just conformance to words that already existed and that were sculpted and engraved intuitively within Moses.
"Take off your sandals, for you are by the sacred valley."

Moses took off his sandals and prostrated himself. He was then immediately told to detach himself from his staff and throw it down.

Moses threw the staff down, and it turned into a large snake, coiling and uncoiling swiftly in front of him. He shrank back in

85

fear. Moses was told to seize it without fear, and it would return to its former state. So the image of the delirious serpent disappeared when it was seized by Moses' hand. God next ordered Moses to put his hand in his armpit and then remove it. Moses did so and saw that his hand came forth white and without harm, which was another sign.

Finally, God told Moses that his staff turning into a snake and his hand turning white were two signs, and He commanded Moses to go to Pharaoh with these signs and give him the message. Moses prayed to God to let Aaron, the brother of Moses, accompany him. The Creator then told him that his request was granted. Both Moses and Aaron were to go to Pharaoh and speak to him with gentle words. (May the peace and blessing of God be on both Moses and Aaron.)

One message, which was to be delivered with soft words, was for Pharaoh. The other message was for the people of Moses and was meant to rescue them from their opposition to the light of prophecy and to remind them of the days of God. Strangely, the mission to Pharaoh seemed much easier than the mission to the Israelites.

We see something very important that is linked to this mission, namely the time when God said, "The hour of doom is sure to come, but I choose to keep it hidden so that every soul may be rewarded for its labors."

Introspective Exegesis

Q: When you said the age of puberty, what did you mean by that?

A: The age of puberty is not only restricted to the age at which a person is first capable of sexual reproduction, and it is not only initiated by hormonal signals from the brain to the gonads (the ovaries and testes). These are only physical manifestations and a magnetism to attract the two sexes to each other. The truth of the matter is that it is the time when the teenager starts looking for the self, because all he or she knows so far is an identity influenced by parents or by the influence of their entourage. It is the reality of the "I," the reality of the "Me," that starts being manifested in the teenager. That's why you hear the words "conflict of generations," but, in reality, it is not a generational conflict. Rather, it is the universal consciousness that starts being manifested through the individual. If you try to prevent that from happening, then we can call that conflict. The conflict is not between generations; the conflict is between: parents who want to narrow down this expansion and to see their self-replication in the kids, and the children of those parents. It is likewise in the culture. You find a person suffocated by cultural traditions. It is the same thing with nationalism. You find people suffocated by national politics. That's why the youth want to revolt and break away from all these identities.

Q: You spoke about the four components of a culture, which are customs, traditions, languages, and religion. For you, culture is another cause of separation. I can see that in the three first components that differ among cultures, but why when you get to the word "religion" did you say "their religion?" To whom were you referring?

A: When I said "their religion," I meant the vehicle.

Q: The vehicle?

A: Of note, there is a difference between the believer and the religious. The religious are known by the name of a religion or a religious sect; the believer is known by the Eternal Universal

Singularity—cosmic consciousness.

Q: What is the difference?

A: The religious speak about the vehicle, preach the vehicle, devote themselves to the vehicle, and create sections (religious sects) out of that vehicle. They create territorial boundaries for that vehicle. Chances are they completely forgot about the destination. The believer speaks about and preaches the destination—the Oneness. He uses the vehicle, but his main concern is consciousness. If you ask the religious what his religion is, he would name it and even be proud of his religious sect. If you ask the believer what is his religion, he wouldn't have an answer to that question, but his actions would incite your conscience to navigate universally.

Q: In terms of influence

A: The religious creates an atmosphere of polarization and provokes others to be on the defensive. The believer creates an atmosphere of universality while standing on common ground.

Q: In terms of territorial boundaries, which we see when it comes to three of the components of culture, namely customs, traditions, and language, do you really think that religion is another type of a territorial boundary?

A: When it comes to polarization, organized religion is worse than any other sectarianism in this life. The person who belongs to a culture and rigidly sticks to it might one day realize his wrongdoing, because after all, it's just a folkloric event of which he is proud. As long as there is a flute, a drum, and some incense, he momentarily feels fine, and chances are that he can break away from that cultural adherence sooner or later. Also, the one who belongs to nationalism and rigidly sticks to its patriotism might one day realize his wrongdoing. After all, he is not after nationalism; he is after his reputation and identity under that nation, both of which he is afraid to lose. However, when it comes to organized religion, a person cannot realize that he is wrong because he has the mentality that he is right and that God is on his side.

Q: How harmful are those boundaries?

A: Before it became physically epitomized in the material world with frontiers and borders, every sectarianism was already an idea in people's states of consciousness. Ideas, when they are based on selfish differences, create boundaries in the external world.

Q: Getting back to Moses, the message was from the right side of the mountain and came from the illuminating bush. Does a mountain have a right or a left side? Also, when you said before, "When culture and nationalism become a part of people's identities, people can hear only one speech from a specific source," don't you think Moses' case was one of them?

A: Does nationalism cross your mind when you hear such a call?

Q: No

A: Do territorial boundaries cross your mind when you hear such a call?

Q: No

A: Does any type of sectarianism cross your mind when you hear such a call?

Q: No

A: A mountain has a peak and a trough; that's for sure. The right and the left were with regard to the human. Actually, there was no right, and there was no left, except for the purpose of showing you that Moses was not listening to his ego, which is always based upon personal desires that are located in the left side of the heart. A human cannot avoid hearing the glory of the voice of his ego, the glory of the voice of the people who control the system, or the glory of his Creator. It all depends on what the person's glorifications and preoccupations are. If a person claims subjectivism, he cannot avoid being victimized by what his ego is saying, which is based upon a previous indoctrination. However, in Moses' case, this voice was boundless; it was not from outside, and it was not from inside. This is the mystery of the two forces; one is centrifugal, and the other is centripetal.

When you empty yourself and free yourself from all those boundaries of culture, nationalism, etc., you can hear the voiceless Universal Message just as Moses heard it. That is your true identity of expansion. The other identities are just causing tightness in your heart and distracting you from your duty toward your fellow creatures. Besides the fact that these voices of culture, nationalism, etc. create boundaries in the external world and characterization in your psyche, they prevent you from absorbing and living the harmony between you (the microcosm) and the macrocosm.

Q: Why, just after confirming the Singularity of the audience was Moses asked to remove his sandals, and where was this sacred valley located geographically?

A: The sacred valley was the heart of Moses. It was a heart that was cleansed of otherness except for the Universal Consciousness. It is also in your own heart and in everybody's heart without exception.

Q: Did you say everybody?

A: Bear in mind that this call was to all of mankind in the pre-existence before they were brought forth from nothingness into existence. It was with the same eternity and the same infinite expansion, but when mankind started being conditioned by time— customs, traditions, habits— and started being conditioned by space, a person's eternity was narrowed to no more than his age of labor, and his space was narrowed to no more than his work environment or where he resides.

Q: Why was a valley referenced? If there was a valley, that means there was a mountain. So where were the peak and the trough located?

A: We spoke about the center of gravity that reflects humility, it is the "I," and we spoke about the epicenter, which is the ego, which is Pharaoh's frequency. Now, the mountain reflects superiority, i.e., vanity. The valley reflects humbleness.

Supposedly, the mountains are what actually stabilize the rotation of the earth. What actually stabilizes the Authoritarian Regime is not in competition with that superiority; it is, instead, in competition with humbleness and humility. Of note, I didn't say humility toward Pharaoh or any other creature, but the humility I mean is the one toward the Sublimity. Therefore, the stability of the rotation of the Earth is not, in fact, the mountains; it is, instead, the valleys. Where Moses is standing is the bottom, your humbleness, your humility before the Sublimity. As such, the search for a geographic location of the sacred valley is just a waste of time.

Q: In terms of the emotions…

A: The "I," is your center of gravity, your humbleness, the trough of the mountain. In reality, the valley represents your intrinsic emotions that are based on humility. They have more power than what seems to be Pharaoh's power. The valleys absorb and drain the mountain, even though the mountain is higher. Likewise, your intrinsic emotions drain and absorb Pharaoh's forces. This means you. You martial your forces when you are in a state of humility. If by forgetfulness you try to compete or resist the superiority of the mountains, i.e., Pharaoh's superiority, you only reinforce that hyper-efficiency against yourself.

Q: The sandals that Moses wore were very thin shoes, but still the Creator told him to remove them. Why?

A: Everybody thinks that he is walking on something solid, but nobody can perceive what is really under his steps. Likewise, when considering the mind, everybody thinks that he is a subjective and free spirit, but nobody can imagines that he has already been conditioned. There is an internal step in the mind upon which the individual counts and relies. So before being externalized, the step was internal and in the mind. If a person's steps are illusions established in the subconscious, the person is not walking on something solid. He is, instead, walking on an illusory false platform, and all of his behavior is based on that condition. If this platform with its condition was removed, the entire structure that was built on it would be demolished.

Q: I assume that Moses did not rely on any illusory platform in his subconscious, such as wealth, a position at work or in the government, possession of weapons, strength of body, or a desire for a celebrity status.

A: The message is directed to you mankind.

Q: How do I recognize these illusory platforms in the back of my subconscious?

A: At the moment when you are vacillating between the external world and your internal world, you are looking for perfection. At the moment when you are looking for idealism, at the moment when you are looking for substantiation, at the moment when you are looking for an identification, at the moment of your search for emotional security, and at the moment when you are looking for some recourse to win a dialogue or debate, all these identities or one of them pops up to the surface of your conscious to tell you, "Don't worry; you are such and such." They involuntarily pop up to the surface of your conscious supposedly and mistakenly to secure your insecurity. Therefore, this is a false platform that you should remove. The prototype for this removal was when Moses was instructed to remove his sandals. In reality, these sandals were in the back of your subconscious and everyone's subconscious.

Q: What do you think I have to do, since they pop up to the surface of my conscious against my will? In other words, isn't that moment already too late?

A: No, it's not. Even though you had some responsibility for relying on them when they were stored as events and formed as emotions, but even at this late date you can always reject the idea that this is your identity and humble yourself with renunciation. That is, you can remove your sandals, which also has implications for the cane or staff, as will be seen shortly. That is the true process of deconstructionism, as noted nowadays and in the recent history by some philosophers and activists. Unfortunately, they limit deconstructionism to collective institutionalism while ignoring the individual characterization. It is also unfortunate that they promote this process of deconstruction while removing the layers without a final equanimity in the state of consciousness that serves as a

93

substratum in the vacuum, as will be seen in the last chapter when discussing the metaphysical world of every individual. This pedagogy is, instead, leading them to the philosophy of nihilism, which will cause a total free fall and will let humanity go astray.

Q: God told Moses to throw his cane down. What was this about?

A: The cane is a symbol of humbleness; yet, it is also a symbol of a hidden force that can nonetheless destroy a person if he relies entirely on it. When the Creator asked Moses, "What is in your right hand?" Moses said, "My cane; I lean on it, and I beat down leaves for my sheep with it, and I use it for other purposes."

In reality, God did not ask Moses what he did with his cane. He simply asked him what was in his right hand. However, you can understand that the idea of what symbolizes security in a person's life comes to the surface of the conscious by itself. I don't mean the conscious of the wise Moses, but I mean the potential Mosaic frequency inside you. As I said, true logic is taught through this gentleman.

Q: And then what?

A: In addition, it was not simply said, "Throw it down," but it was a sort of detachment. As such, God asked him to detach himself from the cane.

Q: What is the mystery behind this detachment?

A: Eastern religion and Eastern philosophy also advocate the idea of complete detachment from desires in order to free the self from misery; for them, attachment to desires is the cause of every pain.

Western philosophy, which is totally based on mammonism, typically advocates complete attachment to desires, even with the price of jeopardizing, traumatizing, and dramatizing the ecosystem—which is the complete anomie of society. In contrast to these two extremes, the intuition taught by the Divinity is neither east nor west; it is neither attachment nor detachment. Instead, its concept is that one deals with desires without being driven by them. When it comes to properties, its concept is that one possesses the material world without being possessed by it.

Q: Would you comment on that?

A: Let's do an experiment. Would you stand here in front of me and hold this cane?

Q: Okay.

A: Now, you have your center of gravity, the vertical shape of your standing body, as a pole; correct?

Q: Yes.

A: You have that cane handy. Try to touch or remove anything from the ground with it in such a way that it will form a right triangle with your vertical, standing, physical body and the horizontal ground forming a 90 degree angle and your cane acting as the hypotenuse. Are you following me?

Q: Yes.

A: We agree that the entire weight of your body is relying on your center of gravity. The vertical position of your body is being supported by your feet, not by the cane.

Q: Agreed.

A: At the time when you are touching the ground with that cane, if for any reason that cane was broken, my question to you would be, "Is the broken cane going to cause you disequilibrium?"

Q: No.

A: Why is that?

Q: I'm using the cane, but my weight is not relying on it

A: Now consider the same experiment with a different position. You and the cane are forming a triangle, but this time your body and the cane form an isosceles or equilateral triangle, a sort of pyramid where your body is relying partially or entirely on the cane. My question to you this time is, "If the cane is broken for any reason, would that cause you disequilibrium?"

Q: Yes, it would.

A: Why is that?

Q: Well, you just said my body is relying partially or entirely on the cane.

A: True, but there is something more important to emphasize. The center of gravity exists under the vertex between you and the cane, and neither you nor the cane is benefiting from it. When a person is in the center of gravity, is emptying himself from the ego and its desires, and is not taking advantage of those desires, like a person who is not using the cane at all, he lives as a hermit, isolated from the world and isolated from the reality of existence, which is the case in Eastern philosophy. This is because, in reality, the struggle with desires has its positive aspects and is meant to create a wavelength in the conscious with a dimension—expansion in the heart. In the present case, there is no dimension. Regarding the other extreme, if a person is chasing after his desires and relying on them (like a person who is relying partially or entirely on the cane), he completely loses his equilibrium, which is the case in Western philosophy, because it seems there is a dimension when a person is running after his desires, but the dimension is only in the external world. Indeed, the internal world is a slave to the emotions, much like a dog chasing after its own tail—it just keeps turning around and around.

Q: In contrast to the previous extremes...

A: In contrast to the two previous extremes, if you deal with the desires without being driven by them, you are the master of everything, and you create a dimension not only in your heart, but also in the metaphysical world.

Q: Why did the cane become a snake?

A: One characteristic of some reptiles, such as chameleons and some snakes, is the variability of their colors according to their surroundings. Nonetheless, they do not control their changing colors. It's an instinctual conversion. Their colors change according to the color of the area in which they crawl. On one hand, an observer considers that these colors are properties of the chameleon; on the other hand, when the same observer notices the changes of their colors and sees the similarities in color in the areas where the reptile crawls, he assumes that these changing colors have some link to that space or that perhaps these colors are properties of that space. Yet, in reality, those colors are neither the property of the reptiles nor of the space in which they crawl, even though an observer sees that with his naked eye and thus cannot deny it.

Q: It's a little obscure.

A: When God ordered Moses to throw the stick, the cane didn't simply become a snake, but it started coiling and uncoiling swiftly in front of him. Now you cannot deny there is a changing color on or in the snake, and you cannot deny there is a stagnant color in the space where the snake is crawling. By the time you admit one color, the animal moves and the color changes. By the time you make a definite decision about a situation, another situation surprises you, although these judgments didn't exist before your detachment from the cane. Are you with me? I'm referring to you, not to Moses.

Q: Yes, I know.

A: Before the detachment from the cane, it seemed it was your property, and that property was static and stagnant. After the detachment from the cane, the state of metamorphoses began.
Now, let's get back to our philosophy, which is neither attachment nor detachment. Here comes the philosophy of the fourth dimension. Whether objects are properties of the material world or properties of our receptivity, we think about objects in terms of sensation via touch, perception with the eyes, and conception in the mind. However, all this analysis is spawned solely from our judgment, and our judgment is spawned from a very narrow, illusory slit. This slit is our conditioning about how to feel the world, how to see the world, and how to think about the world; in other words, it is our attachment to the world. If you attach yourself to the world, you will be conditioned by your agenda regarding how you want to see and deal with the world, even though the world is, in fact, in a constant metamorphosis. Therefore, your attachment is creating stagnation and decay in your state of consciousness, because your stagnation is contrary

98

to the metamorphosis of the universe. On the other hand, if you detach yourself from the world, you will realize that the world is in a constant state of metamorphosis. This is the reason Moses shrank back; I mean the Mosaic frequency inside you shrinks back. This scares you because you are dealing with the unusual, and the unusual frightens your conditioning.

Q: Yes, but why did God ask Moses to seize back the cane?

A: The attachment to the cane, I mean the attachment to the material world, conditioned your perception in certain ways. After the detachment, there was something very important, i.e., the eyewitness that occupied the state of consciousness when the detachment took place. Then there was a seizing back of that material world. God did not tell Moses to attach himself back to the cane, I mean to the material world. Instead, He told him to seize it back. So here you can understand the difference between dealing with the world with devotion to the world and dealing with the world with devotion to the Creator of the world.

When you are dealing with the world, you are dealing with your fear about not being able to control the speed of the light of this universe and the changes of this universe. Therefore, the changes in and of the world create turmoil in your emotions. In contrast, when you are dealing with the Creator of the world, you are also dealing with the metamorphosis of the world, but this time with the evenness and composure of your emotions.

Q: God next ordered Moses to put his hand in his armpit and then remove it; it became white. Where is the mystery?

A: When people living under oppression go for changes, whether within their local community or within their nation by participating in a revolution, they always carry something. Most of the time, they weaponize their ideology and have the intention of revenge. They can carry an ideology, a new pedagogy, a new regime, etc. In contrast, God asked Moses to go with nothingness, an empty and open hand. Not only that, He also asked him to go with mercy, compassion, and love. In this way, the white color symbolized by his hand, before it became epitomized in the external world, was already present in his heart.

Q: After the message, Moses preferred the company of his brother Aaron. Why was that?

A: Moses was forming his cabinet and choosing his councilors. As we know, or we don't know, Aaron was older than Moses. The elderly person is calmer than the young one. So Moses did not choose Aaron because he was his brother, a family member, but he chose him because he was calmer and more mature.

Q: With regard to the psyche, what is this all about?

A: That is your special intellect in your mature mind, which you consult before rushing to a hyper-decision.

Q: There was something mentioned about Doomsday.

A: Psychiatry can be defined as the science of reducing mental suffering and enhancing mental health. To date, the field has been primarily concerned with the first part of the definition. For example, in the Index to the *Standard Edition of the Complete Psychological Works of Sigmund Freud* (19), the word "neurosis" has over 400 references. In contrast, "health" is not even listed. The imbalance tends to be true of contemporary texts, as well. This situation is understandable because psychiatry originated to deal with disordered function. The question, "What is the function of a healthy person?" which require the further question "What is the purpose of human life?" is not usually asked because it is assumed to be answered by simple observation of the everyday active ties of the general population ^{2} (18, p. 122)

Underlying all of our activities are purposes that give meaning and direction to our efforts. One might go to college to become a lawyer, or save money to buy car, or vote to elect an official; all of these actions are vitalized by purpose and if the purpose is removed, the activities may cease. That being the case, what is the purpose of human life, itself? What answer do we have to the question, "Why am I?"

There is a special intellect that distinguishes between right and wrong with regard to this material world. There is also a special intellect that distinguishes between good and evil with regard to the Day of Judgment. So when you choose your intellect, I mean inside your mind, try to choose the right one, the one that extends to the life hereafter.

CHAPTER 11

Moses was there to deliver the message to Pharaoh. It was very simple, maybe the simplest dialogue ever expressed in this existence within the siege of government. He just told Pharaoh that there is God above him and that Pharaoh should not enslave the Children of Israel.

Before entering the kingdom, Moses went through all sorts of security systems, e.g., weapon detectors, cameras in every corner. Once he reached Pharaoh, it came as quite a surprise to many to see Moses back in the administration. Deep within Pharaoh's mind, he knew that Moses was a peaceful gentleman, but Pharaoh was trying to create guilt feelings by surrounding himself with his body guards, by searching Moses, etc. On every TV station, the corporate media's propaganda was talking about Moses, the fugitive, finally surrendering to the authorities and so forth.

In reality, Moses was not truly dialoguing with Pharaoh when he was talking to him, as will be seen shortly. Moses knew that Pharaoh was blinded by his own vanity and prestige, so Moses was, in reality, talking to the good potential frequency inside Pharaoh. Let's consider it as the Mosaic frequency existing inside Pharaoh. Also, Moses was quite careful about which name of the Divinity he would pronounce when he spoke to Pharaoh. As such, Moses used the name that is not among the ninety-nine names that have characteristics. (This is not the right place to go through more detail about those ninety-nine names; if someone is interested in them, he can surely find them). He instead used the name God, which in the old scripture has the meaning of the Absolute, the Deity, or the Owner. Moses used this name in an attempt not only to provoke humbleness and mercy in Pharaoh's heart, but also to share the Universal Singularity without polarizing himself and without putting Pharaoh on a defensive platform. In addition to that, Moses was so careful that, instead of sticking to these names, he used their reflections in this universe.

Then Moses was asked by Pharaoh, "Who is this God?" Moses replied, "The Lord and Cherisher of the heavens and the Earth and all between." When Pharaoh tried to look for a specific name, Moses then said, "Your Lord and the Lord of your fathers from the beginning!" Then Pharaoh said to the people who surrounded him, "Surely, the messenger that was sent to you is a madman."

Moses replied by saying, "The Lord of the East and the West and all between." To which Pharaoh responded, "How about previous centuries?"

Here, Pharaoh tried to make Moses responsible and relocate a force from the unreachable, i.e., the Absolute, to the reachable, i.e., Moses, in such a way as to start another kind of strategy by which to defy him. In response, Moses chose the deprivation that is surrounded by richness and the illiteracy that is surrounded by wisdom. As such, he then said to Pharaoh, "The knowledge of them is with my Lord in a book. My Lord does not err. Neither does he forget. It is He who has made the Earth your cradle......"

Pharaoh was, in reality, looking for a challenge or an adversary, since the existence of the Authoritarian Mentality focuses on gladiatorial dialogues and actions. However, Moses did not give Pharaoh this chance and responded by showing him those expansions of time and space with which Pharaoh was unable to deal.

The next strategy of the Authoritarian Mentality is typically one of squeezing people with regard to hope and fear. In other words, the Authoritarian Mentality attempts to create guilt in someone's conscience, and the guilty person then has to seek Pharaoh's forgiveness and pardon, which then reinforces

Pharaoh's control. Simultaneously, the Authoritarian Mentality attempts to create a desire or hope, which requires thankfulness and gratitude to Pharaoh, which in turn reinforces Pharaoh's domination.

Pharaoh quickly jumped to the hope section by saying, "Didn't we cherish (adopt) you as a child among us, and didn't you spend a good length of life among us? And you did what you did (referring to the death of the Egyptian) while being ungrateful?"

Look how Moses responded. He said, "I did it, and I was wrong." Moses denied neither his former infraction nor his being adopted by Pharaoh's wife. He merely said, "Is this a good pretext for you to enslave the whole nation of Israel?" (Moses didn't want to provoke Pharaoh's rage by mentioning Pharaoh's carnage and slaughter of innocent children and how Pharaoh had ravaged the world.)

Pharaoh responded by resorting to the next strategy of the Authoritarian Mentality, which is forced imprisonment and torture. Pharaoh said, "If you take any god other than me, I will certainly put you in prison."

Moses responded by asking, "How about if I show you clear and convincing signs?"
"Show us your signs, if what you say be true!" thundered Pharaoh.

Then Moses did exactly as he had been instructed. He started with his right hand, i.e., with force being reflected through a dead branch that turned into a large snake, and he then proceeded to the whiteness of his left hand, i.e., with the sign of mercy.

Seeing those signs, Pharaoh said to the people who surrounded him, "This is indeed a sorcerer well-versed. His plan is to expel you from your land and take away your technology." From the depths of his subconscious, Pharaoh referred to two hidden realities without being fully aware of their significance. One was his unsecured platform, which was camouflaged through the sorcery by which his regime survived. The second concerned monopolization and was referred to when he said that Moses wanted to take away their technology. However, God didn't show Pharaoh a new technology through Moses; instead, He showed Pharaoh the same power with a different source.

If Pharaoh claimed democracy and freedom, why didn't he accept the technology of Moses? The Authoritarian Personality does not consider freedom to be freedom when it is in the hands of someone other than Pharaoh or people indoctrinated with the Pharaonic dogma. Democracy is not considered to be democracy when it is in lands other than Pharaoh's. Civilization is not considered to be civilization when it comes from a "foreign" source.

The Pharaonic regime claimed flexibility and an open- minded mentality. However, it dealt only with its own fabrications and was scared to deal with the unusual. Fear comes from the one who wants to monopolize people's emotions; once he sees the unexpected, he uses force and extermination.

Pharaoh's counselors of state said to him: "Keep him and his brother in suspense for a while, and dispatch messengers to the other cities to send for the best sorcerers to come here for a contest." Deciding that Moses and Aaron should be taught a lesson, Pharaoh acquiesced to this advice and plotted with his court to stage a contest pitting Moses and Aaron against the best magicians of the nation.

Moses agreed to the contest and suggested a time and place that appeared to favor the Egyptian magicians, although it turned out to be one reason for their defeat. Moses suggested the forenoon on the day of a festival. He chose the national holiday and the place where people glorified Pharaoh and his regime.

Introspective Exegesis

Q: It seems clear externally, but internally within my own psyche it's very obscure.

A: What you were doing during your migration from Pharaoh, not the external Pharaoh, but your own self-aggrandized ego, was forming your own internal and eternal government, which includes both your physical world and your metaphysical one, which is the one that the majority of people throughout the pages of history have neglected, and to which they haven't paid attention.

You eliminated the illogic logic of dictatorship within you by killing the Egyptian. You attempted to correct the false feeling of sympathy to that quarrelsome man who was from your own community and who was the man who asked you to defend him. You migrated from the ego, which was Pharaoh, to the "I," which was the Mosaic frequency inside you.

Q: I'm just wondering about the return to Pharaoh's administration. For what was that meant?

A: When you bring the divine message to your ego, most of the time the vain ego refuses it and does exactly as Pharaoh did in responding in an oppositional manner and in deviating from the

106

truth.

Q: Why is that?

A: The ego wants to live with an identity. The ego wants to be known. The ego wants to show off. The ego wants to command. The ego wants to conquer. The ego wants to enslave others. Are you with me? If you are not vigilant, the ego will drag you to Hell. Do you see the reason why the majority of people, whenever you talk to them about anything, anything whatsoever, whether it is an ideology, an organization, an institution, or any curriculum, surely listen and respond, act and react. However, when you talk to them about God, they back up, and they start yawning—some of them with mockery, some of them with hatred, and some of them with vanity that strives, God forbid, to place them even above God. Do you know why?

Q: No.

A: The only mirror that tells them who they really are is that mirror. The only diagnosis, the only gauge that tells them who they are is that reflection, but they don't want to know who they really are. When they approach any ideology, any belief, any curriculum, or any organization, they approach it with the slightest identity, already without conscious awareness. At the same time, they are seeking an identity from that approach. However, when they approach the Divinity, the reality of the "Me" disappears. There is no "Me." The reality of the "Me" vanishes. The false identity is disclosed, because in order to feel the Sublimity you have to have the courage to approach it with effacement. That's what scares people.

When they approach anything whatsoever other than the Sublimity, they approach it with an image in the back of their subconscious that serves as a substratum in the vacuum of their life, which is, in reality, only an illusion. This image is usually collective, but when they approach the Sublimity alone, they don't have any image of the self. There is no popularity; there is no audience from which to gain applause; there is no collective ambiance. Instead, the responsibility relies on individuality, and that's what scares people.

Q: How about the scientists?

A: That is the most dangerous dynamism in human history. Science is science when you don't know something and you keep searching with the vehicle of navigation that is called "wonder." Science that comes out of the void into existence is no longer science. In some cases, it even becomes paralysis.

When a person puts science as a condition for his acceptance of the Absolute and the eternity, it is as if he is looking for an intellectual, narcissistic monopoly. Since he doesn't have the guts to dive into the ether by himself, he has to make recourse to the so-called science. In reality, deep inside his psyche, he is not looking for science; he is, instead, scared to be in the mystery.

Q: So this dialogue between Moses and Pharaoh is, in reality, a monologue between the "I" and the ego.

A: That's right, but it is a positive monologue. Before you think about a revolution, try first to have a self-revolution and a self-coup d'état.

Q: Why did Moses choose the name God or Deity, and why did he mention the reflection of these names in time and space?

A: Try to understand that you have been conditioned by the temporal instead of the eternal. You have been conditioned by space—I mean the environment in which you live.

Primordially speaking, you belonged to eternity; you belonged to the cosmic consciousness; you belonged to the splendor of the universe. However, you have been conditioned by this material world, its boundaries, and its obstructions. So in order to free yourself, you have to be vigilant about the first divine name that was used during the discourse that took place in the pre-existence between God and His creatures. That is the same name. It is free from any characteristics. It fills the vastness of the universe within you and creates a common ground and a common shelter between your belief and other people's beliefs.

Q: When he turned to his councilors, why did Pharaoh, I mean the ego, say: "Surely, the messenger that was sent to you is a madman.

A: First of all, you can see that even if Pharaoh externally denied the truth, deep inside he knew that this was the truth when he said, "The messenger that was sent to you..." Unconsciously, he admitted that Moses did not fabricate this message on his own, as you can clearly see when Pharaoh made his statement in the passive voice. This means Someone else sent Moses, but that was too heavy for Pharaoh to accept. In addition to that, you can understand that the ego is scared to make its own decision and always tries to look to its surroundings to agree with it. The ego looks to its surroundings for some collective agreement to support it and for some pretext that will serve as a buffer to diminish the pain of the truth that, on the one hand, popped up to the surface. Unfortunately, and on the other hand, the ego camouflaged this truth.

Q: Why did Pharaoh make the following statement to Moses? "If you take any god other than me, I will certainly put you in prison."

A: This demonstrates that if you don't follow the ego with its desires and vanity, it will threaten you with illusions. In other words, if you don't obey it by showing your own pride and vanity, you will be sad, down, and in the jail of misery. This is how the ego threatens you with these illusions, just like Pharaoh did to Moses.

Q: What was behind Moses' demonstration to Pharaoh and his councilors when he showed them the signs?

A: This is your monologue and role towards your ego. The ego wants attachments and monopolization. When you show your ego your detachments, it surely becomes just as scared as Pharaoh became when he saw the snake with its changing colors. In reality, the ego doesn't want to deal with the metamorphosis of the world. That's why it wants to create policies, curricula, protocols, institutions, etc., all of which suit the ego's state of stagnation. When you show it your detachment, the ego causes a state of flux, and it becomes frightened.

Q: How about the hand?

A: It is the same thing. The ego wants to grasp; the ego wants to hold; the ego wants possession; the ego wants to become aggressive and hostile if anybody wants to challenge it. At this point, you are showing the ego your dispossession by opening your hand. You are showing it your white hand with mercy and love for your fellow creatures.

Q: Why did Pharaoh feel that his strategy was taken from him when Moses showed him those signs? Why did he feel that he and his sorcerers were being expelled from the land?

A: When the ego with its envy sees similarities in otherness, it feels threats to its power. The feeling of being expelled from the land is showing you that the ego is an epicenter without any center of gravity in the first place, but the ego doesn't want to be reminded.

Q: Why did the magicians say to Pharaoh, "Keep Moses and his brother in suspense?"

A: The illusion and the ego always threaten you if you don't agree with them; these are the fears to which you have been accustomed. These are your habitual feelings. If you ever decide other than the usual, you get scared. Yet, in reality, these are merely illusions. Don't worry about them; they will pas

CHAPTER 12

Before any doctrine takes effect in the population, it has to start from the doctrine of self-esteem. This doctrine of self-esteem permitted Pharaoh and his magicians to infiltrate any dogma they wished. Therefore, there is initially an injection of vanity into the population, which leads the masses to be in the epicenter. Once a person is in the epicenter, he or she becomes captive.

Pharaoh's counselors of state said to him: "Keep Moses and his brother in suspense for a while, and dispatch messengers to the other cities to send for the best sorcerers to come here for a contest." Deciding that Moses and Aaron should be taught a lesson, Pharaoh acquiesced to this advice and plotted with his court to stage a contest pitting Moses and Aaron against the best magicians of the nation. In anticipation of celebrating the crushing defeat of Moses, the contest was fixed for the day of festivity in which Pharaoh celebrated his national holiday with outpourings of patriotism.

Meanwhile, the magicians were doing a very good job through the sponsored media. They used all their efforts to dirty the reputation of Moses and his brother with commercials, propaganda, etc. Their focus was on three dimensions: the Theo-ethical dimension, the psycho-ethical dimension, and finally the socio-ethical dimension.

Before any doctrine affects people's behavior, it has to be indoctrinated into their minds. For this to happen, the potential victim has to be unconsciously predisposed to welcome the doctrine, a process that is achieved through a type of hypnotherapy. The result of the indoctrination is not that a person has a choice, a chance to think, or a moment of reflection to make a decision. Such a state is contrary to the meaning of indoctrination. Rather, indoctrination implies that the moment of reflection is completely eliminated from a person's consciousness. Any "decision" he makes must be immediate, reflexive, and without proper reflection. This "decision" must then be followed by unintentional actions that are accomplished by automatic behavior and that are executed without conscious awareness or control. We may call it conditioned reflex therapy, which includes a conditioned stimulus leading to a conditioned response.

When an individual is sitting in a darkened room, he tends to experience a moment of unconsciousness. A similar process occurs during dreaming. When a person dreams, his closed eyes point inwardly into his unconscious world, and he is deprived of any conscious control over the content of his dream. During his usual waking state, when his eyes are recording snapshots of the material world, his will, intention, emotions, and actions are influenced by the stimuli of the external world. When he sits in some darkened room in front of a movie screen or cubic box (television), his psychological resistance and defenses are lowered; he assumes a passive state of reacting, instead of acting, and he experiences a moment of unconscious acceptance in which someone else is stimulating and controlling his emotions.

At that particular moment, the functional heart of the spectator, which is the center of his sentiments and stimulations, is no longer located in his thoracic cavity. Likewise, his brain, which is the main control panel for responses that distinguish between right and wrong, is no longer located in his head. Both heart and brain relocate to the confines of the cubic box in his living room or to the silver screen that hangs at the end of the movie theater.

Both are now under the control of the one who manipulates the plot, characterizations, and scenario of that movie or television show.

Dreams are usually reflections of a person's daily activities. When a person wakes up, the dream is over. However, in cases involving the darkened room, the cubic box, and the movie screen, the person who experiences the moment of unconsciousness as a passive spectator wakes up with a new and different doctrine from the one he previously had. Obviously, this does not happen from a single occurrence of watching a movie or a television show. However, with repetitive exposure to the same movie or show, or with repetitive exposure to a theme that spans shows, a person wakes up from his stuporous state with an urge to do something. He wakes up with new stimulations and responses. He wakes up with an attitude or set of attitudes that has been borrowed from the scenario that was infiltrated into his subconscious during his state of passive viewing and vicarious living.

When people are watching a movie, they seem to a casual observer to be in an external place, sitting on their chairs in front of the screen. However, the reality is that they are inside that movie, vicariously living the actions, emotions, and attitudes that are being fed to them. The whole movie is taking place inside their subconscious. Prior to viewing the movie, everyone has his own reactions, emotions, and attitudes. Each person is an individual. However, after the collective indoctrination of the movie or television show, almost all of the individuals in the viewing audience have experienced a common set of emotions, attitudes, and identifications. Distinct and different individuals have been merged into a collective unconscious that has been primed by a common set of vicarious experiences. Someone else is now controlling their identifications, emotions, decisions, and behavioral reactions. They are now the voluntary servants of the magician's indoctrination.

The word "habit" denotes a disposition to behave in a particular way, and the behavior that results from a habit becomes second nature. A habit may be analyzed as a series of successive steps. Initially, the individual is exposed to a discriminating stimulus to which the individual has been previously conditioned. This discriminating stimulus serves as a green light to initiate a particular behavioral response. If the desired behavioral response occurs, the individual receives positive reinforcement. If some other behavior results, the individual is punished or deprived of stimulation. With repeated exposure to this behavioral paradigm, the person becomes conditioned to respond in certain ways to particular stimuli, and a habit is established.

The intellect of a human being has a special characteristic that primordially distinguishes between good and evil, both with relation to this world and the next world. Pharaoh had to modify that characteristic and create in people's minds an intellect that only distinguished between good and evil with regard to material consumption in this world. When his people were finally indoctrinated, they had to find their values of life solely within the parameters of the consumer-producer system. There were no longer any alternative solutions or values.

The process is as follows. A person is given two or three true introductions with a false conclusion that has nothing to do with the previous introductions. The second introduction possibly corresponds to the first, or the third might correspond to the second, but the final conclusion has nothing to do with these introductions. For example, Mr. X is always punctual; Mr. X is a genius in mathematics. Therefore, Mr. X is always smiling and is very happy with his life. When we look at this logic, we may accept punctuality as a beneficial behavior, and we may accept math as a good science, but the overall logic is entirely and

115

absolutely false. There is no logical sequence that flows from the introductory statements to the final conclusion.

Let's consider another example, one drawn from the consumer-producer system and the magician's use of the media. Advertisements often depict people without X and Y being unhappy, stressed, overweight, socially challenged, involved in family conflict, and being otherwise miserable. In contrast, people with X and Y are shown as being happy, ambitious, successful, glamorous, socially and sexually desirable, and the life of the party. Two somewhat more specific examples of this may help elucidate the point.

- Miss X is miserable at the present moment and doesn't enjoy her marriage because she was raised in a strict family. (The magicians don't use the expression "family with moral values." Instead, they use the word "strict," i.e., like a military base or prison.)
- If Miss X wants to be happy later in her life and to avoid being miserable, then in the name of personal freedom she has to succumb to immorality and be able to satisfy such and such materialistic desires.

Thus, the magicians spin their web; the conclusions simply do not follow from the introductory statements. However, given the passive and vicarious experience of living through the cubic box and silver screen, people suspend their analytical reasoning and buy into the magician's illogic. The consumer- producer system is promoted, and the individual is exploited. Consumerism becomes the driving force in people's lives, and the fishing hook in the mouth of the consumer is embedded ever more deeply through the consumer's emotional slavery. Of note, this process applies not only in the Theo-ethical, psycho- ethical, and socio-ethical domains, but also in every sector of industry, and it reinforces the jeopardy in which the three spiritual dimensions are placed.

When this doctrine takes effect, the Pharaohnic system operates carefully. The magicians who are mainly behind this process are

not going to put people on an unsecured platform and then let them go astray. That would completely destroy the system. Instead, they remove the people from their intuitivism and in the name of freedom infiltrate the system with the magician's institutions, organizations, democracy, civilization, and technological interface.

Returning for a moment to the movie theater and its undermining of the Theo-ethical dimension, the scenarist often programs a conflict into a particular movie or television episode. They place a character, as well as the spectator who lives vicariously through him, in a critical, intense, and highly pressured situation, such as poverty, weakness, insecurity while facing natural disasters, being attacked from outside, etc. Primordially, a human being spontaneously calls upon his Lord during such situations, although still having to deal with the material world. At this point in the story, the magicians try to eliminate the call upon the Lord and portray deliverance as coming from the system with its police state, institutions, and sophisticated technology. When this scenario is done repeatedly, it infiltrates the mind of the spectator without his even being aware of it, and the result is that the call to the Lord is eliminated, being replaced by seeking refuge in the regime and its idolatry. Additionally, the magicians somehow find a way to joke about and mock the person who still has faith in his Lord in the middle of a crisis. However, when it comes to nationalism and reliance on the state, they create prestigious images, the demeanor of a gentleman in men and a poised allure

117

in women. They even glamorize criminality.

As for the psycho-ethical dimension, which is subject to hope and fear, they fabricate a scenario in such a way as to encourage individuals only to focus on and to fear the authorities. By getting the spectators to identify with criminal elements, they encourage the individual to steal, kill, lie, falsify, etc. So long as external supervision is absent, a person can do anything he wishes. In other words, it's not against the law to break the law, but it's against the law to get caught.

Morality is now externalized, as are those restrictions that were originally and intuitively engraved in the person's state of conscience, and right and goodness now lie solely in the hands of the authorities and the judiciary. When this scenario is repeated over and over, the impact is absorbed by the spectators who now focus only on the authorities.

The magicians create an atmosphere of neediness, desperation, insecurity, and sadness whose only amelioration appears to lie in achievement in the material world. The harmonious life becomes constricted and restricted to materialistic desires, and relationships among people become mere toys to be momentarily enjoyed and then outgrown and discarded. Concepts such as husband and wife don't mean anything when compared to money. Parents and children don't mean anything compared to the fulfillment of materialistic pleasures. Neighbors don't mean anything anymore.

As for the socio-ethical dimension, the magicians try to provoke fear in the world. They create situations that lead to mistrust, fragmentation, etc., and these situations are reinforced with slogans and watchwords. "Don't talk to strangers." "Don't trust anybody." "Don't let yourself be intimidated by people." "Don't

118

show dependency on your neighbor." "Don't even rely on your parents, and don't even trust your friends because they are trying to take advantage of you." "Men, don't even trust your wives; you have to be careful." "Women, don't ever trust men; they are all a bunch of sexual exploiters."

Insecurity is felt; the platform is removed; confidence is spoiled; uncertainty is infiltrated; vertigo dominates. Now, S.O.S.—help!

Why do conflicts in movies and television shows always have to be resolved with violence? There are other ways to resolve these fabricated conflicts. Let's imagine that the same conflicts are resolved with forgiveness, compassion, gestures of generosity, a tender voice, hugs, and arms around the shoulders. If these solutions to conflict are repeatedly transmitted to every individual sitting in the room, then when a person wakes up from the movie and becomes conscious, he is predisposed differently than if he is repeatedly exposed to violent solutions. If by coincidence he is confronted by a similar conflict in his external world of reality, he is likely to act with the same tender voice, hugs, and arms around the shoulders that he witnessed while being manipulated during his state of unconsciousness in front of the movie. However, expressions of compassion and sensitivity do not favor Pharaoh and his magicians, since their main concern is to damage and fragment societies in order to control them and to reinforce their police state.

The solution promoted by Pharaoh and his magicians is typically one of violence. As such, their scenarists portray conflicts as only being settled by such solutions as putting a hand in the pocket, withdrawing a gun, and shooting someone or otherwise physically assaulting someone. When an individual is repeatedly exposed to these sorts of actions as being the solution to conflict, then when he awakens from a movie and is confronted by a

119

conflict similar to what he has witnessed in the movie, he is predisposed to seek a physical solution, to find resolution in a gun and bullet, and to apply for a firearms license just to feel self-confident.

There are two stages to the above brainwashing by invisible hands. The first stage consists of provoking angry sentiments in the hearts of men, and the second stage involves an individual's physical reaction to later conflict.

There is a climax that is predicted and projected by the one who controls the minds of the passive viewers. This climax reinforces the habit of aggression and illusory strength that is conditioned into the viewer. Once the climax is achieved, feelings of heroism, prestige, pleasure, victory, and security are felt by the people who are watching the movie. However, one cannot reach that climax unless one goes through the conditions of the whole process programmed by the scenarist.

The process and its conditions usually consist of eliminating someone, knocking someone down, or murdering someone. In other words, the predicted climax that is incorporated with heroism, victory, joy, and peace can only be reached when some conditions apply, conditions which necessitate the elimination of some person, a group of people, an entire community, or even an entire nation. If you don't knock someone down, you are inadequate. If you don't show people your power and kill, you are cowered. Therefore, you are weak; therefore, you cannot be happy; therefore, you are not a hero; therefore, you are not going to have a happy life. This entire package is recapitulated in the implantation of dualism and the gladiatorial mentality, especially in the minds of innocent children. As Pharaoh once said in a speech, "If our citizens are enjoying one hour of freedom, it's because of a war that we have won." Even the toys and video

120

games that are produced by the giant corporations show children that a person cannot be a winner unless he kills someone. A person cannot feel happy unless he eliminates someone.

This whole process deviates to a precise destination with an invisible objective. After a person has seen and experienced the danger outside, he believes that there is nothing that can help him and that can secure his unsecured life except the police state. There is nothing that can protect him from these terrorists unless he gives up the civil liberties that are in his intuitive state of purity. This is the reason everybody is scared of his shadow and why people can't deal with each other without some organism as an intermediary.

When a person is outside in his external world of reality and leaves the darkened room of illusions, he is scared to behave otherwise than how he has been programmed. He is scared to act alone and needs a group of people to agree with him and to assist him. Even if a funny situation occurs in front of him, he cannot laugh unless a group of people from his community is present and is laughing. What we have here is the construction of a dependent personality disorder, a personality disorder characterized by an excessive need to be taken care of and protected.

People don't know when to feel happy and when to feel sad anymore. Everything comes from that which is external and not from the self. When people watch a movie that provokes happiness, they think they are happy. When they watch a show that provokes sadness, they think they are sad. They completely ignore that everything is meant to condition and "teleguide" their unconscious from a distance.

If one follows the history of the cinema back through previous decades, one can hardly find one movie without graphic

121

representations of killing and murdering, where blood pools as a simple, thick, red liquid. In the end, the hero is happy only after killing one or two people or even a whole town. Then, after such "heroism," victory, happiness, peace, and relaxation are felt. The hero picks up a smoky weapon of lung destruction, puts it in his mouth, and demonstrates the demeanor of a gentleman. That's why every boy and girl, whether here or abroad, once influenced by the weapon of mind destruction, starts using a smoky weapon of lung destruction in order to become a celebrity and hero. They always glamorize the stylish woman with a cigarette in her lips.

What makes this process all the more effective is that this so-called hypnotherapy is done when people are exhausted and feeling helpless and hopeless from the stress cycle of their daily activities, either at the end of the day or at the end of the week.

If the muscles are frozen or paralyzed without exercising them, weakness and sloth result, and then other malfunctions develop in the metabolism.

It should be remembered that all feelings come from the brain and that they are chemically induced. However, their enrichment is from the power of intentions from the self; they do not come in an automatic, robotic manner. When the brain runs out of some chemicals or is subjected to too much of other chemicals, the person then experiences anger, lack of sleep, irritability, anxiety, depression, etc.

As noted above, what really maintains the equilibrium of these chemicals is the power of intentions. Human beings are meant to act and react on their own. In other words, if the brain does not exercise, it is frozen in the same way that unexercised muscles are. The only difference is that in muscles the results are concrete, while in the brain the results are abstract. Furthermore,

122

when the magicians are in charge of provoking a feeling, which is the stimulus that leads to a conditioned response within an individual, the individual is then completely deprived of any force. How can a person in this situation develop or reinforce his intentions or the strength of his character? That which is chemically induced in the brain and then becomes replaceable with various over-the-counter aids and prescription drugs, such as opioids, GABA (gamma- aminobutyric acid), serotonin, dopamine, norepinepherine, etc., is not going to develop will power or intentions.

Introspective Exegesis

Q: You mentioned something about the attempt to jeopardize the three dimensions, i.e., the Theo-ethical, psycho-ethical, and socio-ethical. Would you elaborate with regard to my psyche?

A: With regard to a human being, the whole of existence consists of three dimensions. I don't mean that in its astrophysical sense, but in its mystical sense, and these dimensions go in a juxtaposed manner. You have the Theo-ethical in the initial place; you have the psycho-ethical in the secondary position; you have the socio-ethical in the tertiary position. The first dimension is the Absolute, which is not in fact a dimension to begin with, but it is a dimension with regard to a human's confession and testimony, not with regard to its primordial object, which is independent of any conceptualization or perception by the human mind, i.e., intellectualism.

In order to speak about existence, we need a space, time, and manner. To be more accurate, we can identify it with the following questions: "Where; when and how?" When it comes to the Absolute, existence is beyond the where, beyond the when, and beyond the how. In other words, the where, the when, and the how dissolve in the Absolute. Now, the conceptualization of the

Absolute was absolute before the testimony and the confession of the creature. In other words, it is not in need of someone to confess it.

Q: Let me stop you here. What did you mean by that?

A: As an example, the sun is a sun whether with or without your testimony. Therefore, when you give a testimony or confession to the sun, you are actually giving it to yourself. It is likewise with knowledge. How much you know about the sun is how much you know about yourself, and how much the entire sun is with itself you ignore. In the final analysis, how much you know about the sun is how much you ignore about your inadequacy. You, for instance, know vitamin D from the sun. The plants know chlorophyll from the sun, and creatures claim knowledge of the sun when, in fact, they are merely claiming their predisposed and limited ability.

Now, what you define from the Absolute is how much your capability is manifested, how much your incapability is ignored by you, and the hidden cause beneath the definite process of identifying the Deity. It is as if you were looking for an identity resulting from your projection of the Deity, in order to secure you in this existence. It is as if you were climbing a ladder of assumption, when you encounter a sudden feeling of vertigo, which leaves you facing a free fall and flowing in the ether. Given that turmoil, you are left grabbing anything that can secure your existence and that can serve as a substratum or platform in the vacuum. During that moment when you find an identity the same as the one who contemplated the sun, and who thought he knew the sun, you think you have found an identity of the Absolute, when, in fact, you have found a projection of yourself in a vacuum. Speaking hypothetically, when you rely on yourself within your imagination, it gives a certain comfort, but practically speaking it leaves you with more free fall than before.

Q: What is the safest confession from humans with regard to the true identity of the Absolute?

A: The identity of the Absolute is a non-identity; it is likewise with regard to a human's confession. It is a fact that there is no identity; rather, confession of incapability, confession of rejection, confession of renunciation, confession of your effacement, and all of these non-identities are, in fact, an identity. That is the impetuous dynamism of navigation; that is the element of absorption; that is the bootstrap of amelioration; that is the autogenic vehicle to the future; that is the substratum in the ether. If by chance there is an identity being manifested along your journey, and you will surely be surprised by a lot of identities being manifested, therein lies a big danger that has faced the whole of humanity throughout the pages of history. One religious person says, "This is it," and another religious person says, "No, this is it." One religious sect says, "No, this is it," and another religious sect says, "Oh no, this is it." One philosopher says, "No, no, this is it," and another philosopher says, "No, no, no, this is it." Then, there is the atheist, the one who decides to be outside the floundering about and who thinks he is neutral and objective. Then there is the one who wants to be supposedly civilized by choosing atheism, but in the meantime he wants to keep his possibilities open; this is the case with the agnostic.

Q: So which religion is real?

A: Who is talking about religion?

Q: You are talking about religion.

A: I'm referring to religion and to its hidden paralysis, but I'm not talking about religion. I am not even preaching religion, especially in this particular place.

Q: Well, I don't know how to name it.

A: I'm talking about consciousness; I'm talking about the universal consciousness, and you can call it cosmic consciousness if you wish.

Q: Sorry. Keep on going.

A: Any confession that professes an identity for the Absolute is, in fact, dragging a person out of his center of gravity.

Q: When we say confession, it is as if we are acknowledging something that was supposed to be manifested one way or the other, but for some reason it was hidden. Stated differently, it is as if there were some reality that was supposed to be known, but it was camouflaged by lies, and then we say, "Enough is enough; reality has to be manifested; now is the moment of confession." Following that, we then confess.
Getting back to our topic, why is there a confession in the first place? Is everybody subject to this confession?

A: We have the macrocosm, which is the entire cosmos, the whole universe. We have the microcosm, which is the miniature tiny world as it could be, and which is parallel to the previous one. Finally, we have the mesocosm that lies between the range of macrocosm and microcosm, which is so far inexistent; it is a sort of specter that has the potential to be immense, just as it has the potential to be inexistent; this is the human being.

The macrocosm is an immensity that is manifested outside you, while the microcosm consists of tiny, hidden, and unknown particles that are synchronizing exactly with the immensity of the universe. Now, the Absolute is neither-nor; it is beyond what was said. It is not outside, and it is not inside, but it is in both at the same time. It is not without, and it is not within, but it is boundless at the same time. You, as a human, are the mesocosm that synchronizes between the macrocosm and the microcosm through your conscious confession of the Absolute. Your conscious confession is your confession of your inadequacy in front of the Absolute. You are the enigma of possibility; you are the enigma of allowance to unite the whole into the one. You asked me why there is a confession.

Q: Yes.

A: The confession allows reality, which is already a potential reality before your acknowledgment, to be manifested and actualized within you. It is more passivity than activity. As they say in quantum physics, it is the science of accepting possibilities. Everything is already there, and your conscious confession as a mesocosm establishes and allows existence within you to unite and to harmonize.

Q: Why is everybody subject to confession?

A: You might as well ask why it is that everybody is subject to looking for an identity. You might as well ask why everybody is subject to deifying something to gain an identity, whether he is conscious of it or not. The answer is that everyone is subject to confession in order to secure his existence with that confession.

Q: Speaking in terms of astrophysics, where is the safest place for humans in this universe?

A: It is his center of gravity. When we say center of gravity, we mean his humility. When we say his humility, we mean his confession that there is no god except God. That confession is a center of gravity that is concentric with the Absolute and concentric with the universe. The whole universe is pivoting and flowing with the speed of light, and if a human is outside his center of gravity, he will be in the epicenter and will be exposed to that flow.

Now, let us get back to our subject. You understand that the role of the magicians and the Pharaonic system in this existence is to drag you out of your center of gravity by way of misleading statements, e.g., "Oh, we are secular; we don't object to religions; it's freedom for (from) all religions that we champion." Such statements obscure the fact that the speaker has no self anymore; there is no "Me" anymore. There is only nationalism; there is only the corporation. Therefore, all a person knows about himself is nationality. He knows a territorial division that claims nothing more than dust, or he knows a position in the consumer- producer system.

Q: What is the difference between the two in terms of energy?

A: We have two forces. One is centrifugal, and one is centripetal. As for the one who is in his center of gravity with worship, his forces are centripetal. His energy is directed inwardly—involutedly; he absorbs whatever rotates in the epicenter. In contrast, the one who is outside his center of gravity, in the epicenter, his forces are centrifugal. His potential energy is outwardly directed; he starts being deprived of everything, so most of his preoccupation is spent searching for the self by borrowing personality, by borrowing words, by seeking admiration from audiences, etc.

Q: What you have said focuses on the Theo-ethical dimension. Now, how about the psycho-ethical dimension?

A: This is the relationship with the self. The system never teaches you how to deal with the self. It never gives you a chance to know introspectively who you are. In other words, it gives you a doctrine of extroversion and constantly fixes your eyes on the system. If you ever get a chance introspectively to be an introvert, you end up fearing the self and returning to the external system. Anyway, this psycho-ethical dimension is linked with the Theo-ethical dimension in order to keep you stable and composed.

Along your journey, you will have a lot of identities being manifested that are projected toward the Absolute; yet, these identities will doubtless affect you negatively by obstructing the flow of the universal energy within you. As such, your vigilance must be the state of effacement, the state of renunciation. There is no god except God. This is your healthy consciousness. The second phase, which overlaps with the psycho-ethical dimension, is repentance for your mistakes. There is a big difference between seeing a mistake as a sin (when it is a sin) vis-à-vis your Creator and seeing it as an infraction vis-à-vis the system. Repentance from sin keeps you in touch with yourself; repentance from an infraction vis-à-vis the system drags you outside yourself.

Q: What about the third dimension, the socio-ethical one?

A: The magicians have to make sure to create an intermediary between people. Have you ever heard them during their broadcasts or movies or whatever? Have you ever heard them telling you to get in touch with your neighbor, get in touch with your father, get in touch with your colleague at work, get in touch with your mother, get in touch with your sister, or get in touch with your brother? You never hear that, but you hear them telling you to call such and such a company, call such and such a service, call such and such an organization, call such and such an institution, etc.

We spoke previously about the neural net. The neural net of Mr. X and the neural net of Mr. Y do not form two neural nets.

Instead, they form one neural net, despite the fact that they are two different neural nets with different opinion etc. Therefore, the flow of emotions is navigating from duality or multiplicity into unicellular emotion, even though people are different. Once an institution is created, the flow of emotions isn't the same; in this situation, the flow goes from one person to a dead institution where it gets evaporated. In such a situation, people are supposedly getting help from an institution in the external world; yet, they are getting disintegrated internally with anxiety.

Q: Would you summarize the three dimensions with regard to emotions?

A: The whole system is built on how to escape the self and to seek refuge in the external system. You hear people saying that they want the truth. Actually, if the truth were divulged to them, they would collapse, and the system would also collapse. The truth takes a person to the center of gravity by showing him who he is, when, in fact, nobody wants to know who he really is. Basically the whole process is meant to drag a person out off his center of gravity and into the epicenter, meaning his emotions are outside him. Despite the fact that he carries his emotions, they become extrinsic. Once he is in the epicenter, he is overwhelmed by fear, and he looks to the system because he feels he doesn't have any other choice. Look at the following chapter. It shows how people cherish the magicians, not because they have any clue about what is logical or illogical, but they follow the magicians in a vain hope that the magicians will bring them victory by which they can close the gap of fear from which they are suffering.

Q: Actually my question is about my limits within these three dimensions.

A: Your first limit has to do with the Sublimity; do not cross the frontier of worship to the sector where you attempt to grant yourself or material possessions the status of Lordship, even if those limits seem accessible, traversable, etc. If you do, your forces rebound and become weakness.

Your second limit has to do with yourself, your position between hope and fear. If you go a long way to the hope section, which triggers happiness, you are then shifted to the fear section, which triggers sadness without your realizing it. You should not take too much happiness, even if it seems disposable. Take a share, and leave the rest.

Your third limit is toward your fellow creatures. As an example, when it comes to communication—conversation communication, which is only one aspect of life even though it means a lot, even if someone is giving you hours by listening to you, do not take his share. Respect the norm of the dialogue. Speak your seconds, and give him back his time. In terms of walking and in terms of driving, even if you have some power to intimidate people, do not take this power; take instead your share.

CHAPTER 13

There are times when a nation is confronted by a flagrant truth, which is in reality a wake-up call—an alarming signal for the government to change its policy or its regime before it's too late, but most of the time, people within the siege of the government reinforce the cover-up campaign, in order to escape from this truth, instead of dealing with this reality. This deviation will only cause more deterioration in the system.

It was the day of the contest between Moses and Pharaoh's magicians

When people live in confusion, puzzlement, and perplexity, each of which is a sign of deprivation, depersonalization, and extirpation of intuitivism, these are signs of a loss of democracy. What is internally missing in every individual is sought externally and collectively.

The whole nation was focused on the upcoming contest between Moses and the sorcerers. Without a single exception, all the TV stations were broadcasting the news everywhere throughout the world. Spectators on their way to the Arena Zero were interviewed, and most of them said, "We may follow the sorcerers if they are the winners." You can tell that most of them did not have any a particular pole on which to lean. In short, the whole nation was following Pharaoh and cheering for his magicians, not because they were loyal and sincere, but because they thought that the magicians would bring them a

132

victory that would satisfy the doctrine under which they had been living their entire lives.

The fiscal agenda was the benchmark of Pharaoh's nation and was no more than an incarceration of thoughts within the parameters of the consumer-producer system, which had traumatized society by obstructing an alternative system. Despite the fact that the synchronized thread between the political philosophy of that nation and the public policy of its population formed a sort of unique global omnipotence, Pharaoh still ignored the fact that he had created a potential urge of deconstruction in every citizen, since everybody was looking for the self. All they saw so far was their digital image, which corresponded to the GDP (Gross Domestic Product).

It follows that reality, with its principles in the objective world, remained intact, meaning that reality could be explored and seized under certain conditions. Once reality confronts the world of simulacrum, it will absorb and consume it for the benefit of the real, as will be seen shortly with what happened between Moses and the magicians.

If people have dealt with illusions all their lives, those illusions become reality, and reality becomes illusions. What passes for common sense is often nothing more than illusion, and it doesn't have an independent existence by which people live. It is, instead, a common sense that is coordinated with the consumer-producer system. Whoever has corporate power, e.g., a think tank, and advertising power can impose his version of common sense, and most people are conditioned to find solutions only in the consumer-producer system. If anything touches or infringes on their interests, their common sense changes automatically or disappears completely. Here lies the ambivalence between their external vision and their inner one. When they contemplate an external event, they wish for the victory of the magicians; when they stare introspectively at their inner self, they feel the fear of being oblivious, and they wish for the system to collapse, but they don't know where else to go.

Generally speaking, any duel that has taken place in human history came from two divergent forces, and each one ambitiously utilized his/its extreme power to dominate and to knock down the other, since both of them were looking to stand on the podium of victory. In the case of this contest between Moses and the sorcerers, we had one force that wanted to prove itself, which was the case with the sorcerers, and we had another force that wanted to prove its renunciation with transparency, which was the case with Moses. One force wanted to show its supremacy with an identity, and another force wanted to show humility with effacement. One force came with the idea of how much we are, and another force came with the idea of how much I am not.

When the sorcerers arrived, they whispered to Pharaoh, "Shall we have a suitable reward if we win?" How bizarre! They came with the idea of achieving victory no matter what, not with the idea of bringing the truth to people.

Pharaoh answered them, "Of course, and you will be among the closest to me.

Moses chose the time, which was the day of festival, and he chose the moment, which was the forenoon.

Now the question for Moses was not who was going to win. Moses was not worried about that. He was focused on how to infiltrate the truth into people's minds. When he looked at that population, he found them already indoctrinated and conditioned. They had been living all their lives through television and the board of education; illusions had become reality for them. When

Moses looked at Pharaoh, he found him intoxicated by pride. Pharaoh's main concern was in protecting his grandiosity.

There was only one chance to compete against the magicians, but there was another obstacle...

The theory of how to beat a lie detector or polygraph had once been restricted to espionage agencies and their minions. These secret agents were taught how to beat the lie detector if they were ever caught by the enemy and subjected to interrogation. They had been taught to beat the lie detector by having repeatedly memorized a set of recitations in such a way that even if their subconscious was interrogated under the influence of a chemical substance, intoxicant, or hypnosis, the enemy still wouldn't be able to get to the truth, since these spies already ignored it themselves. However, Pharaoh eventually realized that the intuitive state of purity rejects lies. Therefore, he had indirectly indoctrinated his people in how to beat the lie detector by crossing the limits of truth without experiencing any guilt feelings.

There is a bypass that is reflected when a person says, "So what," and this creates a running jump that allows a person to leap over the polygraph. Built upon fabricated pretexts, this attitude of "so what" is actually believed by the secret agent, and this belief allows him to welcome lies and bad acts without any measurable trace of guilt. Lacking guilt and anxiety about lying, the secret agent is able to avoid being caught in a falsehood when hooked up to the lie detector. Because his lies amount to no more than a "so what," he can say or do things contrary to reality without being disturbed and without having the slightest feeling of being wrong. Therefore, there is no change in his nervous system, respiration rate, perspiration flow, and heart beat, and he is able to duel successfully with the polygraph. However, when the secret agent has established that bypass, in some measure he is no longer able to identify the truth for himself, and he has become a captive of his own lies.

The magicians once knew that they were spreading lies and baseless propaganda through the corporate media and newspapers. They once understood that their illusions had no existence in fact and were only the end result of their fabricated anomalies. They once knew that their lies had an existence only in the imaginations of people who wanted to deal with illusions. However, like the secret agent who has established a bypass based upon "so what," the magicians eventually established their own bypass, which allowed them to maintain the belief that what they were doing was right and that they were guiltless. Having built this bypass, they believed their own lies, pretexts, and fabrications and were routinely able to beat the lie detector.

God gives everybody his wish, whether he is good or bad, as long as he puts his trust in his ideology. God may give a disbeliever or a polytheist victory over a believer who has some doubt in his worship. This is not because God favors the pagan, but because the disbeliever is sincere with his lies and the believer is insincere with his truth.

Moses was aware of this dilemma. After all, he had been raised in the House of Solipsism, and he knew about the bypass. Therefore, he tried to remove the bypass from the magicians' state of consciousness by changing the audience for whom the magicians fabricated pretexts. He shifted the audience from the Pharaonic system to God. Furthermore, he did not direct the duel to himself; instead, he directed it to God, and he slowly and articulately said to them: "Woe to you! Invent no falsehoods against God, or He will destroy you with a scourge. Impostors will surely come to grief. The forger must suffer failure."

They disputed one with another over their affair, but they kept their talk secret. There was doubtless some hesitation inside the magicians' conscious states, even though they didn't externally demonstrate that hesitation. The false pretext that feeds the bypass that usually allows lies to be infiltrated was probably removed, and the magicians became momentarily and uncomfortably aware that what they were doing was dabbling in wrongful fakery and illusions.

Moses was doing everything in a punctual and careful manner, and he was meticulously calculating within himself to avoid the inflated self-abuse of confidence. He remained humbly directed toward God and directed toward that nation with mercy.

The magicians tried to deflect his words by responding with the camouflage of compensatory self-confidence and ego defense mechanisms, both of which were a self-protective response to a perception of psychic danger. In this way, they avoided any conscious awareness of conflict. They then immediately rushed to intimidate Moses with a question, "Will you throw first, or shall we?"

"Throw," Moses calmly replied.

The magicians threw down their magic ropes and sticks, and they cried out with patriotism and national pride, "By Pharaoh's glory, we shall win!" They bewitched the people and terrified them with a great display of magic. They cleverly made it appear to the entire gathering that the ropes and sticks had turned into live serpents, wriggling and writhing on the ground! Everyone was struck dumb with horror.

Moses was in a very critical situation. He was not there to show off, to gain celebrity status as a hero, or to demonstrate pride in his ethnicity, all of which are things that most subjugated people throughout the world attempt to do. Moses was there to be as transparent as possible, in order to infiltrate the divine attributes through this transparency. He was there to send people to God and not to himself. Therefore, he was fearful for the nation, not fearful of that nation or of what the magicians had done.

He waited for the magicians to throw first in order to give every single person in that nation a chance to become aware of his idolatry and false pride. He waited the necessary time for the people and magicians to glorify the idolatry of patriotism and nationalism. He then had to show them his inexistence, while giving them the slack to stand more securely on their illusory platform.

All of a sudden the Lord spoke to him: "Have no fear Moses; you shall surely win. Throw that which is in your right hand. It will swallow everything that they have faked here. What you have is real. Theirs are only magic tricks. A wizard shall not succeed no matter how much he may attain."

The moment his staff touched the ground, it became a huge snake, much bigger than those of the magicians, and began to swallow what they faked.

What the magicians had thrown in the arena was initially in their subconscious and was initially a delirious serpent in which they didn't believe, but in which they pretended to believe. The sorcery existed only in their imaginations and in the imaginations of those who were predisposed to accept these illusions. What was projected outside their state of mind was just an illusion that was fed by a temporary pride. In contrast, what Moses threw was a reality that was fed by life from the Creator. What happened back then was a duel between reality and lies.

Usually the iconoclast only removes an external idolatry, or he

138

only removes its internal existence. Moses calculated in such a way as to remove both internal and external idolatry at the same time. That is why he selected the national holiday for the contest in the Arena Zero. It was a choice that ensured Pharaoh's personal presence. It also led to an upwelling of patriotism and nationalism throughout the whole country. Moses had maneuvered them into experiencing the highest of highs so that their subsequent fall would be great enough to accomplish the destruction of both internal and external idolatry.

Consider how the Divine Media spoke so meticulously about that event. God did not say that the snake ate or swallowed the magicians' reptiles; He said that it swallowed what they faked. In other words, the magicians threw nothing more than ropes and sticks. It was only an illusion that these ropes and sticks became reptiles. When Moses threw his staff, it did not eat or swallow everything, but it only swallowed the fakery, camouflage, and illusions. The ropes and sticks remained on the ground as mere ropes and sticks. This was what really struck the magicians. In reality, Moses eliminated the multiple personalities from the magicians and from the nation, but he kept their real selves in place to experience the fear of this sudden awakening.

"The sorcerers fell down in prostration." By this statement, we understand that the magicians were originally standing or relying on camouflage to support their survival. Once Moses removed this camouflage from their state of consciousness, they suddenly experienced vertigo and fell down.

They bowed their heads and pronounced, "We believe in the Lord of the Universe, the Lord of Moses and Aaron." With this statement, we see that even though their prostration was initially involuntary, their subsequent confession was voluntary.

Pharaoh exploded with rage against the magicians and said:

139

"How dare you believe in him without my authorization? Verily, he is your master, the one who has taught you witchcraft. This is a plot you have contrived to turn the people out of the city. But you will see."

Introspective Exegesis

Q: That was a big event, but I'm just concerned about my psyche.

A: Now is the moment of your contest with Pharaoh's magicians. Notice that I didn't say with Pharaoh, who is in reality the ego's illusion. Today is the day of the internal revolution; today is the day of the internal coup-d'état. Now this coup-d'état has nothing to do with Pharaoh. It has nothing to do with changing the system, but it has to do with illusions.
You have emotions that are extrinsic; those extrinsic emotions were formed because of some audience other than the Sublimity occupying your consciousness. The accumulation of extrinsic emotions forms the existence of the ego. The ego is an epicenter, not the center, and the normalization of abnormality causes the existence of the illusions of the ego. Thus, we have the ego that is an epicenter, and we have its survival with false pretexts that are the illusions. Now in order to eliminate the ego, you have to deal first with its illusions.

Q: How far does this effort go?

A: This process is more passivity than activity. People rush to demonstrations. They rush to make a revolution to change a system etc. Yet, Pharaoh is inside them with his political philosophy, and they don't know that.

Q: What are the steps?

A: Never come with the idea of changing a regime. Never come with the idea of "We" and "Them." Never come with the idea that you're going to show them how much you are, because this is just bluffing yourself. Instead, come with the idea of how much you are not, and let the universal consciousness flow. Never come with the idea of rescuing your subjugated people from oppression; instead, come with idea of universality, even if it seems that your particular community has been inhumanly treated. Go for the universal common ground. Then, when you achieve your goal, you will spread love and mercy. If you neglect that, you might achieve your polarized goal, but later on you will find enemies instead of lovers.

Q: And then what

A: It seems it's a big mission, but it's very simple. Just shift the eyewitness from creatures to the Singularity in the same way that Moses did with the magicians. Just warn your illusions that are dragging you to the ego, i.e., Pharaoh. Just remind them about the power of the Creator, and avoid the ego defense mechanisms. It is just a reminder, and that's what the ego dislikes, and that's what Pharaoh hates.

Q: And then what?

A: If you are sincere with yourself, you will see how the illusions collapse and come into your favor, just like it eventually did with the magicians. Your passivity and your surrendering to the Sublimity will drain any external illusory force to your center, and that force becomes yours.

Q: I'm not quite sure of what you just said.

A: The illusions in the mind of the believer become reality, and reality in the mind of the disbeliever becomes illusions. Therefore, you should understand that illusions and reality are not

141

independent aspects in life. As you can see, the reptiles from the hand of the magicians and a reptile from Moses' hand were all reptiles, but the difference was in the state of consciousness of every pole. It was reality in Moses' mind, and it was fakery in the magicians' minds. In other words, it was reality in Moses' mind because the Sublimity was occupying his mind, and it was illusion in the magicians' minds because Pharaoh was occupying their minds. In the final analysis, the unique snake that swallows the fakery of the others was, in fact, reality swallowing illusions. Stated differently, Moses did not destroy the magicians; he gained them to his side. In other words, they joined the Oneness; they joined reality.

Q: Is that all about the reptiles?

A: This is the victory of metamorphosis against rigidity; it is the disappearance of rigidity in front of flexibility. Consider the snakes; they were all crawling and coiling, but the difference was in the states of consciousness. In Moses' psyche, it was surrender to the metamorphosis and the changes of the universe. In contrast, in the magicians' psyche, it was stiffness with a prearranged and fabricated metamorphosis. One pole was adapting itself to the changes of the external world, which was the case with Moses. In contrast, the magicians were attempting to convert the external world to their own agenda

"Of old We sent Moses, with Our signs, and an Authority manifest, to Pharaoh, Haman, and Korah; but they called (him) a sorcerer telling lies...Now when he brought them the truth, from Us, they said, 'Slay the sons of those who believe with him, and keep alive their females,' but the plots of unbelievers end in nothing but errors and delusions!"

CHAPTER 14

The more concentrated a system becomes globally, ultimately forming one single vertex that is completely based on mammonism, the more it becomes driven by the forces of evil, and the more its citizens becomes centered in that vortex.

We see how a person's entire life is centered in the work nexus; he is so influenced by the company's policies that he becomes an automaton and a piece of robotic machinery that is totally deprived of its own intention, its own emotions, and its entire existence.

Under Pharaoh's regime, people were treated inhumanely; they were his slaves. People didn't have time for themselves. Their nights and their days belonged to Pharaoh. They were forced to do hard labor, building huge monuments and structures such as the pyramids. On top of that, Pharaoh's soldiers were lashing them with whips under a very hot sun.

On the other hand, the one who was financing and controlling the economy was Korah, which he did through the Federal Reserve. Besides ever harsher persecution, a propaganda war was unleashed against Moses, who was for free trade but against usury. One of Pharaoh's chiefs had particularly excelled in that game of slander.

Now let us consider the think tanks, which were also known as policy institutes. They were private bodies that conducted research and engaged in advocacy in areas such as social policy, political strategy, economics, science and technological issues, industrial and business policies, and the military. Their primary role was to sway popular and political opinion in directions useful to the think tanks' corporate sponsors. These think tanks were staffed by erudite researchers who produced editorials, TV news pieces, papers, media releases, legislative material, etc. They represented the corporate philosophy of economic rationalism, which favored the corporate takeover of all public enterprises, from health care and education to water and electricity, and which favored an agenda that included decreasing or abolishing government regulations on big business, decreasing corporate taxes and taxes for the rich, destroying the unions and increasing corporate profits. The IMF, the World Bank, GATT, NAFTA, APEC, FTAA, and WTO all took their cues from these think tanks.

In that society, a baby was born and raised for the purpose of serving a production-oriented economy. From an early age onward, a child was victimized by an image that was previously inserted into his mind without his awareness. This child didn't go to school to learn knowledge, but to conserve and reinforce the image that was previously implanted inside him. As such, all his efforts were for the sake of seeking refuge in the work nexus of the consumer-producer system and for the sake of his personal obsession with his almighty capital, even at the cost of jeopardizing his spiritual life. His thoughts were centered in the work nexus and consumerism. Therefore, the ripples of his thoughts spread from the center of the work nexus to the periphery of consumerism. His happiness was measured by his degree of consumption, and his sadness was measured by the degree of his inability to consume, i.e., his deprivation.

When and if he bothered to reflect about this system in which he was enmeshed, this only provoked fear and a gladiatorial mentality, because the system could only provide him with a fabricated, illusory, and collective pseudo- uniqueness that did little to satisfy his hunger for that true uniqueness of being of which he had already been deprived. At best, the identity offered to the citizen by the consumer- producer system was only a position at work or the ownership of some material possessions. This identity was not really his own, but was an identity that was owned and assigned to him by the system.

The decisions in Pharaoh's government were spawned from the axis of mammonism. This axis coincided perfectly with the center of the citizen's thoughts. The ripples of corporations from this center spread toward the periphery within the government through the vehicle of usury, and those ripples affected the thoughts of those individuals who were subject to that doctrine.

There were close to thirty economic indicators in Pharaoh's government. All of them reflected or diagnosed the health of the economy. There was, however, a certain interference with and manipulation of the figures produced by those economic

indicators. Take, for example, Consumer Confidence. Its surveys reflected the national mood about current business conditions and measured consumers' degree of optimism. As a second example, consider Consumer Credit, which measured the amount of installment credit that consumers had outstanding, which was the differential between new credits extended minus credits paid down. Finally, Gross Domestic Product (GDP) was the hallmark of the Commerce Department's effort to provide a comprehensive accounting of product demand and of the factors of production. These three economic indicators were built as a system of interlocking sector accounts.

Now, our main concern is not with the release of these posterior economic indicators and how they supposedly gauged the health of the external economy. Rather, we are concerned with their anterior existence within the psyche of the population.

Take, for instance, Consumer Confidence; it interfered with a human's optimism. It may sound like its numbers were an objective measure of a spontaneous urge from a person. However, this dogmatic urge to consume and to buy was a strategy provoked by the magicians and their commercials, in order to give the consumer the goal of achieving an illusory rank in society by the acquisition of materials. Failure to do so meant succumbing to a dramatic fall in which a person would become oblivious, sad and isolated from the admired society. Therefore, in reality, when they used the words "national mood," the mood of business was initially spawned from the mood of the individual, and this mood of the individual was not as spontaneous as it seemed. Instead, it was an implanted

doctrine of consumerism that became second nature and that resulted from a "teleguided" pseudo-spontaneity.

Consumer Credit was also known by a pseudonym, which was Measuring Consumer Debt Stress. This calculated measure was provided by the Federal Reserve Board. This measurement led to more rigidity in terms of affiliated ratios, such as Holders of Consumer Installment Debt and such labyrinthine indices as Consumer Credit Delinquency, Consumer Bankruptcies, and the Willingness-To-Lend measure. This last mentioned measure indexed the extent of developing consumer credit problems and the restrictions that banks took in terms of providing loans and issuing credit cards.

The GDP used words like "Product Demand" and "Factors of Production." In reality, it was supply and demand, not in terms of monetary counterbalance, but in terms of the demand for products and the factor of production. However, before becoming that, it was a stimulus and response within the person's psyche. The stimulus was intuitive when it came to necessities, and it was implanted when it came to a pleasure- seeking that was induced

146

through propaganda. In either case, the response, which was the supply (products) that was supposed to synchronize with the stimulus, was completely false, because propaganda converted pleasures into perceived necessities.

On the internal front, regarding the three data and how they affected the emotions in a juxtaposed manner, we first look at the GDP. When we say a factor of production, we are saying a factor of consumption, and if we say a factor of consumption, we are saying that which spurred an individual to the acquisition of the material world. If we say what spurred the consumer, we are talking about the implantation of desires that were then converted into perceived necessities. With regard to Consumer Confidence, when we say the mood of the businesses, we are saying the optimism of the consumer and his joyful temptation. Finally, Consumer Credit referenced the mood of the consumer's emotions during this process, which reflected his state of suspension of his emotions during this process, because the emotions had become the property of the banking system during that length of time, during the journey.

Of note, both the GDP and Consumer Confidence indices were released either by the Commerce Department or by a simple institution from a university, but the Consumer Credit numbers were released by the Federal Reserve Board. Why was that? We shall see.

Let's narrow it down to the departure point, the destination, and the journey within the two wavelengths. The departure point was the optimism of the consumer to achieve something with obsession, which represented consumer confidence. Although it was an origin, it was preceded by a clandestine dynamism of consumption, which was the stimulus. Now, here came the role of one aspect of the GDP, i.e., the achievement of the material world, which was the response to the stimulus. (So far we have

147

been talking about the unperceived, implanted seeds before the departure point, then the departure point, and finally the destination, but we have not yet talked about the journey.)

Now, what was the supposedly comfortable roadmap with its resting stations that lined the way from the departure point to the destination, and what was the provided vehicle during that journey? The roadmap with its resting stations was the credit installment with which the consumer seemed comfortable. He seemed comfortable because he was dominated by his obsession to reach the destination, while all the time ignoring the unexpected mental and financial punishment that would accrue in case of delinquency during his journey. With regard to the provided vehicle, in reality, there was no vehicle because it was a skidding process without motion. Instead, the consumer's payment of interest rates was fueling a vehicle that did not move or didn't even exist because it was a process of stagnation.

The consumer had decided to achieve his happiness no matter what. He wanted to achieve an acquisition; he wanted to achieve a destination. At that point, the banking system came with a strategy that was called "buy now and pay later." So the destination became shortened to such a point that there was no distance between the departure point and the destination. In other words, the time of the desire itself became the time of acquisition. (However, it's totally God's prerogative to use words such as, "You want something to be, and it is.")

At this point, there is something that we have to emphasize, which is that there was an unknown trade here; the acquisition was handy for sure, but the heart belonged to the banking system. By the heart, we mean that the flow of emotions during that period of time was controlled by the banking system. It gave a person the material world, and the person gave it his heart. It promised people, "Don't worry; you'll be happy." As people

148

were driven by a desperate consumption to fulfill their desires and fantasies, they were enslaved by the borrow-now-and-pay-later mechanism, resulting in their total subservience to the usury and interest rates of Korah.

GI stood for Government Issue; a GI was something that was issued by the government, like a machine or a manufactured product, and then ultimately became the property of the government. These were soldiers of the war. They didn't think; the government thought on their behalf. They didn't feel; the government supposedly felt on their behalf. If they ever had any intuitive sympathy, they had to suspend that sympathy and instead vicariously borrow hostility from the government. If they ever had any compassion, they had to eliminate that compassion and instead vicariously borrow harshness from the government. They were automatons.

The financial center, whose goddess was the Federal Reserve, was one axis, and the thoughts of the citizens within the work nexus were another axis, although the latter axis perfectly synchronized with the former axis. Such a flow consisted of two concentric circles, positioned in a conic form (like a pyramid, but circular); the vertex with a small circle was at the top, and this circle was constant. The large section was at the bottom where its axis coincided with that of the vertex, and this large circle was in a constant flux, being either in expansion or in constriction. The manipulation of the debt mechanism was spawned from the axis of the small circle of the top, and the manipulation of people's emotions transpired from the axis of the large section in the bottom flow, either toward the periphery with a controlled expansion or back toward the axis with a controlled constriction.

The ripples from the center, while undulating toward the periphery, constituted a battlefield manned by citizens who were

149

civilian soldiers. Those GIs didn't carry guns, but they carried something more dangerous than guns. They carried stress, anxiety, and a constant gladiatorial mentality.

In the Pentagon, the government had as its agenda to engineer a war on the battlefield. Before it could send its soldiers to war, the Pentagon had to prepare them in a training camp, and then it supplied its GIs with sufficient weaponry and a uniform of combat that allowed them to camouflage themselves. In the case of confrontation and the visible wounding of these soldiers, they had the privilege of being transported to the nearest hospital.

With regard to financial prospects, Korah had his fiscal agenda. Before he sent his civilian soldiers, i.e., consumers, to the battlefield of the consumer-producer system, he had to train them. This training was initially accomplished through his magicians, who instituted a basic training program utilizing the cubic box (TV) in the individual's own house. In this way, the civilian soldiers were armed with ideas of consumer consumption to the point that those ideas became an obsession and that obsession became a form of hypnotherapy. The uniform with which Korah supplied his civilian soldiers was nothing more than a pajama of somnambulism. If these civilian soldiers experienced any irritation of their cells, and doubtless there was irritation of their cells, e.g., stress, depression, anxiety, and chronic back pain caused by mental spasm in the battlefield of the consumer-producer system, then those civilian soldiers were wounded with invisible injuries, which were worse than the visible injuries sustained by the Pentagon's GIs. These civilian soldiers didn't get the same privilege as the GIs in terms of transportation to the hospital; instead, they had to transport themselves.

Statistically speaking, more than 75% of Pharaoh's population consulted doctors (psychologists or psychiatrists) for psychological distress.

The Federal Reserve controlled interest rates by either increasing or decreasing them one quarter of a percent at a time, which affected transportation, mortgages, loans, etc. In turn, these fluctuations in interest rates caused fluctuations in hearts, leading to either happiness or sadness. As such, a person's emotional state and level of contentment were controlled by the Federal Reserve.

We can now understand why Korah was waging war against Moses, i.e., because Moses was for free trade and against usury. Moses was for trade that flowed freely between people, not for manipulated trade. Moses was for intuitive democracy, not the "teleguided" democracy that was controlled by monocracy.

Introspective Exegesis

Q: You mentioned something about ripples from the center toward the periphery; would you explain what this circle is and what that cycle is?

A: The circle is the periphery that is sealed by the consumer-producer system, and the cycle refers to those participants in that process. You have desirable products from corporations, and then you have magicians in the corporate-sponsored media tricking people. (How can one implant desires in people's psyches, and how can these desires be converted into necessities?) Then you have the consumer who is a victim of those sectors; at the end, you have the Federal Reserve—the god who is the big manipulator of the economy and of people's emotions.

Q: Getting back to my psyche...

A: Try to distinguish the difference between property and deprivation in terms of time. True property is primarily inside your mind and is related to your time, your emotions. If you own your emotions, you own everything external in the material world. If you are deprived of your emotions, you are deprived of everything in the external world, even if the acquisition seems handy to you.

Q: Would you comment on the words "property" and "deprivation" in terms of time?

A: Do you remember the dimension and the climax? With regard to the physical encounter between a male and a female, and with regard to food on the table, do you remember the dimension? In other words, within those actions, before reaching the climax, something is developed along the way. It is the same thing when it comes to the acquisition of something from the material world. The norms of life require that you have to cross segments of time before reaching your acquisition, and when you are crossing those segments of time, you are crossing dimensions in space. When you are crossing those dimensions, you are developing the unknown; you are developing your emotions. Your emotions are you, and you are the emotions, and that is truly your existence. Now, when you buy something before its time, in other words, you can't afford it, but someone is making it available to you before its time while suspending the flow of your emotions, that segment between the time you sign off for the credit installment to the time of hopefully the final payment, in reality, that time does not belong to you. If that time does not belong to you, your emotions do not belong to you, and if your emotions do not belong to you, this means that there is a big segment deducted from your age and from your eternity.

Getting back to our topic, when the banking system shortens your distance by making an acquisition handy before its time, that distance has the potential flow of your emotions in time and space. Because of your attachment to your obsession, that attachment is suspending the flow of your emotions. It is obstructing your absorption from the universe. It is blinding you from seeing true nature and from accepting the law of possibilities, because all you see is your obsession, and all you trust is the banking system that is taking the place of God. In addition to that and speaking about equalization, all regimes without exception tried throughout the pages of history to equalize the inequality between or among people. They have never and will never succeed, because they have no clue about the true existence. In this modern life, they speak about the upper class, the lower class, and the middle class. In reality, none of them exists under such a regime. With regard to the upper class, I refer to wealth that is seen as criminality in the eyes of the poor, which is not to say that this characterization is always true. As a result of this perception by the poor, the rich often live in fear. In contrast, the upper class often sees poverty as fomenting a possible attack by the poor against them and their possessions, which again is not to say that this perception is always true, and the rich also see the poor living with the hope of revolt. Finally, the middle class; it is an illusion that they can possess their desired objects and hopefully reach upper class status through credit. In other words, they can reach wealth through deprivation. Look at that mockery!

In contrast to the previous metaphors, The Divinity spoke only about the upper class and the lower class. The Divinity never mentioned the middle class whatsoever, but that inaccessible symmetry of inequality is, in fact, the territory that belongs to both the upper and lower classes without penetration.

Q: Without penetration? How's that?

A: That territory is the territory of trade and interaction between the upper and lower classes. This is where the sentimental emotions reside and need to be exercised. It is a zone of no interference with the results. Primarily, it is concern, compassion, generosity, sympathy and so forth; it is the duty of conscience that brings those two classes to the arena of togetherness. Once he consciously expresses his emotions, he is in someway stabilizing every aspect of the ecosystem. When that happens, there is the creation of jobs, free trade, transnational corporations, recruiting, schools, etc. In other words, all these external infrastructures are built and linked to people's psyches and feelings.

Throughout all the divine books, none of them ever mentions the word "unemployment" or the words "job creation;" these are only fabricated words of the external regimes to keep the population in a state of phantasmagoria. The Divinity speaks about charity, generosity, care, love, etc. Why? It is because every structure in the external world is built according to the internal impulses of each class, and the thread linking the upper class and the lower class follows the same trace. In a society where emotions are programmed, feelings are suspended, and sentiments are stocked, the upper class is, in reality, devouring the lower class. That doesn't mean, however, that the lower class is completely innocent. In the final analysis, where is the vehicle that links the upper class with the lower class? There is no vehicle other than greed, a constant state of alert, security, cameras, and no trespassing signs (violators will be prosecuted). The rich live with fear because they feel the poor are tempted to attack them, and the poor live with the temptation to revolt against and attack the rich whenever there is an opportune occasion that can be seized.

CHAPTER 15

There is Moses' existence within the individual's psyche; there is Moses' existence within the siege of a hegemonic nation. In addition to that, we are going to see Moses' exclusion from the organizations. Furthermore, we will see his position in the macrocosm, despite his existence in the microcosm within every person. We will also see how this enigmatic role functions in the whole cosmos. This is the deconstruction of the institution.

On the front page of that morning's newspaper (actually it was not on paper; it was a tablet), which has one copy here in the terrestrial world in the heart of every individual if he wishes to read it and a parallel existence in the celestial world; we find the following engraved words:

"Moses asked the Creator to give him some words of extolment with which to praise Him, the Universal Consciousness. God said to Moses, "Say there is no god except God."

Moses, surprised by this simplicity, then replied, "Oh my Lord, everybody says that. I am looking for something very unique for me only."

God told him in return, "Oh Moses, if the seven heavens and what they contain and the seven earths and what they contain were put in one balance and 'No god except God' was put in one balance, 'No god except God' would outweigh the rest."

The hegemonic system with its global monopoly was built in such a way that if you tried to fight it, you only reinforced its efficiency against you. This was because the system was a network and couldn't independently function apart from the participation of people's emotions. (Obviously, we are not talking about emotions that represent the true self of the individual; instead, we are talking about superfluous emotions that were apart from the neural net.)

The system was a doctrine in the minds of the populace that enabled the political structure to function smoothly, and the whole network was generated by a hidden popularity and prestige in such a way that if a citizen got out of that circle, he felt oblivious and sad. Within such a framework, the system infused people with a pseudo self-esteem, and their pseudo self-esteem synchronized with the system. Their emotions turned out to be eccentric and precarious with regard to the nucleus of the self, and they were subject to influence from an externality. However, when people craved self-esteem to prove their participation in this existence, their extraneous and precarious emotions, in reality, reinforced the system against them, despite the fact that their emotions were inside them. In other words, they were slaves of their own emotions and had a false self-esteem; they had emotions inside them of which they were totally deprived.

Moses' potential frequency existing within everybody was not a part of this system with its network, even if it seemed to live under that system. This frequency's identity was the cane—the symbol of humility before the Sublimity, which is the only distinctive antithesis to the Authoritarian System. In contrast, those citizens' identity was self-esteem—vanity. That's why they were part of the network. The whole country was obsessed with an extreme devotion to and adoration of celebrities, actors, singers, athletes, politicians, TV anchors, columnists, and talk show hosts. That was the way to be in constant connection with the admired society and to gain, or at least to simulate, a celebrity status.

Throughout history and especially in modern society, men have been actively fighting for human rights, civil liberties, and so forth. This is not to discredit those people's efforts, even though they could be loyal in the face of the many atrocities generated by Authoritarian Systems.

The origin of any chaos is from a human's psyche, so before the appearance of any external problem in the objective world, there was already turmoil in the psyche of the human— the subjective world.

When people are dealing with these problems by creating organizations, associations, and religious institutions, they are really dealing with the symptoms and not with the causes. This method of dealing with the symptoms creates more symptoms and distances the person from the causes. The true process is meant to deal with the causes, not with the symptoms, and it can only be enlightened by an effort from individuality, not from a collectivity, not through intellectualism, not by decrees or bylaws. It cannot be enlightened by dry repertoires on arid shelves, which is the modus operandi of non-profit organizations, symbolic organizations, and religious institutions.

This process is meant to originate from an individual's breath—I mean an individual's intention—with his effort of exhaling and to spread as if with the wind. When it is centered with a name of a person or a name of an organization, it becomes hampered by rules, ways, time, and space; it finally ends up consuming its unknown and otherwise fruitful results.

If one's center of attention is external, whether from a prestigious person, i.e., an activist, a philosopher, a religious person, etc. or from an organization, even if it is the name of a religion, then all these methods suspend and consume the next stage. It is another small pyramid where people stare at the vertex of a stagnated goodness.

Now before the appearance of an organization, intention was the property of every individual with a centrifugal force, permitting everyone to exist, his existence being his participation with his individual intention, not the collective intention. His individual intention is not restricted within time, space, or manner. It can be anytime, anywhere, and anyhow. After the appearance of an organization, an individual's intention becomes deprivation and the property of the organization. The individual's intention becomes suspended with a centripetal echo from outside and no longer touches the spirit. Instead, it is touching the extraneous interior emotions that are not part of the nucleus. Furthermore, the time, place, and manner of goodness become the property of the organization, and this is followed by the deprivation of individuality.

The survival of an organization is either through a financial prospect or through protection by some prestigious one. Are there any exceptions left among the gentle people who are sincere and do good for humanitarian purposes? My answer to that is that these people are surely gentle, but the organization is an idolatry of paralysis. Therefore, its individuals are subject to fall into the work force. What I mean is that, primordially speaking, the duty of conscience includes both the instant decision of a person and the involvement of his sentiments from his heart. After the appearance of the organization, the individual duty of the conscience becomes restricted to his instant decision; it completely excludes the participation of his heart. That's why you see a lot of institutions, organizations, policies, and rules, and yet everybody is miserable.

If you let goodness spread through your renunciation and transparency, the principles keep spreading and flowing; you can

158

then seize them and share them. If you center them within an organization, their unlimited reach is delayed, paralyzed, and stagnated at some point; it is another type of monopoly. For some reason, people love to name their protocol, and they love to be named. They love to make history.

Now, let's get back to the breaking news.

Moses was looking for his autonomous uniqueness, which was not to be shared with anybody. God told him to continue developing his uniqueness under the Oneness of universality. However, the most important thing hadn't been said. From the rigidity of the system to its bureaucracy, from a financial organization to a non-profit organization, and from an organized religion to a religious institution, individuality was blocked. That was why Moses was looking for his autonomy. He was directed to the center of gravity.

As we know or we don't know, there are seven heavens. In some teachings, there are seven cosmoses. Moses was on the sixth heaven.

Introspective Exegesis

Q: What was Moses' question with regard to deconstruction?

A: The process of deconstructionism in the eyes of the philosophers is, first of all, the deconstruction of the collective institution while ignoring the individual characterization. Secondly, these philosophers focus on deconstruction without any alternative solution except human instinct. This brings people to the philosophy of nihilism.

In contrast to the previous view, the true meaning of deconstructionism is harmony with the universal flow. Cosmic consciousness is comprised of two phases; the first phase is the process of deconstruction of the individual institution, which is

the confession of "There is no god." The second phase is the reconstruction without a prearranged narcissistic agenda, which is the follow up confession of "Except God." It does not mean that there is a time that is spawned between the first and the second phases; instead, one phase overlaps the other. There is no before and after; there is no without and no within.

Q: We cannot deny that Moses was aware of that before asking God that question, or at least we assume that he knew. Still what was the reason behind his question?

A: If we go through a deep investigation, we discover that one of the reasons that Moses spoke, and the manner in which he spoke, was coming out of suffocation, out of pressure, out of rigidity, out of complexity, out of subjugation, out of collectivity. These were all caused by his surroundings and this terrestrial constriction. The second reason was that the majority of people were brainwashed and that there was nowhere to escape. All people thought alike; all people spoke on behalf of a corporation or an organization, and those institutions were all restricted in time, space, and manner. These were the basic reasons Moses wanted to be withdrawn from the rigidity of the system to the cosmic consciousness and its splendor. Now do you know who was asking this question?
This is the reality inside you that is manifested all the time; this is the reality of your autonomous uniqueness that is searching for the Universal Singularity, just as thirst searches for water. This question is manifested every moment within you. Now, there is the possibility of hearing this dialogue, or I should say of hearing this question or not. Everybody has this question manifested, which is the fact of looking for the self. However, most people prevent and misdirect the question, and not everybody knows where to find the self. The majority of people find the self in a corporation. Others find the self in an organization. Others find the self in religious

institutions. As such, all they can hear is the echo of their obsession reflected from the labyrinth in which they reside.

Getting back to the noble gentleman, when God told him, "Say, 'there is no god except God,'" Moses was aware of that, but he was provoking the shifting question from the physical world to the metaphysical world. That's why he said, "My God, everybody says that; I'm looking for something unique." It's not because he found it small, but he just wanted to show everybody's existence in the celestial world.

Q: I'm still thinking about center and epicenter in terms of the emotions.

A: Imagine that you have the potential center of a sphere within you; yet, you haven't centered yourself in this core because you are still denying your state of humility in front of the Sublimity. At that point, when everything rotates and flows around you, those rotations are, in reality, events that are happening. Your emotions flow with the same precarious norm around the nucleus, which exists as a potential but hasn't yet been developed. Those extrinsic emotions are you, and you are those emotions. They spin, and you spin; they rotate, and you rotate. They cause you dizziness, but, in reality, they make you feel obliviously distant from the self, distant from the core, and depressed. All you find yourself doing is spending unnecessary time searching for yourself. In contrast, when you are in the center of this sphere by accepting the state of humility before the Sublimity, you are concentric with the Sublimity and the whole universe, which was in reality God's response to Moses when He said, "There is no god except God." At that point, your emotions are intrinsic. In reality, they dissolve within your behavior like sugar in water. We don't even have the right to say they are intrinsic. You feel the self and the harmony with nature.

Q: Is there any physical example?

A: Imagine a spinning circle, or I should say a sphere. When you are in an independent center of this circle, are you affected by the rotation of this circle or by what is flowing in this circle?

Q: No.

A: Now consider yourself as an epicenter or an epicycloid, far from the center, on a radius stretched by distance. Are you affected by the rotation of this circle or what flows within the circle?

Q: Yes, I would be.

A: In the latter case, you are affected, controlled, and absorbed. In other words, you are subordinated. In the former case, you are affecting, controlling, and absorbing. In the latter case, you a slave; in the former case, you are the master of yourself.

Q: What is the distance from the core?

A: The distance is the gap that can be caused by unconsciousness or mechanical actions while one is an automaton, but it gets severe when denial of humility and the seeking of vanity take place. As far as you are concerned, it is the distance of the radius from the center. Here, the spinning and the rotation severely affect you proportionate to your distance from the nucleus.

Q: When you talked about institutions, organizations, civil liberties, etc., why did you portray them as being unfruitful, being disadvantageous, or perhaps not fully harmonizing with life in general?

A: Getting back to the center, picture yourself in that center. Now, picture yourself on a small tiny radius with one million micro units of distance from that center. It's like no distance. Now, move that radius with one million micro units of radian (angle in the center of the sphere), which is a tiny arch forming an angle from the center in that sphere. Now stretch that same radius to an unlimited reach toward an infinite periphery. You

realize that as far as you go with that radius and as big as the degree of the radian seems to expand, nevertheless it doesn't change the number of degrees, but it does change the dimension of the arch. Do you now see what kind of effort you provide when you are in the center in terms of rotating that micro-unit of radius—yourself? There is almost no effort; it's like the motion of a finger, maybe less than that. Now picture yourself at the end of an unlimited reach of a radius far from the center, and see what kind of effort you have to provide and what distance you have to go to accomplish certain things within that arch. See how precarious you have become? Not only that, see how exposed you are to the danger of the pivot of the sphere and how precarious you have become!

It is exactly the same process as having an abnormality rectified by institutions and organizations in the external world, i.e., the objective world, while being far from the individual's center of gravity. When the abnormality is rectified in the internal world, i.e., the subjective world or human psyche, it's almost impossible to compare.

If you measure the degree of the radian, whether from the center of the sphere or from an epicenter, you find it is the same. It is 25 degrees close to the center, and it is the same 25 degrees far from the center. However, when you measure the arch within the center, which does not even exist, and you measure the arch from an epicenter toward the periphery, you find an immense difference. As far as you are from the center, that's how gigantic the dimension of the arch becomes. This is similar to the solution.

It is one solution but with a different approach, as we shall see.

Q: I'm curious about it.

A: From a subatomic standpoint, the world, or I should say the universe, is in constant metamorphosis. Our feelings and our emotions are likewise in a constant flux. This book, for example, that is in your hand is different from what it was a few hours ago in terms of its particles. Now, when an organization or an institution is dealing with the epitome of an abnormality that is externalized and is the reflection of what was previously in a person's psyche, the organization or institution is, in reality, dealing with time. Once it finds a solution to that problem, it has found a solution to something that happened years and years ago, because by the time it supposedly finds a solution, the world has already moved with the speed of light, and the emotions will follow the same trace. At that point, they find themselves in contradiction with what they had already institutionalized, and then they accept this contradiction and swallow it, because they are afraid to show their inadequacy and their initial paradoxical decisions. Then the false pretext comes when they say, "We know that the system is not perfect, but at least we are not anarchists." Well, they could be right somewhere. In other words, there is flagrant anarchism, which is the case in some third-world countries, including among them the pashas and the sultans of societies. There is a camouflaged anarchism, which is the case with the high-tech countries. In the final analysis, they are all the same.

Q: You mentioned the word "concentric" a lot, maybe more than a lot. Sometimes you refer to it as the link between a human being and God, and sometimes you refer to it as the universe or the macrocosm. Are you able to define the difference if there is one, or is it the same?

A: Be careful. The word "concentric" is primarily with God.

Being concentric with the universe is the result of the previous axis.

Q: Is it possible to list some similarities between these principles that synchronize the microcosm and the macrocosm?

A: Gravity is within all things and affects all things; there is no escape from its force. It cannot be altered or interrupted by any presence or counterforce. It controls energy, as well as matter; time slows down, and space is warped by its pull; it creates order from chaos in structuring the galaxies, the stars, and the planets. Now, do you see the power of gravity?

Q: It is gigantic!

A: Yet, the greatest force of gravity is emptiness; gravity is created by a vacuum, another word for emptiness. Now, here comes the symmetry between the microcosm, which is the human being, and the macrocosm, which is the universe. The greatest force in the human being is his center of gravity, and his center of gravity is his voluntary worship—his humility before the Sublimity. At the same time, his center of gravity is his emptiness, his renunciation of self-attributes, and his divestitures of the ideal of the ego "L'ideal du moi". Once the ego, in its vanity, starts identifying with cultural, territorial division, then wealth, beauty, knowledge, corporations, organizations, etc.—all of the above stand as obstacles and obstructions between him and the flow of the universal energy.

We are confronted in our lives by weaknesses, we feel inadequate etc. These feelings of insecurity are not there for a bad reason, they are there to let a human being be in touch with the self vis-à-vis his real existence—to be centered and concentric first with the Absolute and then with the universe while being in that state of flux. But because of the human's misconception, he wants to

165

escape this reality to overcome his insecurity and fear with a supposed security. Now here comes the appraisal process of: "I want to prove to myself how much I am, and I am..."

Q: I am...?

A: When you are positioned in the "I" there is no image, and the fact that there is no image scares you and deprives you of the credit, because the credit at this time is flowing in the ether and keeps you wondering, searching, navigating, and exploring. That is the state of metamorphose, and yet it is your beneficial state of absorption. Nonetheless, that credit belongs to someone—the Absolute, so you, through your false analysis, want to seize it, come up to the visible world, and claim it, in order to give yourself a sense of security. At that point, here comes the formation of the ego with its constituents.

When the "I" doesn't accept voluntarily the state of humility with worship—effacement, it is subject to a sort of vortex—turmoil in the mind. When you look at the diameter of this vortex, you find the top larger than the bottom in terms of how it seems in the eyes of the victimized person, i.e., an expansion through his false perception. Once this whirlwind gets to the bottom, it starts getting narrowed—in terms of how it becomes constriction and starts ejecting—ejaculating what is in the bottom, such as the sand or the dirt are ejaculated by a physical whirlwind. However, in reality, it is an entropic and metastable psychological energy—the state of volition that the concerned person had stored extrinsically but from which he doesn't benefit. Now look at the bottom, and visualize how the "I" starts transferring its energy to the ego while still being deprived. Once the ego is formed with all its constituents, there is a momentary stability that is followed by turmoil. Here the ego experiences more free fall than before, and then it starts to reinforce itself with pride and vanity. This is the moment when the ego starts to stare—in some cases at the external government as

166

though it were sacred, e.g., when it is a protagonist that is driven by nationalism, and in other cases it stares worshipfully at non-profit organizations etc, e.g., when it is an antagonist driven by activism. Yet, in both cases, it ignores completely the return to the self—the "I."

Q: My last question to you about Moses' presence in the sixth cosmos? I am very curious about this mystery.

A: I will remind you of that.

CHAPTER 16

Holidays are another strategy of obscurantism. If people wish for deconstruction, they have to think about the days in which their happiness is spawned. The whole year has been compressed into one day; their role is to decompress.

The word "democracy" is a hypnotic, collective word that the majority merges into in order to compensate for the lack of an individual's true democracy.

The nation goes into a supposed state of precision in any given set of circumstances, and that precision is seen as advancement, as an achievement. This precision narrows down the whole into the few and the few into a singularity. We have a day for everything. We have a day for love; we have a day for one's birthday; we have a day for mother; we have a day for women; we have a day for father; we have the day for amnesty; we have a day for forgiveness etc. The precision is that the one day of celebration results in 364 days of condolences. In other words, the nation is not orbiting around a 365-day calendar; it is instead orbiting around one day, and the remaining 364 days are pending days and are days of slavery and exploitation where everybody is waiting. Everybody is staring; everybody is waiting in line; everybody is expecting. Meanwhile, death is approaching.

It happened in a seaside town where they had been prohibited from fishing on the Sabbath day. Fishing was tolerated on other days, and the practice of not fishing on the Sabbath was usually observed. This routine resulted in a habitual pattern in their daily activity, a pattern in which all the people were driven by a habit that was restricted within time and space. For some unusual reason, the fish stopped coming up to the water channels and pools on all days with the exception of the Sabbath day. On the Sabbath, the day of prohibition, the fish continued to come up to the water channels and pools and did so openly. At this point, some people, a section among that community, probably thought it was the right time to use their stratagem. They prepared their nets and containers on the day before the Sabbath and did so in such a way that they could hold the fish. The next day, on the Sabbath, the fish were eventually caught. On that precise day (Sabbath), they were supposedly respecting the prohibition, and the day after the Sabbath they would pick up the fish.

The community (the nation) was divided into three sections. The first section was comprised of the breakers of the Divine Law. The second included those people who felt responsibility and who rushed to cure diseases and to prevent cataclysms by preaching to others against violating the prohibition. The third section was composed of the lurkers who had a personal interest in these kinds of tribulations.

Introspective Exegesis

Q: Was there any reason behind the prohibition against fishing on the Sabbath?

A: This prohibition against fishing on the Sabbath was related to the dimensions of time and space by which humans are habitually characterized, which in this case were the Sabbath and the shore. It was one among other methods to exercise self- control with regard to time and space vis-à-vis the Invisibility. Thereby, these people of the town, if they respected the prohibition, would surely develop their will power and their strength of character

169

based on the Invisibility and not based on pressure from a visibly external other.

Q: With regard to the emotions...

A: As was previously mentioned, extrinsic emotions represent the ego, an epicenter, and intrinsic ones represent the "I," the center of gravity of human. Sometimes you don't realize when you are in the center of your time, which makes you the master of your time, and sometimes you are in the epicenter of your time, which makes you a slave to your time. What drags a person from being in the center to the epicenter is not necessarily anything bad; it is the routine, and that routine is in Pharaoh's hand.

Q: It's a little foggy.

A: You are surprised by some good feeling; yet, you completely ignore the source of that feeling. From where is it coming? There is a memory trace encoded from that whole situation. Afterwards and unconsciously, you attribute those feelings to that day when you felt good. You attribute those feelings to that moment and to your involvement with whatever was going on. Then that day, that moment, and that involvement become a whole package of precision, which is a memory trace. At some other time, you will attempt to gain that same ambiance and pleasant feeling by attributing the situation to that same day on the calendar, and you then think you are getting the same feeling again.

Now, the first spontaneous feeling that you originally had was one that you did not program. You did not prearrange it; it just happened that day at that moment, and it could have been the result of other unknown factors that had nothing to do with that exact day. That feeling, in reality, was true because your eyes were innocently facing the horizon of non-expectation without any prearranged agenda. In contrast, the second feeling, the one that you predetermined, prearranged, and attributed to that day and to your involvement is not real because your eyes are no longer facing the horizon of nothingness. Your eyes are only facing your expectation, and you think you are having some happiness. Actually, you are simulating happiness with a reactivated memory.

Q: How's that?

A: A reactivated memory is retracing a date, and a day in the year is a segment from eternity. In this world, you are crossing galaxies with your intentions and behaviors in the terrestrial world before they become visions in the metaphysical world, as will be explained later. This process is achieved by planting the seeds of goodness, not by simulating the crops. However, when you stand still with a calendar date through the retrieval of your memories, you are, in reality, skating in one place and simulating a feeling that does not even exist.

Q: And why not?

A: Try to understand. A few minutes ago, or maybe a few seconds ago, your feelings were different than they are now. When you try to grasp a memory of certain feelings through the process of retrieval, you are simulating a feeling, and that feeling brings you back to a particular date and situation in your psyche. In contrast, the situations in the external world, in reality, are never repeated, even if they do seem alike. Each situation means something different from one moment to another and from one person to another. Therefore, in the final analysis, the situations outside you are flowing and are different from one moment to another, giving you the potential to navigate in the ether while bringing different beauties from the galaxies.

171

Here you are creating stagnation in your psyche; the stagnation of your emotions becomes contrary to the flow of the universe. Then comes stress, and you have no idea of its origin. One moment you find yourself saying, "Of course, I'm having fun," and another moment saying, "No matter how I try to be happy, there is always someone who tries to spoil my day, to spoil my party, etc."

Q: I can confess to that.

A: Now, that one particular day will supposedly secure a constant feeling, and that feeling has a day on the calendar. Once it becomes known and named, it creates a precision, and that precision becomes the focus of the contemplator, which is you. Now, because of the fear of the scattering and the possible loss of that feeling, a person wants to create an anniversary. If he does, then he has narrowed and reduced a day that had every possible sentiment and that was originally flowing eternally with the laws of the galaxies into a very tiny day. Let's create a day that symbolizes love; let's memorialize our birthdays; let's create a specific day to express sympathy to our mothers; let's create a specific day to express sympathy to our fathers; let's make a day to glorify one's culture; let's create a day of forgiveness, amnesty, etc. This system annuls and completely suspends the whole rotation of the Earth in the galaxy, which is, in reality, the cosmic expansion within a person's psyche. What should be expansion is reduced to no more than a tiny, dead nexus.

Originally, humans were given three hundred and sixty- five days a year under the solar calendar and three hundred and fifty-five or fifty-four days a year under the lunar calendar. He was given the whole cosmos in which to exercise the flow of his emotions.

Q: Would you comment on that with regard to Pharaoh?

A: A human's presence at a particular moment in a particular

172

place is for a reason, and this causality is the main factor in stimulating his joy, or at least in attempting to avoid sadness and misery. Therefore, the audience that controls his time and space is the same audience that controls his metamorphosis, his state of comfort, his pleasure, and his emotions. If his emotions are controlled by someone else, then a person lives the life of an automaton, and he is completely deprived of his existence.

All those days mentioned previously had a hidden connection to the consumer-producer system and gave a certain relief from long-term psychological pressure and social fragmentation. Each of those days had its own festival, each of which was organized according to Pharaoh's protocol.

Time and space had fallen into Pharaoh's hand, and God wanted to remove them from the monocracy, the collectivity, and place them in a people's democracy—individuality. That is why this prohibition against fishing on the Sabbath was revealed to the people of this town.

Q: Could you in some way explain the mystery behind the prohibition?

A: We are not talking about the logic behind the prohibition or the obligation even though we have discussed that already regarding the prohibition, which is in reality one drop from its mysterious ocean. Instead, it is a matter of accepting this regulation from the Invisibility, rather than from a visibility. When people waste their time arrogantly challenging the Creator regarding His rules without paying attention to the mystery, it's like the proverb says: "I show him the moon, and he is looking at my finger."

As an allegory, can you hold two baguettes or sticks long enough to reach the sky, to reach the galaxies infinitely? Now, try to join them both while overlapping each other. Now, on the end nearest to you, close to the extremity of both of them, try to nail them in such a way that they become sort of a pair of scissors that are not equilateral. Put the nail one inch from the extremity nearest to you. Now, look when you open the pair of scissors where you have put the nail; if you open it one inch on your end, it gets opened thousands of kilometers or maybe more on the other extremity. Are you following?

Q: Yes, I am.

A: This is exactly what happens when either you open yourself to a moment of abstention by not crossing certain limits or you open yourself to a moment in which you fulfill an obligation from the Divinity. You are opening an eternity not only in your life in the terrestrial world, but also in your life in the celestial world; in both cases it's an opening process.

In general, if a society crosses prohibited frontiers but then experiences remorse of conscience, their return is a sign of a healthy society. Their recognition of those infractions leaves the principles of reality intact. Nonetheless, most of the time there is encouragement to refrain from repentance. Why? If people return through recognition and repentance, their emotions, even if they reflect infractions, are converted to strength and remain intrinsic with regard to the core, and they strengthen their characters. If they don't return but still do accept the fact that their error is an infraction vis-à-vis the Creator—an audience beyond time and space, then their emotions become extrinsic and burdensome, but their reality (nucleus) remains intact. If they don't return and they normalize their infraction with the attitude of "so what," then their bad emotions become intrinsic, and they damage their nucleus. It is like a virus that penetrates the hard drive in a computer.

Q: You are actualizing this phenomenon; my question to you is, "How applicable is this story in our current lives?"

A: Regarding the abnormality, you may call that infraction, sin, etc., the nation is always divided into three sections. You have those who are driven by or follow their passions; they cross the limits, whether toward God or toward people. You have those who preach, advise, etc. Finally, you have those who, when they promote the normalization of the abnormality, have a personal interest behind these tribulations. So basically these three sections figure and appear at any given time.

Q: Who is behind this encouragement not to repent and return?

A: Such encouragement usually comes from the lurkers. They supposedly defend citizens' rights under the guise of freedom and democracy. They wait for emotions to be externalized, and then they can sell any product and create any method they want, because the citizens are oblivious, due to the superfluous

emotions inside them, and are looking to recuperate the self. Therefore, they may buy or accept any ideology that promises to secure their existence. Also, those lurkers serve as mediators between the people's extrinsic emotions and the big companies, because everything is related to the consumer- producer system. When this pattern of abnormality is done repeatedly, it becomes legitimized and institutionalized; it becomes part of public policy and political philosophy. At some point, it finally becomes statutory.

With each normalization of an abnormality, a corresponding organization, association, or institution is created. Whenever that happens, the individual begins to seek externally for that which he has lost internally. This is done through consumerism ("You have to buy to feel happy.") and spending money. If there is no money, the banking system provides temporary freedom and relief to the needy person. However, as soon as that money becomes available, people are once again controlled by usury, and the stress circle also inevitably begins once again.

Q: What are the repercussions?

A: Some of the repercussions of this system are experienced by the physical body (psychosomatic illnesses). Once this happens, society is transferred to the chemo system. In other words, for each distress or damage to the physical body, a chemically-induced agent of relief will be manufactured (e.g., dopamine, serotonin, etc.). Eventually, the society will even seek to cure its loss of spirituality through over-the-counter (OTC) remedies and prescription antidotes, resulting in another pharmaceutical industry being created and manipulated by the lurkers.

Q: Would you comment further on the fact that when abnormality is repeatedly legitimized, the abnormality ends up becoming part of public policy and political philosophy?

A: The whole system is meant to create a second personality within you, i.e., one that works for the system against you. In other words, the system hijacks your mind through conditioning, and it hijacks your immune system with antigen. In the end, it tries to make you comfortable with your stress and to make you comfortable with your disease. You work; you borrow; you satisfy an implanted desire that is not even yours. Then once you become sick, you happily buy those antidotes and gladly live with a diagnostic label.

Have you noticed how people in this society identify with such and such sickness? You may hear people saying: "Oh, I'm diabetic;" "Oh, I'm asthmatic;" "Oh, I'm bipolar;" etc. If you analyze their words, it appears that they are satisfied with lives that are identified with whatever illness they claim to have. When they say, "I am," it becomes part of their extension, part of their life; it becomes their very identity. Further, once they accept that identity, they tend to sacrifice their future budgets to insure the continuous use of pharmaceutical remedies.

CHAPTER 17

In the previous chapter, we spoke about deconstruction, or decompression, in terms of eliminating a day. In this chapter, we are talking about construction in terms of seizing time from eternity through individual intention. When people lose their individuality, in terms of their individual intention, their compulsions become offensive, so do their actions.

On the front page of the morning's divine Scripture, the following breaking story dominated the news.

The harsh sun made the desert hot and dry. Moses prayed to God for water for his people. In return, God asked Moses to strike a rock with his staff. Miraculously, twelve springs gushed forth.

It seems that every domain and every sector of life becomes a battlefield. This is because mentalities have been militarized and every acquisition from the material world becomes a weapon.
Duels in the arena between two gladiators have never stopped in societies. The only difference between now and then is that in ancient times the duel was a physically concrete act performed on horses or elephants and with swords, javelins, and shields. In some ways, the fact that such duels were physically concrete acts made them more genuine and sincere. The pain and anguish of the loser were immediately apparent and real to any observer, and innocent bystanders were seldom struck down by an errant thrust of a sword. However, the modern duel is frequently a much more abstract affair and is usually camouflaged by technology and by the word "civilization."

(We must not forget to add that such a people's revolt exists internally, but its manifestation is oppressed by so-called amendments, civil unions, and reparations, which act to tranquilize any unexpected revolt that might be a surprise to the authorities.)

The gladiatorial mentality spreads outward with surprising rapidity. It starts in a single ego, spreads to immediate family members and neighbors, and then is extended to the tribal level. Eventually, it is manifested on a national level.

Introspective Exegesis

Q: What did you mean when you said that when citizens are deprived of their individual uniqueness, their compulsions become offensive; they fall into a conditioned pseudo-uniqueness?

A: We are here reaching the stage of intention with regard to individual time, not collective time, which is the penchant or the inclination from which the person acts intentionally. We have one person who is behaving from the core—the reality of the self, and we have another person who is behaving from something outside the self, a sort of borrowing of an intention.

Q: Are you speaking about the time or the inclination?

A: That inclination itself is with regard to the individual's time, not to the collective time.

Q: Are there any concrete example?

A: When you leap, do you need a penchant, a trampoline, on which to stand or not?

Q: Yes, I do.

A: When you have something solid, e.g., an immobile trampoline, under your feet, once you leap your action rebounds and leaves residues, traces in your body. There is first of all the muscular contraction, and then there is the development of some muscles, such as the quadriceps in your legs, the gluteus in your lower back, etc. Now consider when you are skydiving with a parachute, and you want to jump to another space while being in the air, or consider when you are swimming on the surface of a deep swimming pool and are not touching the ground. Are you able to jump under both circumstances?

Q: No, I'm not.

A: Why is that?

Q: Because I don't have an inclination, a penchant, on which to put my feet.

A: It is similar with intention. There is one intention that bursts from the self and leaves residue, which is a sign of possession and joy. It is not muscle development, but the development of will power. On the other hand, there is an intention that is simulated or borrowed and that doesn't leave any residue except feelings of deprivation and turmoil, both of which make a person feel oblivious.

If a person is deprived of himself, his autonomous uniqueness in terms of his individual intention that is spawned within his own time, he falls into the collective pseudo- uniqueness where every individual has the same intention as everybody else. In such a case, people don't see and feel their individuality; they only feel the

180

collectivity. They feel the corporation; they feel the organization; they feel the institution; they feel nationalism etc. It's even the case that they feel their religion. That's why they become hostile, aggressive gladiators. In other words, it's like everyone is saying: "Where am I? Who took the 'I' from me? I see something, but I don't see myself. I feel something, but I don't feel myself."

Q: You included religion. How come people don't feel the self even in religion? I don't understand that.

A: You have the destination, and you have the vehicle to that destination. The destination is God, not in terms of distance or in terms of time, but in terms of focus. This is undoubtedly the dominant impulse of consciousness. The vehicle is a religion that claims to take you to God, and it cannot be ignored or neglected. Otherwise, there is no journey. Now when the vehicle becomes the dominant impulse of consciousness, being more dominant than the destination, people start worshiping the vehicle (the religion) instead of the destination (God). They don't feel the self, and theybecome gladiators like the others.

Q: Would you be more specific about collective time and individual time?

A: Collective time is an infinite series of separate moments in space. It is the planetary orbit that is measured by 12 months. When it comes to individual time, it is also an infinite series, but one that is happening in the brain, in the psyche, as it is happening in the external world. However, this time we don't say a series of moments because we don't know yet. We have the right to say there is a series of events that is happening and that can be seized by a person through his consciousness and intention, and this series of events then becomes that person's individual time within his own psyche. However, this same series can be neglected through automatism, and we don't have the right to credit any quantitative time to the mechanical individual—the automaton. It is the unknown moment that occurs without any chronometric measurement. Since a person is bombarded by billions of bits of information in his brain, he is only percolating or integrating a few hundred from this gigantic quantity.

Q: Would you comment on the difference between the two, I mean individuality and collectivity?

A: Herein lies a big mystery. We have the existence of individuality within diversity. This existence has to do with time, despite the fact that there is a time that implies generality. Still there is a unique time that is seized according to everyone's intention. When we say time, we are referring to two things: the quantitative and the qualitative. The quantitative is, chronometrically speaking, referred to as twelve months. With regard to qualitative time, we are speaking about the role of human beings—the intention within the moment.

The moment is an expression for your state at a given time. This state does not attach itself to the past or to the future; it is an existence that is seized by you and that is so far considered to be like a specter, like water without form and without color, especially during its (water's) state of evaporation. So the form and the color of water are not from water; instead, they are from the container. It is likewise with your state. It is the involvement of your intention in that particular moment that gives you an unpredicted identity.

Consider the example of a very small balloon that is no more than a dot; it doesn't contain any air. When you start inflating it with your breath, it expands to allow the air that was originally outside it to come inside it. It is similar with that time that was originally

182

outside you; it becomes inside you. In reality, there is no outside, and there is no inside. However, this is a vast topic; let's just leave it as it is.

Q: Would you in some way clarify how to seize the moment?

A: When you have the Absolute in your mind as an observer, you get unpredictable intentions that synchronize widely with

the universe. When you have an institution in your mind, you get across between routine and constriction; nothing is new. When your intention is concentric with The Absolute, you come across intentions that are yours, and nobody else has them. Even if another person has the Creator in his mind, he will likewise get intentions that are his, and nobody else has them. Even if sometimes somebody else's intentions seem similar to yours, they still have different results in each person according to his or her predisposed situation.

Q: Metaphorically speaking, I can see that you linked the 12 springs to the 12 months. Could you go into details and their links?

Also when the statement was revealed about the 12 springs, it suggested that water was coming out of the rock as the result of pressure. Was this pressure related to an effort from a human being or from nature?

A: It was from both. You are the enigma between the microcosm and the macrocosm. All you have to do is to let it be with just a small gesture of conformity regarding the physical world. All you have to do is have your presence of mind (intention of conformity) when it comes to the metaphysical world.

We cannot ignore the fact that there was pressure from the water that Moses released that had the potential to pierce and break a sort of dam, thus quenching the thirst existing within mankind. The water was ready to gush out; it was just waiting for one gesture. There was also pressure from the spiritual aspect (the Sublimity). The pressure that results from reaching humility with love has the potential to pierce and break any institution, to break stubbornness, to break the dogmatic conditioning to which people have been adapted, and to reach people's hearts. Thus, the Sublimity was likewise ready to burst in people's hearts; it was just waiting for a person's individual intention. In the physical world, the water was prevented by the rocks from reaching the people's thirst; in the metaphysical world, the Oneness of God that gives a person his uniqueness was prevented by the idolatry of the institutions. It was prevented by conditioning; it was prevented by the collective intention.

The water did not come by itself, but it was provoked by people's thirst. In addition, the sort of laser of the Oneness of God that is beyond time and space was not ignited (animation) by itself, but it was provoked by the individual's intention.

Q: Do you know how I feel? At the moment when I grasp this reality, I sometimes feel that it slips from my hand.

A: Certainly it needs concentration. Don't forget that you are building your eternal self. Don't let it escape your mind. A soul is inside you and is going through sequences of life, going through stages of life.

There was a time when a reality inside you asked for its uniqueness, despite its coexistence with multiplicity. Do you remember when this reality asked God for the universal remembrance?

Q: Yes, I do.

A: There was a time of the eclipse of holidays, when this reality inside you tried to eliminate the collective holiday within the self and disperse it to the splendor of 365 days a year. Do you remember that?

Q: Yes, I do

A: Now it's the time of collecting, of gathering, which is a reality inside you having the potential of seizing the moment out of the 12 astrological months in which the majority of people are supposedly subject to their planetary influence (Neo-Platonism).

Q: How is one moment seized from 12 months, and how does it compensate for the 12?

A: Let's get back to our allegory. The striking of the rock was in the physical world. The intention was in the metaphysical world, which is primarily in the psyche. The striking broke the rock in the physical world; intention broke the characterized institution in the psyche. Now here lies the mystery: God did not ask Moses to strike the rock 12 times; instead, He asked him to hit it once. Here is another mystery: God did not ask Moses to use a jack hammer or explosives; instead, He asked him to use the weakest link, which was Moses' cane (a symbol of humility). Are you following me?

Q: Yes, I am.

A: It is likewise with intention. One moment with humility under the supervision of the Sublimity compensates for the feelings that flow with the orbit of the 12 astrological months.

185

Q: Are you saying that the 12 zodiac signs become one?

A: You can say that, but that's not exactly what I meant. Let's get back to our previous analysis regarding emotions. We have the "I", which is humility, the center of gravity in the center of the universe. We also have the ego in the epicenter. The emotions of the "I" are in the center, and then they dissolve without being stored. Nonetheless, they flow with the law of the universe and absorb what rotates in the epicenter, resulting in tranquility. The emotions of the ego are in the epicenter; nonetheless, they also flow with the law of the universe, but this flow is precarious and is subject to and absorbed by what rotates in the epicycloids, resulting in turmoil and deprivation. Do you now understand the difference between someone who is subject to the planetary orbit and someone who is concentric with the universe by being primarily concentric with the Absolute?

Speaking about astrology, every person is supposedly influenced by his zodiac sign; every person has his personal characteristic according to the zodiac sign corresponding to the time of his birth. This influence comes from the orbit and the pivot of the periodic irregularities in planetary motions. All of this has to do with what flows in the epicenter. Despite this planetary orbit, the center is not affected, which means that the center of gravity is not affected.

Q: So?

A: You asked me before about why the position of Moses is in the sixth heaven. This is the place where the Mosaic frequency within you that puts you above the planetary influence of the 12 astrological months to which most people are subject. You will be the owner of the Milky Way and not owned by any planetary orbit.

Now, the majority's logic is derived from the special intellect that distinguishes between the terrestrial world's right and wrong. Therefore, their logic cannot rise above the biosphere because they have been conditioned by the logic of the consumer-producer system, which allows them to see solutions to their problems only within the parameters of the consumer- producer process. Now, do you see the fortune of the individual's intention?

The majority of people throughout history were preoccupied by asking for their rights, their civil liberties. They demonstrated, burned things, and committed sabotage in the streets. They screamed, went on strike, made revolutions, etc. They thought this was freedom. However, sometimes these revolts were actually engineered by Pharaoh and his cohorts, who were using a strategy of: "Keep your dog hungry, and he will follow you." They cursed Pharaoh; yet, they voluntarily deprived themselves of their moments that they could have seized from the eternity without using anybody or any institution as an intermediary. Their intention belonged to Pharaoh; their emotions belonged to the corporation. They preferred to give their entire age and their eternity to Pharaoh; yet, they demonstrated against Pharaoh. Look at that. If you had spoken to them about cosmic consciousness, the only arena of mockery that was left for them was mocking their Creator.

CHAPTER 18

The first sign before the collapse of a hegemonic nation is the disappearance of Korah. As such, on that fateful day, the financial center (which was the symbol of globalization) collapsed.

T he Divine Media had previously reported many times something about Pharaoh's federal funds, which were of course manipulated by Korah. Here is the text of the scripture: "Korah was so rich that the keys to his treasure were too heavy for even several strong men to carry."

When he was asked by Moses to give charity and to avoid charging people usury, Korah argued that his wealth was due to his own cleverness. When he was asked at the World Trade Organization to keep a balance between the high-tech countries and the countries of the Third World, Korah reacted with the same attitude, and he indirectly said that before he would do as Moses requested he would convert the whole world to his own politics, globalization, and New World Order.

Korah publicly displayed the glitter of his immense wealth, usually through such tentacles as celebrities, actors, singers, athletes, politicians, TV anchors, columnists, talk show hosts, etc. Those who coveted the worldly life said, "How wonderful it would be if we possessed the like of what Korah has been given. Surely, he is a man of great good fortune."

People who had faith in God and in the Day of Judgment said to him: "Do not exult in your riches, for God does not love the exultant, but seek by means of that which God has given you to attain the abode of the Hereafter. Be good to others as God has been good to you...for God does not love the evildoers."

He replied, "These riches were given to me on account of the knowledge I possess."

Analyzing that year's Discretionary Fiscal Budget, the Federal Pie Chart was as follows: 17% for Labor, Health and Human Services, and Education; 13% for Veterans, Housing and Urban Development, and independent agencies; 06% for the Departments of Commerce, Justice, and State; 15% for other parts of the government; and 49% for the Department of Defense.

Now entitlement programs such as Social Security and Food Stamps represented non-discretionary spending; in other words, Congress could narrow or expand eligibility, but it couldn't directly determine the level of spending. On the other hand, the Pentagon consumed almost half of discretionary spending, while education took up only about 07%.

In the breaking news, the Divine Media's morning edition reported that something catastrophic had happened to Korah's World Financial Center. The report was as follows: "We caused the earth to swallow him (Korah), together with his dwelling, so that he found no one to protect him from God, nor was he able to defend himself; the ungrateful shall never prosper."

At the exact moment of the collapse of the World Financial Center, Pharaoh's administration raised the country's nuclear alert codes from Defcon (Defense Condition) 6 to Defcon 2. (As the degree of the alert increased, the lower the Defcon rating became. Defcon 1 was the highest alert.)

The Federal Pie Chart for the Discretionary Federal Budget that was mentioned previously was related to the antecedent year up to the time of the collapse of the World Financial Center. However, the total outlay of federal funds after the collapse of the World Financial Center was increased to 54% just for military spending and was reduced to 46% for non- military spending.

Furthermore, on a worldwide basis, Pharaoh's single nation used 40% of the world's natural resources, leaving the rest of the world only 60%. Other statistics claimed Pharaoh's nation was using an even higher percentage of the world's natural resources. (These higher figures could be authentic, considering the clandestine nature of Pharaoh's nation's monopoly; it's hard to verify the real figure.) Such disproportionate consumption caused gigantic instability, and this instability was only accentuated by the fact that many of these natural resources were taken illegitimately.

Pharaoh's nation accounted for 47% of the world's total military spending. Some claimed that Pharaoh's military spending was naturally so high because Pharaoh's nation had the highest Gross Domestic Product (GDP) of any country in the world. However, Pharaoh's share of the world's GDP was only about 21%.

Introspective Exegesis

Q: You are talking about wealth; then you are talking about the collapse of the World Financial Center; then you are talking about the military. Where is the link?

A: The country was owned by Korah, i.e., by the banking system. On the internal front within people's psyche, Korah represents passions when they exceed their limits. Haman represents the military and its derivatives agencies. On the internal front within people's psyche, he represents the ego defense mechanisms. Here you see the peak of mammonism and its collapse, the latter of which is synonymous with Korah's disintegration and Haman's sudden interference in the siege of the government.

Q: Would you go gradually and explain how the system got to that peak?

A: When you look at Pharaoh's system of mammonism, it was, in reality, invading itself by monopolizing everything. It was confiscating and devouring; it was a system of obesity. The system was invading its own structure by overcharging people and by working them much more than it was supposed to. When the system supposedly became so powerful, its omnipotence rebounded at a certain point, just like someone with obesity. The obese person cannot move easily; he is hijacked by the self. This is what happened in Pharaoh's nation; two things were prominent, i.e., obesity and violence.

Domestically and realistically, obesity had nothing to do with over-nourishment, nor did it have anything to do with the neurotic aspects of depression. Those were etiologic agents that can be classified as being in secondary or even tertiary positions. The main, although unspoken, cause had to do with the system of three deteriorating strategies that were infiltrated into people's minds and that led the population to become obese. For example, obesity resulted from being an executant but not a participant. This was like the case with the GI that stands for Government Issue, where the individual's emotions were completely suspended. We have the first jeopardy, which was under the words "don't worry." The words "so what" constituted the second jeopardy. Then at the end, we had the last jeopardy under the words "who cares." This whole recapitulated package was under the false banner of freedom.

Q: How did it work?

A: Initially, we had the "don't worry" phase, which was the disappearance of individuality by merging and dissolving it into a pseudo-collectivity; the individual became a mechanical executant, like an automaton, but was not a participant in his emotions. There was a corporation that consumed individuality, or you could say that the corporation devoured individuality and that it then became obese. It was as if you were saying that the corporation was pregnant by those executants. It was as if you were saying that the corporation gathered a state of metamorphosis of the emotions and stagnated them in its womb. Once those emotions were gathered, they fed neither the company nor those victims of extirpation; they became, instead, astray and suffered a miscarriage.

In every sector of industry, you had the phenomena of obesity and pregnancy. We don't refer to this process as exploitation; we are far beyond that point in our discussion. We don't refer to slavery; we have already passed that point, as well. We don't refer to a society of consumption; we are also beyond that term. Instead, at this point, it had become a completely sterilized society. It was like when people wanted to use mules or horses beyond their capacity to work on farms. To accomplish overworking the animals, they sexually sterilized the animals. Have you ever seen a horse that no longer looks like a horse, but it is built and developed like a bull even though it still has the physiognomy of a horse? It's because it was sterilized and was deprived of its sexual desires. Similarly, society became sterilized. However, despite being sterilized, society did not lose its sexual desires (that domain was even promoted), but it was mentally sterilized.

This all came from an injected vaccine that immunized the

192

individual from his conscience and made everything permissible. There were no rules, no limits, and no frontiers. All those regulatory limits were seen only in the external world. The individual did not conceive them within his intellect or his will power.

Q: What about the phase of "so what?"

A: Surplus in any aspect of life creates a burden, and the burden creates pain. A mistake in any aspect of life creates remorse of conscience, and that remorse creates pain. That pain, intuitively speaking, is not there to remain as pain, but it is there to let the individual feel it and to let the individual fight it. That pain is there to regulate human beings' character, much like the immune system regulates the body, by having the person being in touch with himself. Now the system of obesity plays with the deviation of that pain; it lets you accept the pain via fun and tranquilizers, allowing you to be joyful under the guise of "so what." However, as long as the pain remains, as long as you consume (and that is the true definition of obesity), you are in fact stopping the pain by simultaneously feeding the pain.

Q: What about the phase of "who cares?"

A: Here was the last disaster. If you have ever done anything wrong, if you have ever neglected anything, this phase tells you not to look behind you, not to try to recoup the past, and not to try to rectify or compensate for your wrong. Just keep on going. It is as if there were a standing jump in the mind, which is a moment of reflection that allows you to be aware and to analyze your acts. However, this standing jump has to be eliminated by the system of obesity. There is also a running jump in your mind that drags you into completely ignoring those acts that should be promoted. This running jump is, itself, a phenomenon of devouring, i.e., a phenomenon of obesity, and it results in a state in which there is no longer any feelings of concern and no longer any universality. It is just me, myself, and I.

Q: You said that at a certain point this omnipotence rebounds and become weakness. Are there any concrete examples? Also, regarding the imbalance you previously mentioned, whether among individuals or among nations, how is it manifested?

A: The balance of existence says that Pole A is allowed to eat 3,000 calories per day and that Pole B is also allowed to eat 3,000 calories per day, assuming that each of them is doing the same amount of physical activity. For some reason, Pole A takes 4,000 calories, which means its surplus is causing a shortage of 1,000 calories for Pole B. These extra 1,000 calories are not Pole A's, but he takes them anyway. Now, the question exists whether or not Pole A really possesses this extra 1,000 calories. The answer is that he does not. He carries them as a burden or sickness, but he does not own them as a force. Consider this example magnified on a large scale. Now, these 1,000 extra calories do not only flow in the body as a sickness, they also create burden, and they create...

Q: If I remember, somewhere before, you were favoring inequality. You considered inequality the zone where resides every sentimental emotion that has the potential to be exercised. Therefore, every infrastructure in the external world is exactly built based on how the flow is of these emotions, and now I see you talking about equality. How can you explain that?

A: The principles in the objective world are intact, and the...

Q: Any examples....?

A: There are no rich and poor in the objective world; there are no

194

beautiful and ugly in the objective world, etc. However, in the subjective world, there are rich and poor, etc. Now this inequality is a responsibility; this inequality is a duty of conscience from both the rich and the poor. From the part of the rich, there should be humbleness, generosity, charity, etc. From the part of the poor, there should be humbleness, respect, etc.

So in the final analysis, if a rich person wants to spoil these principles by abstaining from sharing his wealth, he is, in reality, just jeopardizing his own subjective world. He is not jeopardizing the objective world, as we spoke about it before in reference to the calories. With regard to the poor person, if he wants to spoil these principles by being rebellious, he is, in reality, just jeopardizing his own subjective world.

Q: How about if the surplus is outside the physical body, such as money, land, or whatever?

A: When the surplus is supposedly in the external world, it appears to be outside the physical body. Here the situation is worse; it seems to be distant from the person; yet, it is linked to him one way or the other. It is linked to him through his mind and through his feelings. That surplus will be transformed to fear if it is not purified, and that fear is...

Q: One second. What do you mean by purified?

A: We will get to that later. Let me finish. As I said, surplus causes a gap. As big as that gap is, that is as big as that fear becomes, and that fear will manufacture unnecessary security, which will in turn manufacture unnecessary armaments to compensate for the gap. As was indicated by one of the previously cited statistics, the reason why Pharaoh's nation accounted for 47% of the world's total military spending was because it had the highest Gross Domestic Product (GDP). In reality, there was no link whatsoever between GDP and military spending, but it had to do with the manner in which GDP was greedily accomplished and the manner in which it was greedily manipulated.

Pharaoh's system of "don't worry" and "so what" and "who cares" showed that the population was in a very sensitive state of fear. While security was all around, in reality, the country was not secured within itself at all, because that supposed security was only in the external world. It was nothing more than a police state that was camouflaged with extreme pleasure; you heard the word "fun" a lot, and then there was quick violence. In such a situation, people shifted with an immediate switch from extreme happiness, which you could have noticed, to extreme sadness, which you couldn't have noticed.

Q: What does the World Financial Center represent in the psyche?

A: This is the answer to your question about purification when you interrupted me earlier. Now do you remember the example about the calories given previously?

Q: Yes, I do.

A: Imagine yourself taking those extra calories, even though you don't really need them and even though they are just going to be a burden inside you, adversely affecting your cardiovascular system, etc. In reality, those calories are forming an extrinsic interiority. In other words, you carry them, but you don't benefit from them. Now transform this small example to a much larger scale. When it comes to money or when it comes to any ownership in general, after certain limits, if it is not purified or purged, this ownership rebounds and becomes weakness and deprivation. The answer to the question of purification is the voluntary deprivation of the

196

1,000 calories. In other words, the answer is charity. That is the time of the mysterious trade. That is the time of the true stock market. Your surplus is going to bring you what you don't have if you act early, freely, and before it's too late. This includes love, compassion, sympathy, generosity, etc., all of which are recapitulated in the word charity. So you are not depriving yourself; in reality, you are just converting and transforming your surplus property into an extended property. You are just extending your property from the physical world to the metaphysical world.

CHAPTER 19

This is the time when a nation starts reaping its own crop while being blinded by its supremacy and, at the same time, blaming otherness. It thinks that it can police the world. The situation in Pharaoh's land became chaotic after the collapse of the World Financial Center. This was the time when the Patriot Act was signed. The contrived acronym of this act was drawn from "Providing Appropriate Tools Required to Intercept and Obstruct Terrorism."

Pharaoh's counselor of state said to him: "Wilt thou leave Moses and his people to spread mischief in the land and to abandon thee and thy gods?" He said: "Their children will we slay; their females will we save alive, and we have over them irresistible (power)."

There was a big and hot debate within Pharaoh's administration between those who agreed with him and the minority who disagreed with Pharaoh's decision.

When Pharaoh's plan to have Moses murdered was put to a vote, there was an honest man among his counselors who spoke out and said: "Would you slay a man merely because he says, 'My Lord is God?' He has brought you clear signs from your Lord. If he is lying, may his lie be on his head; but if he is speaking the truth, a part at least of what he threatens will strike you."

On the other side, The Israelites started an internal revolt within themselves and told Moses that they had been hurt before and after he came. In other words, for them there was no difference between being under Pharaoh's nationalism and being with Moses' prophecy—their situation did not improve.

To establish a utopian government requires massive effort, because such a government starts internally within the individual and then grows externally as an outward, governmental collectivity. Bringing back the Theo-ethical, psycho-ethical, and socio-ethical dimensions and centering them from the epicenter to the center of gravity are the biggest fears of any external government in this world.

Moses replied to the Israelites: "Chances are that your Lord will destroy your enemy and will make you successors to see how you will act."

Introspective Exegesis

Q: What is behind the historical verse: "Verily, never will God change the condition of people until they change what is in themselves?"

A: If only people would understand the meaning of this last expression, perhaps they would then avoid an eternal waste of time. As simple as it sounds, the conditions of the external world will never be changed unless people change what is in their psyche.

Q: What was behind those words when Moses said, "Chances are?"

A: The probability statement is not referenced to God; yet, it is referenced to God at the same time, as will be explained shortly.

Q: Moses also said that there was a probability that God "...will make you successors to see how you will act." He said successors, but he did not specify whom to succeed. He left that part of the statement blank. Why?

A: He meant it was up to the people to decide. However, Moses did not modify the eyewitness, i.e., the One who sees "how you will act," because the Singularity of the eyewitness is One Who is God. The only issue here to be resolved was whether people voluntarily wanted to have their Creator as their eyewitness or whether He was their eyewitness in spite of their wishes. In the former case, every move of theirs became a personal strength and part of the development of the self.

Q: How about if people desired to have the institution of a governmental regime as their eyewitness?

A: God was still their eyewitness anyway, however much His being an eyewitness to their actions may have been involuntary on their part. In such a case, each of their actions and behaviors became a reinforcement of Pharaoh, which confirms our earlier statement that the gap, differentials, and emptiness between the "I" and the ego belonged to Pharaoh, to Haman, and to Korah and his dead institutions and corporations. The power that the citizen gained depended on his choice regarding the eyewitness and the government over him. What each citizen developed right then could unknowingly have been a reinforcement of Pharaoh. If the future eyewitness was simply another name for a Pharaonic system, then what the citizen developed in that present moment was his self-esteem, which would have been epitomized by a future Pharaoh, by a future police and military state under the name of Haman, or by the passions inflamed by a future Korah with his usury-driven banking system and his external corporations.

Q: I'm just thinking about something... If my memory is correct, you said before that Moses was not sent to Pharaoh as an adversary, and when you spoke in the same chapter about the psychological aspect, you stated that Moses was a conflict provoking impulse. So why did Moses say to the Israelites, "Chances are that your Lord will destroy your enemy." Why did Moses use the word "enemy?"

A: Moses was not talking about the external Pharaoh, and he never considered Pharaoh as an enemy, Moses was talking about the internal Pharaoh—the ego with its grandiosity; this is the biggest enemy, and it is within us before the appearance of any possible enemy outside ourselves.

Q: Why did the Israelites feel there was no improvement either under Pharaoh's regime or under Moses' prophecy?

A: This is the biggest disaster of people when they join a religion while escaping from nationalism. They always have the same agenda, conditions, protocols, etc., the same ones they had before with nationalism. That's why they never succeed. Their collapse is apparent from one moment to another, and you find a lot of them in the pashas and sultans of societies. (Actually these people took God's place without realizing that, and they think they are religious.)

Q: Let's get back to our event with regard to the psyche. What are all these events from the collapse of the World Financial Center to the Patriot Act and homeland security?

A: The World Financial Center represents the condensation of wealth within the government and within a person's psyche. It represents the condensation of addictions—collapsed pleasure. Following the collapse of the World Financial Center, there was a takeover of the government by military reaction, and within the person's psyche the same type of takeover occurs via the ego defense mechanisms. On the governmental level, they signed a Patriot Act against supposed terrorism from abroad; yet, the consumer-producer system itself was a terror. Within a person's

psyche, a Patriot Act is a pretext generated by ego defense mechanisms, a psychic danger enabling the person to avoid conscious awareness of his internal conflicts. Yet, his addictions still cause him anxiety. When one speaks about homeland security in the siege of the government, in reality it is homeland insecurity. Individually speaking, it is the imbalance between hope and fear that creates a gap leading to angst.

Of note, human beings are motivated by hope and fear, which are two forces that are attractive and repulsive at the same time. These two forces intuitively exist within a human, regulate his behavior, and give him a feeling of a tranquil existence.

Q: How do they function? What do they trigger?

A: Hope triggers pleasure, approach, leaning, loosening, and relaxation. Fear triggers anger, sadness, abstention, contraction, and remorse.

Q: I can understand that hope and what follows are beneficial, but do you consider fear, anger, and what follows as something positive?

A: This is the biggest mistake of modern psychology. They consider fear, anger, sadness, and remorse as something bad and negative. As such, they try to eliminate them. Actually, they will never succeed; they just create an imbalance in a person's life by promoting an escape from reality. People cannot be devoid of their impulses because their impulses are a part of their intuitivism. If there is no fear in you, you will approach every dangerous situation without having the slightest feeling preventing you from that approach. If there is no anger inside you, there is nothing to incite your reflexes to defend you from external danger. If there is no remorse inside you, you aren't able to recuperate and compensate for your past. However, we have to emphasize something here. If fear goes beyond the limit, it isolates a person from the joy of existence; it gets to a severity where the person cannot have any pleasure in food, any pleasure in sex, or any pleasure in approaching life in general; this is a suicidal state. As such, fear has to be counterbalanced by hope. Also, if anger goes beyond limits, it becomes psychoneurotic. Thus, anger also has to be counterbalanced by hope. If remorse of conscience goes beyond limits, it creates desperation and depression. Therefore, the middle ground is the healthiest position.

Q: You said something about the two forces, attractive and repulsive. Are you able to comment on that?

A: The force of hope, which is in fact pleasure, is so powerful that it can drag you to the extreme. If you enter that extreme, you are then shifted against your will to the fear section. If you see a person leaning a lot to his passions while thinking it is a permissible happiness, you find the same dimensional repercussion occurring as in sadness. As much as you see him supposedly being happy, you expect him to be sad. As much as you see him being happy, you find him sensitive to anger. The role of the person is to maintain himself in the middle while taking advantage of the two forces.

Getting back to our analysis, pleasure is not with hope, which only leads to a supposed or false pleasure. Pleasure is with the force you provide by abstaining from going too far to the extreme. This is where pleasure resides. Also, your refusal to go too far into fear, which can trigger anger, gains for you a force that is itself a pleasure. If the two forces drag you one way or the other, you vacillate between extremes and experience disequilibrium. Do you now see the whole posterior spectrum of the collapse of the World Financial Center, the signing of the Patriot Act, and the anterior link within the person's psyche?

Q: Are you able to list any repercussions on the physical body from any neglect of these two forces?

A: The immediate variability in the state of consciousness between the two extremes is the cause of many physical diseases, such as: the flow of blood sugar in the brain, which is influenced by the stress cycle; the constant release of adrenalin, which provokes the heart to beat faster and causes high blood pressure; diabetes; and a lot more. You can say that almost all diseases originate from this neglect.

Of note, hope and fear are feelings, but they are conducted involuntarily from the cerebrospinal axis of the nervous system. Nonetheless, they are regulated voluntarily by a person's intention and by the development of his will power. We have previously seen that feelings are chemically induced in the brain; we are now speaking about their extension in the body.

There are 12 cranial nerves in the brain that are grouped into 12 pairs of sensory devices; they regulate a great variety of bodily functions. They innervate the smooth muscles of the blood vessels, the heart muscles, etc. These are autonomic nerves that are divided into two types, which are sympathetic and parasympathetic. The sympathetic nerves trigger muscle contraction; on the other hand, parasympathetic nerves trigger muscle relaxation. The study of anatomy is limited here, but the study of theosophy is helping us navigate. Getting back to hope and fear, we said that a person is responsible, and now regarding those 12 pair of nerves, we are saying they are autonomic.

Q: So where is the catch?

A: I was getting to that. If you go to the extreme of hope or pleasure, even though the parasympathetic nerves trigger muscle relaxation, and even though you think that pleasure is an arena of relaxation, in fact, you have provoked the other side to occur, which consists of the sympathetic nerves that trigger muscle contraction. That's why you hear a lot about the following symptoms caused by stress such as: headaches, stiff neck, insomnia and fatigue, rapid heartbeat, and other repercussions on the physical body, which include stomach, legs, and chronic back pain caused by spasms etc. Furthermore, once a person experiences these symptoms, he then thinks that he needs more pleasure in order to relax, when in fact, he is unexpectedly and exponentially increasing the severity of the muscle contractions by the sympathetic nerves, which causes even more spasms. It keeps going, and then afterwards the person will be swinging loosely and rapidly from slackness to stiffness and from supposed happiness to unexpected sadness.

As previously noted, when there is no force insuring the avoidance of extremes, a person vacillates between a total floppiness and a total spasm. In other words, here come the states of sloth and fatigue, and then everything is transferred to chemical regulation. In other words, antidotes have to regulate a person's state of comfort. That's why you sometimes see a person vacillate between marked jolliness and a totally different and opposite mood. This simply illustrates that the physical body has run out of some chemical OTC or prescription remedy.

CHAPTER 20

This was the end of the empire; this was the crop that was harvested from the seeds of tyranny. We can now see the real image of the emperor and how the military network was becoming dust; we can see how grandiosity was becoming humility; we can see the "Emperor without Clothes."

A s his efforts to crush the believers reached a feverish pitch, Pharaoh became increasingly intransigent. It was, however, Pharaoh's last breath. Angel Gabriel came down that day (may the peace and blessing of God be on him). He was the angel who had been disguised as a man in the beginning of the story, the one who had previously infiltrated into the White Solipsistic Palace. He had warned Pharaoh about the possible, upcoming disaster, and he had kept Pharaoh's response written. Pharaoh had said, "The one who pretends to be God, he deserves to be drowned in the sea." Gabriel brought this note with him to show to Pharaoh.

The Divine Media reported as follows: "We sent an inspiration to Moses: 'Travel by night with My servants, and strike a dry path for them through the sea, without fear of being overtaken.'"

Why didn't God ask Moses to strike a dry path for them in the beginning when He gave Moses the power in his cane? Why did He wait?

The first divine words to Moses that required an action from him were, "Remove your sandals." A human being supposedly walks on the ground and on what is solid, but he ignores what kind of illusory platform he has under his feet in the back of his subconscious.

If the initial instructions to Moses had been to rid his people of the illusions they were carrying in their subconscious minds, illusions that flowed from Pharaoh's obscurantism and gloomy doctrine, they would never have been able to walk on that which was solid. To avoid this, Moses was first instructed to rescue his people from obscurantism. In other words, before a footstep can actually strike the ground, it has to be intended in the subconscious.

Once Moses had established an internal government, God then asked him to project outwardly what was already in the internal subconscious. In other words, people would be walking on a dry path that had already been established in their psyches.

The establishment of a utopian government required substantial effort from these humans, but the splitting of the sea necessitated a much greater effort than that which humans were capable of achieving. Such an act was not in the hand of any person, but it was done by God's mercy.

By not ignoring them, Moses made an interval within the obligations and prohibitions related to the Divine Law. In return, God made a safer path for him on which to walk. With regard to this, the Divine Media reported the following: "For surely ye shall be pursued. Then Pharaoh pursued them (by) his forces." There was no doubt that they would be pursued.

Why did God use the word "by?" It seemed as though there was something pushing Pharaoh or dragging him against his will to a particular place. God also used the word "forces." So, what were those forces?

There are two probabilities. Either an external force dragged him, which was impossible if his claim to being a god had been true, or an internal force propelled him. The latter was the case.

When the dialogue took place between Moses and Pharaoh in the White Solipsistic Palace, Pharaoh was convinced that what Moses came with was absolutely true. This can be shown by noting the conversation between them in which Moses said: "You are well convinced that these things have been sent down by none but the Lord of the heavens and the Earth as eye-opening evidence, and I see you indeed, O Pharaoh, to be one doomed to destruction."

Moses said these words clearly to Pharaoh, but Pharaoh's self-aggrandizement did not allow him to accept this reality. With great effort, Pharaoh pushed down this authentic impulse, just as he had done when Angel Gabriel came to warn him. In both situations, Pharaoh knew he was lying, but he preferred to hide within his lies.

In order for the Pharaonic regime to survive, it had to establish a bypass as a special characteristic in the minds of the people. This bypass was under the words "so what." It was a response that unhesitatingly arose in the subconscious of Pharaoh and his people and that permeated all of the activities of that sovereign kingdom, including those pertaining to the exercise of its powers and duties throughout the entire world.

If a person thinks that he is wrong, then he is creating a "standing jump", we can say a moment of reflection. However, a person doesn't want to believe that he is wrong. As such, in such a situation, he often creates an immediate pretext to give himself slack. This way he can beat the lie detector and create a "running jump." Unfortunately, the forces of a "running jump" dragged Pharaoh to the water of death.

When for the second time Pharaoh started a campaign against Moses, he knew it was a lie. Nonetheless, he fabricated one piece of propaganda after another and infiltrated fear everywhere in the world. He even proclaimed to his people: "Leave me to slay Moses, and let him call on his Lord! What I fear is lest he should change your religion (Constitution), or lest he should cause mischief to appear in the land!"

This propaganda dominated the administration and the subconscious of Pharaoh and his counselors to such a point that everybody was afraid of Moses and his followers. This domination then became an obsession, and this obsession then became a form of hypnosis. (Hypnosis is a tool of psychotherapy that is occasionally used, not without controversy, with the aim of recovering repressed memories, an action which may be done to dirty the reputation of the believers.)

If Pharaoh's memories or his subconscious had been properly diagnosed, he would have been found to be in a state of fear and blindness. When he verbally accused Moses, Pharaoh was not lying about his feelings; he was lying about Moses. Ironically, this internally fabricated fear of Moses became a self-fulfilling prophecy that resulted in events that later justified an external fear that was reality-based. Pharaoh's government had established an illusory path on which it eventually walked without ever being aware of how it had sealed its own fate.

As was seen with regard to the magicians in the Arena Zero, if a secret agent is repeatedly indoctrinated with a certain recitation, he won't be able to differentiate the true story from the fabricated one. This was similar to what happened to Pharaoh in the end. If he had been put under a lie detector, he wouldn't have been found to be lying because he had come to believe his own propaganda and was captive to his own lies.

We can now understand the forces that drove Pharaoh to chase after Moses and his followers, the most important of which was his denial of the Divinity. This denial provoked him and his administration to act as though they were God. Needing to maintain this charade, Pharaoh was incapable of showing or even admitting that he was a loser. He could not reveal his fragility or express his inadequacy. A second force that drove him was the propaganda that he had fabricated against Moses and his followers.

When Pharaoh reached the sea in his pursuit of Moses and the Israelites, he couldn't stop his chase or retreat. Why?

It was already too late for Pharaoh. He was controlled by those internal forces—compulsions that he had previously developed. That's why before his collapse all his thoughts were about the militarization of space, waging wars in different countries, and infiltrating his troops in more than one hundred and twenty-five countries, while believing those countries loved him and were his allies, when, in fact, there were only puppet allies in the vassal leadership of those countries, leaving the rest of the population of those countries to hate him.

Why did God choose the night for Moses and his followers to travel out of Egypt? If one meticulously analyzes God's words, one may be surprised by a fortune.

God told Moses to "travel" (*Isra*). *Isra* is a verb that means to travel at night. It stands as an independent word in the scripture. In addition, God told Moses to travel "by night." In other words, Moses was to travel at night by night, suggesting that there were two nights. The illumination of the first night referred to the illumination of the state of consciousness. If Moses and his followers did not enlighten their subconscious with servitude to

God and distance themselves from obscurantism, they wouldn't be able to see. The second night was the external night.

Among Moses' followers there were people who accepted God with fideism, i.e., a total and complete faith that is not subservient to reason or the intellect. This was a special characteristic, which involved an intellect that refers neither to the understanding of the senses nor to reason. These people were transiting with spontaneity. There were other people among the followers of Moses who had accepted God through technology and reason. However, if their technology was not present or functional, these people faced fear, vertigo, and destabilization. This group among the followers of Moses saw the approaching army of Pharaoh, screamed in fear, and said, "We are besieged and overtaken."

Look how the First Admirable reacted to this fear. He said, "By no means, my Lord is with me." He didn't say that God is with us, and he didn't say that his technology was with him, even though he had that power handy—the cane.

It was not a matter of choice, not a matter of intelligence, and not a matter of technology. It was a matter of being either in the center of gravity or being in the epicenter. Even if Pharaoh had been in the middle of the believers and right next to Moses, he would have been absorbed and overwhelmed by the water. Likewise, if one of the followers of Moses was left behind and overtaken by Pharaoh's army, he wouldn't have been drowned with the Egyptians, even if he had been immediately next to Pharaoh. This interface had nothing to do with geography, but it had to do with the center of gravity and the epicenter.

As the waves of the sea began to split into two halves with a thunderous uproar, each side began to rise up as high as a mountain. A safe path across the seabed opened up. The internal government walked peacefully across the seabed while the water stood stationary on each side like huge, foaming walls.

When Pharaoh was fighting for his life, Angel Gabriel (may the peace and blessing of God be on him) came to Pharaoh and said: "Pharaoh, do you remember me? Aren't you the one who wrote this expression and told me to show it to everybody who pretends to be God. You see I kept my promise; I'm showing it to you."

The military network that spoke on behalf of Pharaoh was defunct. His dynasty had gone astray. At that moment, when the reality of the self spoke, with his last breath Pharaoh finally said: "I believe that no god exists except the Lord in whom the Children of Israel believe. To Him I give up myself."

The poor emperor apparently didn't know that he had been without clothes since the very beginning, or perhaps he knew he was naked, but he didn't want to admit it. His illusions became his reality. The majority of his counselors helped him maintain his illusions by pretending he was clothed, and they didn't dare to bring this matter of his nakedness to his attention. Perhaps some of them were preoccupied with picking up the crumbs left from his meals. Others were scared of him because of his hubristic attitude. As a result, they faced the inevitable consequences.

"This day We will save your body, so that you will become a sign for your successors."

Introspective Exegesis

Q: In general, what can you tell me about this event in the psyche?

A: All that we see at this stage was just conformity to what was

212

already anterior in the psyche and now was posterior in the external world. It is as if God was showing everyone what was taking place in the subjective world, and now its epitome was visible in the objective world.

Q: Why was there a transit? Why was there motion from both sides, I mean from Moses and Pharaoh? Why didn't God specify a destination for Moses?

A: Speaking about the unspecified destination, Moses was going toward his nomination and Pharaoh was going toward his perdition. God did not use the word "escape" concerning Moses' case; He merely told him to travel, and there was freedom of choice on Moses' part. However, when God spoke about Pharaoh's pursuit, His words showed that Pharaoh was dragged by forces—the running jump. In other words, there was no standing jump to create a moment of decision. This also demonstrates that the domineering person is not living his life as independently as he claims.

On a governmental level, Pharaoh's hegemonic nation was not, as it claimed, a living democracy. Its aim was always to monopolize, invade, conquer, and spy on other nations, all the while fearing that a challenger existed somewhere. (As you can see, that was why Pharaoh named his space shuttle "Challenger.") This hegemonic nation's existence was always creating an enemy in the subconscious and then combating this enemy to prove its existence, when in fact Pharaoh had created this supposed enemy by himself, which was Moses even before Moses was born.

Q: Now let's get to this event in terms of the emotions.

A: This was all taking place in each person's psyche. Bear in mind that Pharaoh's potential of collapse and Moses' potential of enthronement were taking place in everybody's psyche without exception; it was up to the person to choose which polarity he would transform from potential to actual. The ego with its constituents would collapse anyhow, anyway, and all the time. So would its extrinsic emotions, because all its structure was based on grandiosity, and grandiosity drags the person from his center of gravity to the epicenter. It was likewise with Pharaoh on the governmental level. In contrast with the "I," which was Moses' frequency, Moses would be nominated and enthroned anyway, anyhow, and all the time, and so would his emotions, because all his structure was based on humility, and humility drags the person to his center of gravity.

Q: What is traveling by night at night within the emotions?

A: Your true emotions that become a part of your impetuous dynamism are part of your behavior; they are intrinsic, not extrinsic. The difference between the two is as if you have a lamp that is located outside your house that leaves the inside of your house in darkness, and you have a lamp inside your house that enlightens your house. The first illumination is the illumination of the mind, and then with that illumination people can function in the objective world.

Q: ....behind the dry path?

A: Once extrinsic emotion is formed, it is always formed with a supposedly secured identity that is sought by the unsecured person. Such a person's logic and common sense will be unconsciously subservient to that identity. As such, he is basically standing on that emotion—a sort of air bubble. Whenever he feels insecurity, he makes recourse to that identity. In fact, this person is not walking securely on a dry path. In the case of Moses, his mission was effacement and renunciation, which is a true stability and equanimity in the flow of the emotions. That's why God told him to walk on a dry path.

Q: What was the difference between the two groups among Moses' followers?

A: There was one group whose faith was through fideism, which is a faith without reason and without interference from intellectual thoughts. There was another group whose faith was based on science and reason. The difference between the two is that with fideism there was no departure point, no destination, and no journey. This was because these individuals absorbed the universe, since the macrocosm and the microcosm were inside them already. Everything was already there through confession, as was previously noted about the mesocosm. Reason became dissolved in such a person; this person was devouring sciences while joyously navigating in the mystery without having an explanation for that journey and that joy.

Q: Let me interrupt you here. On a few previous occasions, you were favoring the journey between the departure point and the destination, and here I see you denying or rejecting this dimension—the journey from the departure point to the destination. How come?

A: The difference between a person who is putting a condition on his journey, which is the case with the scientist, and the one who is not is inside them. The latter person is navigating within his "globality," and his science is not a condition but a bootstrap instead. Now along his journey, the scientist will have a whispering voice in his mind that is telling him, "You cannot navigate or transit unless 'the because and the therefore' are present." In contrast, for the one with fideism, there is no whispering voice in the first place; therefore, there is no condition; therefore, there is no stagnation. Are you following me?

Q: Yes, I am.

A: The "because and therefore" were fabricated by creatures according to their handicaps and inadequacies. Because they felt emptiness in the vacuum, they fabricated a substratum. Now when it came to frightening situations in the external world, what popped up to the surface of the conscious was what the individual had established previously. You have one person whose faith is through fideism. For him, there was no "because," and there was no "therefore." There was, instead, a bootstrap. You have another person who was a scientist and whose logic only functioned according to specific circumstances. So when the "because and therefore" did not synchronize with the external circumstance, this person faced a tremendous fear. This is what happened.

Q: Why did Moses say, "God is with me?" Why didn't he say, "God is with us even though his brother Aaron I assumed was with him?"

A: Do you remember when we spoke about the neural net? We said that the neural nets of two people do not form two neural nets; instead, they form one neural net? It is similar with groups or populations from different regions; despite the diversity of people, there is still one neural net. When Moses said, "God is with me," he meant that the Sublimity was with the humility, that the humility was the center of gravity, and that the center of gravity was first of all concentric with the Sublimity and was then followed by being concentric with the universe. Although Moses had a lot of followers, e.g., his brother Aaron, still Moses did not mention people's diasporic diversity or their voluntary interference, but he mentioned the potential of humility existing within everybody, which is in reality one, which is the neural net.

Q: You said it was not a matter of choice, and it was not a matter of geography. Rather, it was a matter of being either in the center or in the epicenter. Would you comment on that?

A: All that is built in the center in terms of the emotions is stable, and all that is built in the epicenter is precarious. It follows that what was reflected in the external world was just an epitome of what was in the psyche. The water was a specter without color, without form, and without any effect; at some point, it could disappear by evaporation. (For some reason and for some people, water becomes life; for some people water becomes death.)

Now the splitting of the waves into two halves with a thunderous roar, where each side rose as high as a mountain, that interspace between the two waves was the balance between hope and fear that resulted from contractive and repulsive forces, and the repulsive and contractive forces were an obligation that had to be fulfilled and a prohibition that had to be upheld. All of this was done through humility that was exposed to the Sublimity. That was the reason God asked Moses to strike the sea with his cane—the symbol of humility.

God could have told Moses to prepare a raft, for example, or a canoe.

Q: How about Pharaoh's confession?

A: You can understand that what spoke on behalf of self-aggrandizement were the constituents of the ego. Once they started disintegrating, the reality of the self was disclosed. In other words, the layers of the ego started peeling, and the reality of the "I" started being manifested. As you can see, this was Pharaoh's confession.

CHAPTER 21

At this stage, the government is no longer holding the throne of its sovereignty. We don't say that it is owned by corporations because we have passed that point already. Instead, it is owned by the victimization of the corporations, as we shall see with the people behind the stock market.

Pharaoh and his army had collapsed, but Moses did not take over the government. Instead, his government was in constant transit.

As was previously said, Moses' government was in transit. He was in a direction facing the Promised Land. God asked Moses to purify himself and to prepare for an appointment: ablution, fasting, and total effacement. In the meantime, Moses placed his brother in charge over his people before leaving for the appointment.

The following dialogue transpired between God and Moses. "What made you hasten in advance of your people, O Moses?"
Moses replied, "Behold, they are close on my footsteps; I hasten to you, O my Lord, to please you."
God said, "We have tested your people in your absence, and Al-Samiri has led them astray."

Al-Samiri was one of the followers of Moses. (In reality, his name was the Samaritan. However, history is sometimes awkward, and the name Samaritan became a symbol of honor, instead of being a symbol of jeopardy as it was supposed to be. That's why we are using Al-Samiri as his name.) However, when Moses was absent, Al-Samiri took advantage of the situation and asked all the people in the region to invest mutually by giving up their jewelry, which he then liquefied, amalgamated, and molded

into the image of a calf's body. In doing this, Al-Samiri was acting on a deep and secret knowledge. He was aware of the presence of an angel on Earth, and he timed his actions to correspond to when the angel passed by. He knew that after the angel's passage, the angel left life with a soul behind him in that particular place. He merely caught a glimmer of the passing of the angel. He threw a glimpse of that passing into the calf, and then the calf gave forth a mooing sound.

Al-Samiri inherited internal poverty and isolation, which spurred him to externalize and then to admire the idolatry of a bull, a bull that had a tendency to fight with horns and that sought the enslavement of others, as well as symbolizing high prices in the stock market. The momentary shape of this bull was the volume of the participants.

In this search, he was aided by the complicity of some people who in the near future would control the large corporations and the banking system, which in turn would be used to control all the other interlinking sub-systems.

The motion and mooing of the golden calf provided Al- Samiri with a chance to control the fluctuations of the market. Through this motion, he was able to impose any common sense he wanted, and then new prohibitions and obligations, which were for the benefit of the wealthy owners of the transnational corporations and the banking system, and which were based upon their convention wisdom, which stated as a fundamental protocol: "Remember the golden rule; he who has the gold makes the rules."

Of course, everybody pretended to be aware of and in control of their emotions, and every nation pretended to be aware of and in control of its investment. However, the reality was that people's emotions followed their hearts, and their hearts followed their investments. Therefore, the one who controlled the fluctuations in the market was the one who controlled their hearts. The one who controlled their hearts was the one who controlled their emotions, and the one who controlled their emotions was the one who established what passed for common sense. The people's emotions were thus enslaved within the labyrinth of the obscurantism of that government and its fabricated common sense. In short, the people had become slaves to their own emotions.

Al-Samiri could not deal with and control individuals within the nation, but he was able to deal with them collectively through their mutual investment.

It was under Aaron's watch that the golden calf was created. As such, the situation with regard to Aaron was quite complex.

In addition, Moses had another lesson for his people upon his return. When he came back, he was already aware Al- Samiri had made the calf and about the details surrounding the calf's construction. In confronting this situation, Moses went to the hierarchy of the government in a careful, step-by-step manner. He not only rectified an error, but he also taught an eternal lesson about how the New World Order was built.

Who was the first to be blamed?

Moses went to his people first, although he knew that it was Al-Samiri who fabricated the calf. Of note, by saying his people, I don't mean a particular ethnicity or a particular religion, for this group was cosmopolitan. Anyway, Moses started at the bottom of the pyramid by saying, "O my people! Did not your Lord make a handsome promise to you (by saving you from Pharaoh)? Did the promise then seem to you long (in coming), or did you desire that wrath should descend from your Lord on you, so you broke your promise to me?"

Look how the First Admirable spoke gentle words. He didn't refer the salvation of his people to himself or to anything he had done, but he gave all credit to his Lord.

The people said, "We did not break the promise (voluntarily), but we were forced to carry the weight from people's ornaments, so we flung them (into the fire), and that was what Al-Samiri suggested."

Clearly, there must have been a major propaganda effort and influence from some group to have caused this tribulation. This can be seen by the fact that the same people who initially responded to the questioning by Moses continued by saying, "They said that this is your god and the god of Moses."

Now who said to the people that the calf was their god and the god of Moses? Was it Al-Samiri, an unknown group, or both? The truth of the matter lies in the use of the plural pronoun "they." As such, Al-Samiri could be included in this group even though Al-Samiri was referred to individually as suggesting that the people throw their ornaments into the fire. The people said that Al-Samiri suggested it, but they didn't say exactly what words he used. It could have been a vague encouragement, but this did not exclude him from sharing responsibility in saying that the golden calf was their god and the god of Moses.

The pronoun was "they," so who were they? They were the wealthy people. They were not blamed because they were rich, but because they were narcissistic, liars, and greedy. These were the people who owned the gold. These were people who controlled the transnational corporations, including the corporate media; they control the whole world today.

It is worth to stop here for a second and hear the mockery of this modern world. Lengthy time is spent on the internet research, conferences have been made, volumes of books have been written, serious discussions were shared among people; all of this to search for the elite that is controlling the world...............

Yet, Moses never directed his dialogue to them. Why? The answer is because this Admirable didn't deal with symptoms, he dealt with the source. The damage that worried Moses the most was not the motion of the calf or the fluctuations in the market, but what would follow that.

(The artificial and fabricated rules that are encapsulated within obligations and prohibitions that become statutory, institutionalized, standardized, and a part of public policy and political philosophy are always established by think tanks—the wealthy people. Any logic and rationale that these bylaws have are drawn from the consumption criterion. Therefore, what satisfies consumption becomes the standard for what is logical and common sense.)

From whom was Moses to obtain accurate testimony and the truth about what had transpired with the golden calf? The answer was his brother Aaron, although Moses already knew the truth before he came back to his people. He already knew his brother had given his every effort to stop the people from constructing the golden calf. Nonetheless, Moses went to his brother and blamed him. In doing so, he was waiting for Aaron to give his statement and to pinpoint his reason for why he had finally stopped his attempts to dissuade the Israelites from constructing the calf. So what was Aaron's reason? Why did he finally stop his efforts?

Aaron's presence was an interference with an abstention. He had reached the limits of what he could do when his continued interference was going to cause further separation and bloodshed among the Children of Israel. When he reached that point, he abstained from further action. If Aaron had not interfered, it would have been a disaster. If he had interfered beyond the limit, it would also have been a disaster. However, his interference was meticulously calculated. He did his share of humility and abstained from crossing the frontier of Sublimity.

So why did Moses confront Aaron? There are two basic reasons. Firstly, Moses was demonstrating that when one adjudicates a situation, one should always obtain and check all the relevant facts and all sides of the story before acting. Secondly, Moses was illustrating that even though Aaron was his familial brother, the more important brotherhood is brotherhood under God's shelter.

At last, Moses went to Al-Samiri and spoke to him in a most unexpected way. Moses said, "What had come over you, O Al-Samiri?"

"I saw what they did not," replied Al-Samiri. "I took a handful of dust from the messenger's (i.e., the angel's) trail and flung it away (into the calf). Thus did my soul prompt me?"

Al-Samiri's answer was quite revealing. It did not have any direct link to the question that Moses asked, but it did demonstrate a great deal about Al-Samiri's obsession with his internal self-obsession. He had become captive to and preoccupied with impressing others with what he had discovered about the passing of the angel, even though he was religious. Moses asked Al-Samiri about the tribulation that he had caused. In response, Al-Samiri told Moses about his strategy! The poor man didn't know prophecy sees beyond time and space. Did he think Moses was in need of a journalist?

There was in Al-Samiri an inner speech similar to Cain's when God said about him, "His soul suggested to him to kill his brother." This type of inner speech or suggestion demonstrated a developing self-aggrandizement of the ego. Al- Samiri's answer was that his soul prompted him revealed the same sort of self-grandiosity. In both cases, there was self- glorification. In Cain's case, his inner speech led him to criminality by killing his brother. In Al-Samiri's case, his inner speech led him to enslaving the people. Both cases resulted in cataclysm.

Al-Samiri deserved severe correction and even execution, but Moses was not just dealing with Al-Samiri, he was dealing

with all of future humanity. "Be gone!" cried Moses, and he condemned Al-Samiri to live as an outcast, telling him to say, "Touch me not!" to everyone he would meet for the rest of his life.

Why did Moses tell Al-Samiri to say, "Touch me not?" He was letting the punishment suit the crime by not satisfying Al-Samiri's desire. This is what befalls someone who tries to convert people to his own desires; he becomes sensitive to and disturbed by any minor gestures or words from others.

During this crisis, before he even released Al-Samiri, Moses didn't let Al-Samiri continue with idolatry dominating his state of consciousness. Moses preferred to purify him first and to eliminate the calf from his mind, which was an iconoclastic mission. Moses said, "Now look at your god, to whom you have devoted yourself."

Moses burned the calf and scattered its ashes over the sea in front of Al-Samiri and all the others. He then admonished his people by saying, "O my people! You have indeed wronged in devoting yourselves to the calf. Turn in repentance to your Creator and slay the culprits (egos) within you."

Why did Moses tell Al-Samiri to look at his god but did not use the same expression when he spoke to the idolaters among his people? He didn't say that the calf was their god, but referred to the calf to which they had devoted themselves. He made this distinction even though both Al-Samiri and a section among the Children of Israel seemed to have had the same intention. After all, some of the Israelites had said, "We will not abandon this cult, but we will devote ourselves to it until Moses returns to us." In saying this, they made their adoration of God conditional upon the return of Moses.

The word devotion does not mean worship. One can devote oneself to something, but that does not mean that the devotion creates obligations and prohibitions other than those existing intuitively. However, if the legitimacy or illegitimacy of these obligations and prohibitions are believed to follow from that to which one is devoted, then the devotion has become worship. There is no record that Al-Samiri ever actually worshiped the golden calf, but still Moses referred to the calf as Al-Samiri's god. If the prophet said it, then it's true.

What actually happened between the elite that controls the world and Al-Samiri was never directly disclosed, but one can infer what happened from the subsequent results. The whole process was meant to use think tanks to modify and create new laws, which were different from the intuitive Divine Law that already existed primordially.

When a stimulus intoxicates a person to the point that he is driven by it, there results a conditioned response, which satisfies the instinctual aim that was previously established in a clandestine manner. For this habitual strength to be reinforced, there has to be a strong link between the stimulus and its response.

The stimulus part of the above equation is affected through propaganda and lies. Do you want to live an eternal life? Do you want me to show you the tree of eternity? Do you want me to show you the kingdom that will never perish? Do you want to remain forever young? Do you want to look great and always feel good? Do you want to keep your money in a safe place? If so, here is the calf. Invest your money and wait for its maturity. Don't you see it is moving with a mooing sound, which is a sign of life? Those same words were previously pronounced by the first teacher, whose name was Lucifer and his nickname is Beelzebub. This is how trust is gained from people, and it opens the door to altering belief.

After this is done, and after the link between the stimulus and the response is reinforced, the majority of people are conditioned and emotionally "teleguided." Since they no longer make an effort to think about what is logical and illogical, they merely assume that the laws they are creating must obviously be logical. Of note, the institution of doctrine is contrary to a person having a choice, a chance to think, or a moment to reflect. The real meaning of indoctrination requires that all moments of reflection must be completely eliminated and that decisions must be automatic and reflexive. Those who are conditioned to certain deviations no longer experience any disturbance with regard to imposed dogma, and they are fundamentally incapable of rejecting such dogma.

In order for these wealthy experts to secure the continuity of what seems to be a smooth mode of life, they have to maintain economic perspectives in conjunction with so-called logic or common sense. Further, this common sense has to be in conjunction with people's consumption. This consumption has to be coordinated with people's desires, and these desires need to be converted into perceived necessities, the lack of which supposedly exposes people to a major disaster in their daily

activity. If by mistake or by forgetfulness a person does not behave and act according to the prescribed mode of life or does not buy those supposedly indispensable materials and irresistible products that are so-called necessities and that are linked to the fabricated common sense, then he is inundated with messages proclaiming, "You have to be; you need to have; you should become; you must ignore; otherwise, you'll be excluded from the admired society."

When Moses told Al-Samiri that the calf was his god, it was not that Al-Samiri was seduced by the mooing motions of the calf and bowed to it, but it was because Al-Samiri wanted to enslave the people by stagnated prices regarding the stock market, which leads to the stagnation of the emotions.

Introspective Exegesis

Q: Why did Al-Samiri choose a calf? Was it really Al-Samiri's choice or was some internal force of which he was unaware dominating him?

A: The bull was a symbol for a person who believed that stock market prices would go higher and who thus bought stocks in anticipation of those higher prices. Bulling the market meant trying to advance prices. Given this understanding, it can be seen that the bull had a tendency to knock down and exploit the poor and naïve, i.e., those who were most adversely affected by fluctuations in the market.

Q: At the risk of being overly meticulous, you said that Al-Samiri had fashioned a calf, i.e., a baby bull, not a bull. Is there a difference?

A: He was giving an impression to investors of a possible maturity, which was a life of security in this domain.

Q: Why didn't Al-Samiri make a calf from earth, from wood, or from his own jewelry? Why didn't he make it from the jewelry that belonged to a distant people?

A: The people didn't have any love for or connection to clay or wood. If Al-Samiri had used foreign capital, there would have been no investment in the idolatry from those people who were present. It was only by getting the people to invest what they loved, i.e., their own jewelry, that he was able to influence them. As such, he asked them to invest their hearts, or at least what was connected to their hearts, i.e., their jewelry.

Q: What was the stock market all about, and who were the shareholders? I hear those terms being used a lot throughout the entire world, even in poor countries.

A: Let's go through that step-by-step. When we say stock, we are referring to storing something...

Q: What was the reason behind stocking?

A: In the old days, some people stocked merchandize for a period of time; when there was a lack of a particular commodity in the market, the stocker took out that stocked merchandize and sold it for an outrageously exorbitant price, a practice that was prohibited by the Divinity.

With regard to the stock market, people didn't stock anything; rather, they collected money from so-called investors to make them believe that they were shareholders in that company. If the company did well, the price of the shares would go higher, and eventually the shareholders would make a profit out of it, and percentage of dividends. However, if the company did not do well, the so-called investors would end up liquidating their position with a loss, in some cases losing their entire investment.

Q: I find this really confusing. I don't know how to put it into words. I mean... How to buy... So what were these so-called investors buying in reality?

A: It was a reflection of what Al-Samiri caught from the angel. In your opinion, what did Al-Samiri catch?

Q: I don't know. You said life...

A: Okay, let's assume that it was life. Did anybody from those investors own that life?

Q: I don't think so. I don't even know if he caught anything.

A: He caught a simulation and flung a simulation, and those investors owned the illusion of life.

Q: Would you explain that?

A: To simulate is to pretend to have something that you actually don't have, and to dissimulate is to pretend not to have something that you already have. One implies deprivation, and one implies possession; one implies absence with a faked presence, and one implies presence with a faked absence. For example, when one is watching a play or spectacle on stage, the performers are just simulating various roles, and those roles that are being portrayed become hyper-simulations and become believable to and acceptable by the spectators. The performers are catching something in the air and then transmitting it to the spectators. In other words, they are inviting the whole into the mutuality of the one, and when the spectators see the hyper- simulations of the performers, they assume that they are true. If we analyze the situation, we realize that the performers are, in reality, deprived of the characters they are performing, and the spectators are likewise deprived of those characters. However, all of them, both performers and spectators, want to live a moment of deprivation, a moment of unconsciousness.

Q: Getting back to the stock exchange, you mentioned the banking system with its usury and the stock market. I couldn't ascertain the difference between the two, if there was any.

A: It was very similar with regard to the investor and the company's agenda. The only difference was that one activity was slow, and the other activity was ostensibly fast. Depositing money in a bank with the aim of gaining interest was slower and yielded a smaller dividend return to the investor. In contrast, investing the money in the stock market was potentially faster and usually yielded a substantial dividend to both the individual investor and the corporation. Now, our main concern is not with the investor or the company, but with an unknown third party. Our main concern is the stock itself and what was meant behind it. What people bought in the stock market was, in reality, what the performer plays on stage. They bought air; they bought simulation, especially in the futures market. Can you imagine? You enter the market with a selling position, and then you buy it back. Can you sell something you don't even own?

Q: Obviously not.

A: It was similar when it came to options in the stock market or the futures market. You entered the market with a selling position, and then bought your contract or your position back. There was disaster waiting to happen in such a scenario. It was not the buying or selling, but what the person was buying and selling. The person was buying and selling a value. If we submerge a little bit into the world of consciousness, the value was the flowing energy that was supposed to navigate freely within people's hearts.

Now do you know who the angel was that passed by and of what it was that Al-Samiri was aware?

Q: I have no idea.

A: He was Angel Gabriel (may peace and the blessing of God be upon him). Angel Gabriel's name in some other places was Holy Spirit. Where was this Holy Spirit?

Q: I really don't know.

A: He was and is the reflection of the Absolute in the macrocosm; in other words, he was and is the flow of animism in the universe. What we mean by that is that every star in the galaxies represents certain feelings in humans that have a potential to be seized and to be developed through a human's consciousness and behavior. When Al-Samiri caught a glimpse from the angels' passage, it was like he caught a simulation of the whole potential flowing energy of the universe with its galaxies, and he reduced it to a dead calf. Further, everything connected to that also became dead and lifeless.

There are cosmic rays—energy in space that synchronizes exactly with human consciousness. If those emotions are not exercising as they are supposed to be, they cause entropy in the ether, and that entropy affects the ecosystem. That's why you hear of all kind of allergies to things from nature, when in fact allergies have nothing to do with nature; they have to do with the predisposed nature of human being. Now what was said is from an astrophysical standpoint. When we go to the mystical approach, if the calf represented death, the investors were connected to that

231

death as well.

Q: When you said buying a value, what did you mean?

A: Before Al-Samiri fashioned the calf, people were looking at each other, and people were dealing with each other. When we say dealing with each other, it could have been in terms of trade, selling and buying or in terms of social interaction in general. When we say selling and buying, we mean that their emotions were flowing with a tendency to develop mutual trust, love, compassion, generosity, and gallantry, even if there was unscrupulousness within that trade. (It is better to externalize the hypocrisy than to simulate perfection with a hidden disaster.) Shall I name them all? I mean the number of sentiments. I cannot name them all because they coincide with the number of the stars in the galaxies. Even if I had the most advanced telescope, one that was 100 generations ahead of what we now have, I wouldn't even be able to name or count a few, because at the time when we count the number of stars, which coincide with the emotions, that number has disappeared in the ether.

After the calf was fashioned or created, people's eyes shifted to the calf—to their investment. They were no longer with each other, and neither with nature. The calf, meaning the investors' emotions, stagnated just like the stock exchange. The value that was supposed to flow among people was now flowing on the screen of the computer, and its fluctuations were affecting people's feelings. Here comes the death of every falling star, which eventually ends up as a meteorite. Do you know where the falling dead meteorites from the stars are located? Their location is in the subconscious; these dead meteorites in the external world are, in reality, people's dead emotions that once percolated, but become extrinsic, and then they died. In the long run, they created feelings of melancholy and angst.

Q: What did you mean when you said in the beginning: "At this stage, the government is no longer holding the throne of its sovereignty….up to…. it is instead owned by the victimization of the corporations, what did you mean by that?

A: We have corporations that consume individuality.

Q: What do you mean by consuming?

A: It is as if you were saying that the corporations gathered a state of metamorphosis of the emotions, and then they became stagnated. Once those emotions were gathered, they fed neither the company nor those victims of extirpation.

Now let's get to something a little deeper, the emotions flow from individuality not from collectivity. When there is collectivity you don't call that emotional expression; instead, you call it instead ambiance. Of note, the nation or the ecosystem is in reality the expression of every individual. Once the individual's emotions are suspended, there is no longer a nation or ecosystem. They, I mean the emotions, supposedly become the property of the one who owns the corporation. Now when all these individuals' emotions become the property of one person or of a group of people, they still have their functionality, but this time with turbulence. This time these emotions are no longer emotions because they cause a disequilibrium in the corporation, not from its fiscal aspect, but from its psychological aspect first, and then later on it will cause its jeopardy regarding the ecosystem.

Q: Getting back to Moses regarding the stock market…

A: Bear in mind that we are talking about facts and whether these facts were perceived or not. Take the example of the World Financial Center; it collapsed during Korah's time, not because of an act of terror or sabotage, but due to the condensation of wealth.

233

In reality, it is collapsing all the time in the psyches of people who have the same mindset as Korah.

Now getting back to the stock market, the stock market is crashing anyway, anytime, and anyhow. Don't wait until you see its collective and posterior crash; think about its individual and anterior crash that is taking place continuously in the mind. What Moses showed to people regarding the burning and the scattering of the calf was not an act of self-satisfaction; it was an act that was going to take place anyway, anytime, and anyhow. Now, when you hear the words 'the time of depression' and people were starving and couldn't find what to eat etc.....these are all scenarios fabricated by this elite.

Q: God asked Moses to purify himself for an appointment. Where is that reflection with regard to the psyche?

A: As we have previously seen, there are times when the Mosaic frequency inside you is looking for its uniqueness by calling the Creator. There are other times when the Sublimity is calling you. It's up to your humility to hear this voiceless call.

Q: Would you be more specific?

A: There are times when you just want to be withdrawn from everything, you become disgusted with everything, and you think something is wrong with you. Actually, there is nothing wrong with you. The majority of people handle this by going on vacation and having fun; there is nothing wrong with that. The exceptional Gnostic (I didn't say agnostic) understands that the call was meant for retreat, a journey without transit. This is a complete government that deals with the material world without neglecting the celestial world. Try to respond to that call by purifying yourself from your complete attachment to the world of decay.

Q: Now what was behind Moses leaving his brother Aaron in charge over his people?

A: This was the complete establishment of the internal government; in other words, this was how the ruler should govern his internal nation.

Q: Ruler? Could you describe his internal mission?

A: This type of ruler is the one who governs the psychological and physiological bodies within the self before controlling anything else outside the self. He is the one who maintains the distinction between the instinctive desires and the implanted desires that become an addiction. He is the one who controls his temper and the army of reasoning that is free from ego defense mechanisms. He controls the military and is not controlled by it. This intuitive ruler (Moses' frequency) accepts the information captured by his workers, i.e., the senses, but he nevertheless recognizes that his senses are limited and makes sure not to follow every bit of illusory information brought to him by the senses. Such a governor is the one who does not object to the special intellect, i.e., his prime minister when he offers him his weaknesses. He even looks forward to this companionship. Now before leaving, Moses consulted his special intellect, his brother, not in terms of asking his permission, but in terms of putting him in charge of the senses.

Q: Would you elaborate in terms of the central nervous system, if that's what you meant regarding this governor?

A: To begin with, we have the central nervous system, which is the governor over the whole body. We have nerve impulses that travel along the body and transmit signals from the central nervous system to the organs. The nerves that carry these impulses are called efferent nerves. We also have nerve impulses that travel along the body and transmit signals from the organs to the central nervous system. These impulses travel along the afferent nerves. We know that these nerve impulses originally travel in one direction. If, for example, information from the genital system (sexual desire) or the digestive system (appetite desire) is transmitted to the nervous system through a nerve, action orders from the brain cannot travel back to the genital or the stomach through the same nerve. There is another nerve, i.e., an efferent one, which carries the return message.

The central nervous system (the governor) should not accept every instinctual desire without the consultation of his special intellect (his knowledgeable prime minister). In other words, when the stimulus is transmitted to him, he must not get confused between what the system wants and what it needs; otherwise, the governor will be dethroned, and his confusion will cause his own coup-d'état. Originally, the brain does not respond to the stimulus until it consults the intellect and makes a distinction between want and need. This happens in one fraction of a second. That's why the return message from the nervous system takes a different nerve alleyway to surprise the conceivers. That is also why it makes a controlled and volitional response to the stimulus. In this way, one avoids becoming an automaton and avoids being dethroned.

Q: If the contrary does apply, what are the consequences?

A: Do you see what is happening in our modern life regarding psychological trauma (depression), it is all caused by the loss of the self—the disappearance of the individual nation as it was initially described when talking about the governor (the internal government) with his senses, i.e., desires.

Take the case of serotonin, for instance. This chemical agent acts as a neurotransmitter, a type of chemical that helps relay signals from one area of the brain to another. It is believed that an imbalance in serotonin levels may influence mood in a way that leads to depression. Now what are the possible problems regarding a lack of serotonin? It could be a low brain cell production of serotonin; it could be an inability of serotonin to reach the receptor sites, or it could be a shortage in tryptophan, the chemical from which serotonin is made.

A long time ago, we didn't hear so much about psychological illnesses to the extent that we do today. In this so-called modern life, everything is conditional, everything is "because and therefore;" everything is systemized; everything is centralized, and people make their journey conditional by relying on what is supposedly scientific evidence.

When it comes to the Divinity, the Creator asked you to do good things based on faith and servitude. There is no "because and therefore," even if you find reasons and explanations along your journey. The cause and effect that you think regulate your life will themselves cause a conditional segment. This segment will cause a block in the brain, and this block will cause malfunctioning or suppression of serotonin or dopamine or another neurotransmitter. Am I making myself understandable?

Q: Earlier you were linking the nervous system to the whole body and its organs, but here I see you talking only about what is taking place in the brain regarding serotonin.

A: Serotonin can also affect the functionality of the cardiovascular system, muscles, and various elements in the whole physical system. However, there is something that I wanted to get to, which is that scientists often refer to the brain's production of serotonin, and sometimes they refer to the brain's manufacture of serotonin.

Let's try a small experiment. You have someone who is

depressed. You share a conversation with him by giving him a chance to talk and by making him feel comfortable, and you find him going on and on. Afterwards, you realize that he feels much better than before, and he admits that. Now here comes the foggy justification: he will say to you: "By talking to you, it always makes me feel better." At that point, you say to yourself, "Well, I must be unique because I have a power to affect people's mood." Then here comes a smart scientist who says that both of you are wrong. The scientist says that while the person was talking to you, his brain simply started manufacturing serotonin, and that's what makes this depressed person change his mood from bad to good.

Q: Who is right, and who is wrong?

A: All of them are right, and all of them are wrong. Getting back to our analysis. The brain manufactures those chemical agents when you don't know, when you don't have "the because and therefore" in your journey, just as it did for the one who started talking without having planned it. If the depressed person had known the results of that dialogue and had started his conversation with that projection, chances are he wouldn't have ascended to a positive mood. Take this example in all other aspect of life, especially when it comes to worship or sacrifice.

Sacrifice is not necessarily an act of giving something as an object. You can sacrifice your time for the sake of another; you can sacrifice a forgiveness. The most important thing is that you don't have an agenda of receiving something in return for the sacrifice you are making. Otherwise, it would not be distance from you, and it would therefore create stagnation, and this stagnation would be a block in your nervous system.

Forgiveness itself facilitates the passage of many chemical agents in the body. Most of the time, especially in an intellectual

238

environment, people tell you that they don't have any scientific

evidence to justify their engaging in worship. However, they don't realize that they are merely consulting their egos when they make such a claim. Further, their egos are just flowing with desires. Now these desires have their time, and that segmented time creates a block in the brain. In our final analysis, who created the serotonin? It is nothingness, and what is nothingness? It is a negation followed by an affirmation that the person freely believes without explanation, and what is negation followed by affirmation? It is "There is no God except God."

Q: Let's get back to the governor (the nervous system) and his nation (the physical body).

A: When the stimulus and response are under control of the nervous system, this is what facilitates the smooth functioning of the chemical agents in the brain and their extension in the body.

Q: What did Moses do when he sought dialogue with the Creator?

A: There were some very important events, very deep. We prefer not to discuss them.

Q: We have a record that God told Moses, "We tested your people during your absence."

A: Yes. During your concentration on your Creator, when your humility has a total link with the Sublimity, you feel a certain sense of tranquility and holy comfort to such an extent that if the kings of the world knew about that feeling they would wage war against you to seize that feeling. Fortunately, this is the secret of the sincere worshiper. When he is seen by people who are competing and chasing after this material world, they think that he is stupid and fanatical, and such criticism gives him a true sense of independence.

Anyway, at that time of your retreat, you find that you don't want to abandon that feeling. You want it to be forever. (I don't say it happens to everybody, but it happens to a few). Here lies the biggest trap, and here lies the question. Is it that you don't want to abandon God, or is it that you don't want to abandon your feelings? If you have a name for your feelings during that retreat, then that means you are leaning slightly or entirely on your feelings.

Q: Is there a problem with that?

A: Originally you approached God without a prearranged agenda, and that's what really kept you navigating without any frontiers and with that beautiful feeling. However, once you relied on that feeling, it becomes a stationary consultation for you. In other words, whenever you want to pray or to approach God with any type of worship, you consult your feelings.

Q: Would you summarize that?

A: There is an immense difference between being with the feelings and being with the Creator of the feelings. It is much better to have the absence of feelings while being with the Creator through consciousness and humility, than it is to have a good feeling with the absence of the Creator.

When you find a name for a feeling, you should be vigilant to put your concentration back on the Giver of feelings. This is what keeps you as an astral gentleman, and yet terrestrial at the same time. This is the biggest disaster of religious people. They begin with the Creator, and they end up being with the ambiance. They then collapse and vengefully project their collapse on external others, all the while thinking that this overreaction is for God's sake.

Now, let me get back to your question. The material world with its attraction and its preoccupation would drain you back again to the competition. The biggest enemies, complicit with the material world in which you are mistakenly seeking refuge and polarity, are your own people, i.e., your own senses and your own internal desires. Therefore, be vigilant over your cabinet.

Q: What was the secret behind Al-Samiri, the one who led them astray?

A: This was the abuse of confidence in religion. Al-Samiri was very religious, even very mystical. When Pharaoh and his army collapsed, Moses became so powerful that a lot of people began to refer to this power as heroism, not prophecy; they called Moses a hero. Moses said that he was a humble messenger of God, but they called him a hero. They wanted to make heroism out of prophecy. They completely forgot what really saved them from Pharaoh. What actually saved them from Pharaoh was the cane, i.e., Moses' humility, and by the time they were saved, a section among them chose superiority. They started propagandizing the pedagogy of, "We are the chosen people, and we ride humanity." Fortunately, the gentleman Moses never verbalized or even felt that expression.

Anyway, Al-Samiri is the abuse of confidence in religion, and that Al-Samiri could be inside you. You think it's your power, but it is instead your disaster.

Q: You mentioned something about the Promised Land. Would you elaborate a little bit about that?

A: When you speak about a promise, you are speaking about a hidden condition. It is as if the father promises something to his son on one condition, i.e., that the son does his homework. With regard to our case, the unspoken condition is an identity, and the identity itself is a non-identity. In other words, it is effacement of self-attributes, i.e., the state of humility. This is the condition; you will see it in more detail shortly.

The true expression revealed by the Divinity was the "Sacred Land." This land was the land of diagnosis; it was the land of gauging; it was the land of either conformity or conflict, depending on the person's intention before entering it. Moses did not enter the Sacred Land; neither did his brother Aaron.

Q: Why was that?

A: When he asked his followers to follow him to the Sacred Land, they refused. Moses did not ask them to invade or ask them to fight. He merely asked them to enter. They, on their part, not only refused but claimed, "A race of giants dwells in this land. We will not set foot in it till they are gone." They also said, "Go, you and your Lord, and fight. Here we will stay."

Given that they were still far from the Sacred Land, why did the excuse of a race of giants come into their minds? Why did the word "fight" cross their minds? This shows you that when they started neglecting humility and developing their feelings of superiority, they started developing adversaries in their subconscious according to the constituents of their grandiosity. They felt superior. They projected their own feelings of superiority onto the inhabitants of that land, even though they had no clue as to who inhabited that land. The second thing they said to Moses was, "Go, you and your Lord, and fight," but who was talking about fighting? Neither God nor Moses had ever mentioned this word. This shows you that when a person gets out of his center of gravity, he starts to feel adversaries, i.e., fighters

242

waiting for him somewhere.

Q: I assume there were some of Moses' followers who followed him?

A: There was his brother. In addition, there was Joshua bin Nun, one of Moses' closest disciples. Caleb also supported Moses, as did a lot of young, sincere believers.

Q: Did they ever enter this land?

A: After their refusal to enter that land, they brought punishment upon themselves, and they became homeless and perturbed for forty years, losing their compass of direction before they finally entered that land. When they entered the Sacred Land, Moses and Aaron were no longer with them and had left this world. They entered that land when Joshua bin Nun was the successor.

Q: What happened next?

A: The Kingdom of Israel was established, but Moses had not come as a king. He had come as a symbol of humility in front of the Sublimity. However, the Kingdom of Israel was built on superiority. It was built on usury, and it was built on seduction. The perdition of that kingdom started from the religious people. The rabbis one day would preach against drinking wine and against illegitimate sex, and the following day they shared in those same pleasures. One day they were against usury, and the next day they collected it. After years in that situation, Moses' identity was completely lost. What remained from it was only heroism, which was what also happened with the prophets David and Solomon (may peace and the blessing of God be upon them). They call them kings. God forbid if these humble prophets came for that purpose. The Israelites had withdrawn prophecy, had drained away the divine message from those prophets, and had left them as

243

bodies without souls, ignoring the fact that the image they gave to their prophets was a repercussion that turned upon them.

When immorality started being legitimized, they didn't know they were dethroning themselves. They didn't know they were looking for someone to command them. They didn't know they were looking for someone to invade them. Thus, they finally gave an indirect invitation and a green light to Nebuchadnezzar to invade them. He caused massacres and burned books, all of which was caused by the Israelites having neglected the teaching of Moses.

Q: Getting back to my psyche. What does the Sacred or the Promised Land represent for me, allegorically speaking?

A: The Sacred Land is inside you, the Sacred Land is the final image of your internal government. Do you remember when God spoke to Moses the first time? He told him he was by the sacred valley. We mentioned that the sacred valley was Moses' heart and that there was no need to look for its geographic location. Actually, everybody has the potential of that sacred valley. God did not tell Moses he was by the sacred mountain. God's words were very meticulous. He merely said the sacred valley, in other words the trough, in other words the humility that has a potential to be absorbed from the Sublimity. It's up to the person to transform potential into actual. Now, that internal sacred valley is harmoniously and exactly linked to the Sacred Land. It's like the Sacred Land absorbs the sacred valley into it if the conditions that Moses, the gentleman, was carrying are met. If the contrary happens, in other words, if grandiosity overcomes humility, if harshness defeats gentleness, if polarization dominates universality, if hatred overpowers love, if rigidity defeats submission, then there is conflict. The potential intuitive sacredness that serves as conformity to the Sacred Land is transformed to conflict.

THE SECOND PHASE
OF HISTORY

CHAPTER 22

We next discuss the second phase of history within a government and within a human's life. In the prior phase, emotions had been the property of the corporations. In this phase, emotions became the property of machines within the corporations. People's animation came from the machines. At this point, the appearance of the Second Admirable, Jesus Christ, became indispensable. This was the time of the potential for reanimation.

At this stage of life, there was no lack of energy, as the whole world was mistakenly claiming. There was no lack of education, as the whole world was mistakenly claiming. Instead, there was an overflow of energy everywhere; there was an overflow of information everywhere; there was an overflow of natural resources everywhere. However, every energy is entropic and metastable, whether within the ecosystem or within people's states of mind. All of society was completely detached from nature, instead of being in harmony with and absorbing from nature. Everybody became allergic to certain things in nature. Humans' intelligence was subordinated to machines, resulting in a type of artificial intelligence (AI). Human life was absorbed from electronic components, resulting in cybernetics.

At this point, we enter the epoch of the gods, i.e., cybernetic interaction. Here we encounter the roles of Jupiter, Poseidon, Uranus, Pluto, Athena, etc., which linked corporations and humans through electronic components, influencing human emotions to such a point that there was a sort of ghost inhabiting human minds with reference to a human's devotion to computers and to the reflected circuit (AI) from computers back to humans.

The Divine Media's morning edition reported the breaking news: Angel Gabriel was instructed to come down. (This was an emergency interference. There was no life anymore. Planet Earth faced a cataclysm, since there was no animism anymore.) His mission was to breathe the Holy Spirit into a woman.

When Angel Gabriel got close to her, the woman said, "I seek refuge from thee to the Most Gracious, (come not near) if thou dost fear God."
Then Angel Gabriel told her that he was a messenger of God by expressing the password. At that point, the woman became receptive to the absorption of the Holy Spirit.

A lot of propaganda against this woman was fabricated about her pregnancy. There were rumors in the streets and in the newspapers accusing her of all sorts of bad things. After seeing this from her people, she vowed to the Merciful that she would not talk to anybody.
When she was asked by people about her mysterious pregnancy and her deliverance, she pointed to the baby, and they said, "How can we talk to the one who is a child in the cradle?"

He (the baby) said, "I am indeed a servant of God. He hath given me revelation and made me a prophet." (May the peace and blessing of God be upon you, Jesus.)

His mission started at his birth and lasted for 33 years, unlike that of other prophets, who were all given the divine message after a certain age of maturity, mostly after forty years of age.
During Moses' epoch, people's emotions became corporations. During Jesus' epoch, people's emotions became cybernetic. In other words, if you tried to deal with humans, you didn't even

247

find them. Instead, you found an answering machine. If by some miracle you found a person, there was no difference between him and the computer. If you looked for a sentimental reaction from a human being, you found the simulation of sentiments. If you asked for humanism, the unspoken words from the person told you, "I'm sorry the computer was not programmed to be compassionate or to display any sympathy on the screen."

This phenomenon was not like before when corporations were dealing with each other. Here, we had electronic devices that were dealing with each other. Human beings were not automatons like before. We had already passed that point. People were, instead, machines in their full forms, dehumanized. People could be next to each other, and they couldn't get in touch with each other except through electronic devices. Neighbors could be next to each other, and they had to email each other instead of facing and touching each other. People could be lovers; yet, they couldn't express their sentiments directly except through texting each other. People felt safer communicating with each other through computers, rather than facing each other. In almost every public service, there was a partition separating humans, and those people in charge stared worshipfully at computers without giving the slightest glance to their fellow humans. Almost every sector of industry had cameras watching, and they had a security service. They had more trust in a camera than in a human being.

Life was so alienated; it was as though everybody was in a flight simulator sitting in front of a screen of his reflected desires and flying toward holographic, simulated images of pretence that did not have any reality. In other words, reality had died, and now they had to reinvent reality through simulation. What was reflected in the mirror of life was a holographic image of simulation that did not have an origin.

As a result of these phenomena, there were two scourges that ravaged the world under the name of civilization and technological interface and the third one is a result. They were blindness, leprosy, and finally death. The whole world suffered from alienation and fragmentation, as if they had leprosy. Nobody dealt with another except through an intermediary or a technological device. Most of them suffered from the blindness of not seeing each other; instead, they saw the rules of Jupiter, Apollo, Uranus, Pluto, etc. as being above human harmony. All of them died in the sense of absorbing their lives from dead idols, electronic components linked to Jupiter Incorporated, Poseidon Limited, Pluto, Athena, etc.

At that point, Jesus' mission came from the Divinity. "I have come to you with a sign from your Lord. I make for you out of clay the figure of a bird and breathe into it, and it becomes a bird by God's (will, permission and power), and I heal the blind and the leper, and I bring the dead to life by God's (will, permission, and power). I tell you what you eat and what you store in your houses. Surely therein is a sign for you if you believe."

We have three segments of his life. One segment was before his birth, and that had to do with his mother. One segment had to do with his entire life, which lasted for 33 years until the day of his ascension. The last segment had to do with the time after his absence.

Shortly before Jesus' ascension to the celestial world, he spoke to his disciples, "Verily, I say unto you that one of you shall betray me, insomuch that I shall be sold like a sheep; but woe unto him….he shall fall into the pit that he has prepared for others."

Now the decision to kill Jesus had been part of a discussion and plot against him that went way back. The main part of the reason was that the Children of Israel started preaching superiority under the guise that they were the chosen people by God. What follows

249

that is the practice of usury throughout the world.

That fabricated dogma of being superior had isolated them in the world while being targeted; the reason why, historically speaking, for a period of time they reach certain level of power which is in reality only a slack, and then shortly after they face a free fall. And Jesus on the other side was preaching humility same as Moses, and was against usury.

The other reason behind that plot was that Jesus was a danger to the pagans who had multiple and visible gods. Jesus was calling for One God. The pagans fashioned definite gods incarcerated within time and space, and Jesus was preaching an indefinite God beyond time and space. The pagans wanted to externalize emotions from people's minds. In contrast, Jesus was internalizing them within people's minds.

As we know, Judas Iscariot was the traitor who was one of the 12 disciples of Jesus. He was, in reality, just the last drop that caused the overflow of the vase. In other words, he was not the main cause of the decision to kill Jesus.

When the night of Jesus' ascension arrived, everything in the terrestrial world was plotted and ready for his execution. On the other hand, in the celestial world, everything was ready, as well. Judas Iscariot was a mediator zigzagging in three directions. In one direction, he was with those who devoured usury. In another direction, he was with the head of the soldiers under the Romans. In still another direction, he was hypocritically among Jesus' disciples.

For the concept of the Trinity. There was no sign, and there was no verse whatsoever that showed or reflected the concept of the Trinity. There was evidence of death; that's for sure. However, this evidence of death became distorted into a fabricated dogma that was made after Jesus' ascension and that existed under the slogan of: "Don't worry; someone died for us." The people behind this fabricated dogma had no idea and no clue about what really happened. Further, the fabricated dogma of the Father, the Son, and the Holy Spirit was originally made as a pre-assumption under the word "maybe," even though its cascade came from the Romans. It then became an obsession under the words, "There is no doubt about it." It then became reality under the words, "Of course." Finally, it became sacred under the words, "In the name of the Father and the Son and the Holy Spirit." This entire false pedagogy was linked and taught by the pagans without anybody's awareness.

The breaking news from the Creator was in the morning edition of the Divine Media: "God has set a seal on their hearts for their blasphemy, and little is it they believe—that they rejected faith, that they uttered against Mary a grave false charge, that they said (in boast), 'We killed Christ Jesus, the son of Mary, the messenger of God'—but they killed him not, nor crucified him. Only a likeness of that was shown to them. And those who differ therein are full of doubts, with no (certain) knowledge, but only conjecture to follow, for of a surety they killed him not. Nay, God raised him up unto Himself, and God is exalted in power, wise..."

Introspective Exegesis

Q: What does the Virgin Mary represent?

A: The Virgin Mary is all about nature. She is the universe telling people, "I don't exist, but my existence is through that spirit by my sound of silence." She is the sun telling people that she is not a sun by herself. She is the sun because of the spirit that is inside her. She is the moon that is telling people she does not exist. She is the mountains telling people we don't exist. She is the rivers telling people we don't exist. She is the seasons telling

251

people we don't exist. She is the stars telling people we don't exist. She is the vegetable world telling people we don't exist. She is the galaxies telling people we don't exist. By her directing people to the baby, she is directing people to the Holy Spirit. Now, what did the baby say? He simply admitted his inexistence, as well, and directed people to their Creator.

Look how the circle is. It started from nature, in that humanity is blinded (I show him the moon he is looking at my finger), and nature is claiming renunciation in reality. It is as if you were saying that the solid is confessing by renouncing its solidity and thereby transforming to liquidity, and then the liquid is confessing by renouncing its liquidity and transforming to a vapor.

Q: Jesus said that he could tell you what you were storing in your houses. What was behind that statement?

A: He knew what was in their minds. The reason he knew what was in their minds was because of the oneness of the spirit of God. The spirit of God doesn't have left and right, up and down, or any dimension. In other words, he felt them.

Q: When God spoke about breathing the soul, He only mentioned it with regard to one type of animal, the bird. Disregard the fact of His bringing people from death to life; I'm just referring to animals. Why was there only the bird?

A: The bird's characteristic is flying, i.e., freedom. That is exactly the reflection of the spirit, i.e., not to stick to the earthy world. There are no boundaries, no frontiers, no restrictions, etc.

Q: What did you mean by the following expression: "At this point, we enter the epoch of the gods?"

A: The first thing you notice in this transferable history starting from Moses' epoch up to this time is the formation of the ego in a voluted way. Geometrically speaking, first you see the emotions that wind around the center—a neural-net with an increasing distance from the center—toward the epicenter. After that phase you see what was intuitively a diasporic frequency becoming dispersed into multiple institutions, and those institutions become sacred, and once they become sacred they are converted into mechanical organisms, i.e., cybernetics that program what is good and evil. At that point, people absorb their lives from those so-called gods without any conscience awareness.

Q: We have a record that the traitor Judas Iscariots' physiognomy was transformed into Jesus Christ. Would you be able to explain that?

A: This is the mystery of the social interaction. People are interacting with each other with vibrated signals within their psyches all the time without ever realizing it. It is the same way as particles are encountered in cosmic rays interacting with matter.

Consider a sincerely good person interacting socially with an unscrupulous person. Without anyone's awareness, those vibrations from both sides create energy in the good person and deprive the unscrupulous person from his energy while creating something negative. When it comes to the unseen intentions, every positive energy is transferred to the one who attempts or does good things to and for people. Every negative energy is transferred to the one who betrays people without him ever realizing it.

Getting back to our story, when Judas Iscariot was planning to betray Jesus, he was in reality developing a negative energy within himself without realizing it.

Q: Let me interrupt you for a moment. People are betraying each other all the time. Why don't they get the physiognomy of the one for whom they are wishing bad things?

A: When we say someone is a materialist, that means he is more driven by materialistic forces or perhaps by animalistic forces. When we say someone is spiritual, that means he has more leanings toward the spiritual aspect of life than the material aspect. In other words, he is struggling with his ego to maintain his spiritual status. However, when we say the spirit itself, we are talking about the core, the nucleus. When it comes to the physical interactions of the materialist person, it is as if you are looking at a dark mirror where you don't see yourself. When it comes to the spiritual person who is struggling with his ego, it is as if you are looking at a mirror where one part is clear and the other part is wavy. When it comes to the spirit itself, you are dealing with a very clean mirror where your image gets reflected back to you exactly the way you are at that same instant.

Let's get back to the issue of social interaction and the vibration resulting from intentions. When we betray (God forbid) the materialist person, we don't see the vibrated reversibility coming back to us right away. That doesn't mean we are not going to face repercussions; it is just taking longer. When we betray the spiritual person, the vibrated reversibility that comes to us is delayed but is faster than in the previous case. When we betray the spirit itself, the vibrated reversibility comes right back to us. Therefore, the supposed advantage we get from betraying the two first cases is the delay and the slowness of our bad karma.

Q: I see where you are going. Could you elaborate regarding Jesus' case?

A: He was the spirit of God; he was the purity and transparency. That's why Judas had an immediate repercussion.

At the same time, Jesus was the spirit of God's frequency within everybody. If we submerge a little deeper regarding our previous analysis, the whole betrayal is taking place within the psyche of a single person.

Q: Is there any physical example?

A: While punching a punching bag with your right hand, the action is exterior, isn't it? At the same time you're punching, try to touch with your left hand the triceps of your right arm from below. What do you feel?

Q: It gets contracted at the same moment as when I punch.

A: Therefore, there is an exterior action with an interior rebound. That rebound is the vibrated reversibility of your action—intention. Call it karma; call it destiny; call it repercussion or whatever you want. It is the same thing with the intentions.

Q: It is still obscure with regard to Judas' physiognomy being transformed to that of Jesus. Also, how does such an unscrupulous person deserve the privilege of being transformed into Jesus' image?

A: When the Creator spoke about this particular event, He said: "They had neither killed him nor crucified him....... Only a likeness of that was shown to them" This part of the statement shows that the Divinity did not deny the execution, but the Divinity denied the execution of Jesus. Now regarding the word 'likeness' in the following verse, we notice that the original verb in the scripture is "*shoubbiha*", and this verb is put in the passive voice. Now the infinitive verb with its active voice is "*shebbaha.*" The verb "*shebbaha*" means "to liken to." When it comes to the passive voice, which is "*shoubbiha*," it means to become "dubious to" or "doubtful to."

Q: I have two questions for you, or maybe three questions. Firstly, why is the statement put in the passive voice? Secondly, when you said, "Dubious to or doubtful to," to whom is the statement being referenced? Finally, is this likeness a stagnant one, or is it flowing with metamorphoses?

A: If the Creator had said, "I made Jesus look like this to them" with an active voice, the responsibility (for this perceived likeness by the observers) would have been entirely on the Creator. However, God said it in a passive voice, because each group and every individual was entirely responsible for its or his own perception, which was spawned from its or his faith. We have previously seen a similar case with Cane and Able regarding the acceptance and the non- acceptance of the sacrifice.

Getting back to your second and third questions, the image of Judas Iscariot during his death did not appear to everybody as a stagnant image. It appeared to every group differently according to their predisposed nature, which has to do with their faith, and according to their good or bad intentions toward Jesus. Jesus' real disciples, including his blessed mother, knew that Judas was not Jesus. Others who had some doubt regarding Jesus' message did not have a definite decision; they were between yes and no according to their faith. Others, e.g., who voted for Jesus to be killed, saw Judas as Jesus, a perception that was based on their projected characterized vision, which in turn was based on their obsessed agenda. Others had no clue and remain in doubt up till now.

Q: Does this perception, which is based on faith and intention,

256

concern only those people who were physically present at that particular event, or does it also concern other, absentee people from different times?

A: It concerns every individual, present or absent, whether during that time or other times. This is to show you that every perception and projection is based on what a person is developing. An intrinsic emotion within a person spawns life, and that life develops a vision, and the projected image outside the self will be based on that vision. In contrast, the extrinsic emotion spawns death, and that death develops a vision, and the projected image outside the self will be based on that vision. This is our explanation of the transformation of Judas Iscariot's physiognomy to that of Jesus Christ. In reality, the transformation never took place, and it did take place at the same time. The transformation was not from the exposed image; it was instead from the projected image that was based on the vision of the perceivers, which was developed through their emotions.

One of the early Christian sects in second-century Egypt was the Basilidians. These people were not present during the crucifixion event, but still they rejected the idea of Christ being on the cross. They deeply believed that someone substituted for him. As another example, the Docetists were also not present at the crucifixion. Despite the fact that they went a little far in their belief, they have one aspect of their faith that is absolutely true when they consider Jesus as a spirit who didn't even have physical body. They also rejected the idea that Jesus was killed.

Q: We have a record of Jesus Christ coming back and dying on earth. How do you explain that?

A: My answer to you is with a question. He will come back. There is no doubt about it, but for what reason?

257

Q: He will establish God's kingdom on earth....

A: Well, that is a part of his extended mission, but what is his first mission?

Q: Nothing that I'm aware of at the moment?

A: His first mission is to kill death.

Q: To kill death?

A: His first mission is to break the cross that is reinforcing the fabricated dogma of death that was made after his ascension. Now if he were meant to be buried on earth like any other prophet before him, it needs to be understood that such a burial is just an element of transition from this world to the other.

Q: What is the frequency of Jesus Christ within my psyche?

A: He represents self-reanimation.

Q: How's that?

A: Do you remember when we spoke about consciousness and the presence of the Observer, and we gave the example of the laser?

Q: Vaguely.

A: Can you visualize a laser coming from a certain direction above you? Once you visualize that, also visualize that when someone presses a button the laser is pointed at your mind and that when someone releases the button the laser stops. Can you possibly imagine that?

Q: Yes.

A: Now, I said, "Someone," but there really is no someone. Instead, it's you. The activation of this laser does not depend on anybody outside you, but it is entirely your responsibility to ignite it. It is just waiting for you to activate it. Furthermore, this laser is beyond time, space, and manner. In other words, it doesn't have a time when, a particular location where, and a specific way you can absorb it except by humility and renunciation. Also, it is neither centripetal nor centrifugal. Now, do you know what that laser is?

Q: Consciousness?

A: Consciousness when you ignite it, but its effect in your heart is the Holy Spirit. It is life. It is animation. It is animatism.

Q: Would you comment on that?

A: When people speak about life, spirit, soul, zest, etc., they are using confusing words in this world. The word "animism," which was taken from "anima" is the existence of the soul everywhere in nature. The word "animatism" is similar to the previous one, but it includes the concept of an impersonal supernatural power in nature. In fact, those interpretations are totally spawned from an atheistic source. This is not the life that was meant by the Creator; this is just a specimen of animism in nature. What we really call animatism is the life that is absorbed from the Creator by responsible consciousness. What is happening in this world is exactly what happened to the Romans with their gods; they saw life in nature, in the sun, the moon, the water, the wind, etc. Then they deified them with icons. They didn't realize that their lives were starting to spawn disintegration through a vice versa reciprocity from those gods. In this modern society, it's similar to the corporations and their rules. They have become gods like Jupiter, Poseidon, Pluto, etc., and people have absorbed their lives from them without realizing it.

259

Q: How do they affect a person during his daily activity?

A: If during business hours a person acts or behaves in a polite manner or verbalizes soft words for the sake of or for the profit of a company, this person surely carries a memory that forms an emotion that is related to that prior politeness, that is if he is conscious. A person who expresses or shows generosity for the sake of a business transaction carries an emotion related to generosity. A person carries an emotion of honesty if he acts honestly, even if it is because cameras are capturing his behavior on film and because he could face severe punishment from his company if he did anything unlawful. These memories are stored and encoded in his subconscious mind, but they do not belong to him. Instead, they belong to Jupiter Incorporated, Uranus Limited, Poseidon Incorporated, Pluto, etc., all of which are the gods that are fabricated from the corporations of the modern, so-called civilized society.

Q: Why is that so?

A: When these supposedly quality memories are stored and form emotions, they are fed by Jupiter Incorporated, Uranus Limited, Poseidon Incorporated, etc. In order for those stored memories to avoid death, they have to be continuously enriched by the same audience (i.e., Jupiter, Poseidon, and Uranus) by which they were formerly energized. As such, their survival is limited to business hours and is conditional. It is restricted within a time and space prescribed by the fabricated gods.

Q: What does the presence of Jesus have to do with this?

A: This gentleman came for this resurrection, which was the removal of dead intermediaries, and which, in turn, allowed direct contact with the Eternal Deity.

Q: What was to be resurrected?

A: The dead were to be resurrected.

Q: Where was this death located?

A: It was located in the subconscious minds of everybody whose intentions and memories were meant for the sake of another audience rather than God, audiences such as Jupiter, Apollo, Uranus, and so forth.

Q: What is the difference between carrying a memory of an emotion of politeness and being polite, or what is the difference between carrying a memory of an emotion of honesty and being honest?

A: At times, it may almost seem that there is no difference, which is wrong. The difference between the two cases is the following. Merely carrying a memory of an emotion of politeness is carrying a burden. That's why you hear the words "depression" and "anxiety" a lot in this society. In contrast, being polite is absorption without storage. The subsequent result is part of your own behavior. You are not merely the man who carries politeness or honesty, but you are the polite and honest man. After a while, an extrinsic emotion disintegrates when it is in storage. The encoded memory that forms an emotion initially flows, and then it dies with a feeling of anxiety, depression, and then fatigue. With regard to being polite, there is absorption without storage, and that becomes a part of a person's behavior. This is the harmony that is felt only by the sincere person.

Q: Well, we see that people are happy with their jobs!

A: We often hear modern man saying that he loves his job. In reality, he loves the time and space where those memories have been stored and survive for a while, which is to say that he loves Jupiter Incorporated, Apollo Incorporated, and so forth. Those memories flow into an eventual death unless the same audience reappears for whom those actions behind the memories were formerly meant. If the same audience is absent, melancholy occurs. Therefore, a person has to go back to the same place and time that spawned those memory traces so that he can energize those dead impulses. This is why people under such influences make a big deal out of the holidays. For example, they are restricted within time and space and are prearranged by an invisible hand. You see people going to work looking like zombies, stepping on each other, or raging at each other on the road with all sorts of hostility; yet, when they get to work, you see a totally different attitude, i.e., a commercial smile and politeness, which just shows you how a person gets incarnated in an extrinsic emotion and behaves with it. In other words, the person is escaping on the one hand and simulating on the other.

Q: Would you give some examples regarding other behaviors?

A: When an individual who is beholden to an audience is withdrawn from that audience, he carries a security but is not secured; he carries certitude but is not certain; he carries politeness but is not polite; he carries generosity but is not generous; he carries power but is not powerful. The same is true for affection, compassion, gallantry, etc. A person who merely carries affection is not an affectionate person. A person carrying compassion is not compassionate and so forth. This is especially the case with organized religion. A person may speak about religion and preach it; however, his absorption may still be from the idolatry of religion, not from God. Further, the idolatry of religion has its effect only during religious holidays or religious ceremonies. Therefore, such religious people's absorption is from the ambiance of religion.

In the idolatry of religion, people's contact is through a fabricated god, and this fabricated god is characterized by time, space, and the manner of the people's behavior. These people are supposedly alive only when that audience and its rules are present, which happens only during set times and places. If the fabricated god to whom the person owes his allegiance is absent, then the person acts in a surprisingly different manner from when the fabricated god is present. In addition, such people carry happiness, but they are not happy. The same thing is true with education; people carry education but they are not educated.

Q: What was the main reason behind people creating icons?

A: The inspiration that spurred people to externalize images, statues, and idolatry was not an influence from Jesus Christ at all, God forbid. It was not part of his teachings at all, since his main mission was focused on iconoclasm. When an emotion is internally extrinsic with regard to the nucleus, it dies and causes such pain that the concerned person wants to externalize its reflection. In other words, he wants to externalize the opposite of what is already painfully flowing in the subconscious.

If the memories that led to an emotion were previously encoded as supposed strength, these false emotions of strength later create feelings of weakness. Because of the pain associated with having these impulses of weakness, the individual externalizes these impulses as images or statues of strength, e.g., as dragons or as dominant personalities expressing heroism etc. When a memory seems to be encoded initially as beauty from the audience of idolatry, its flow in the subconscious is the opposite, i.e., ugliness. As such, a concerned person externalizes ugliness with a flimsy mask of beauty in order to justify his internal ugliness through external admiration.

The flow of these dead impulses in the subconscious causes such disturbance and melancholy that a person rushes to idealize, externalize, and eternalize these deaths with an image or statue of a dominant personality or a leader of a country who epitomizes the opposite of what was initially in the subconscious. Inadequacy, fragility, ugliness, and weakness are all idealized and eternalized by statues. As we can see, even Jesus Christ was made into an icon and deified. The reasons behind that were that people not only felt the death of their fabricated god, which was their devotion to the institution, but that the crucifixion itself was constantly transmitting death to their emotions.

Q: What are the consequences of all of this?

A: Once a person has externalized an impulse into an image or statue for the purpose of eternalizing death, and once he has shifted his inward view to his outward view by looking and admiring that image or statue, a person finally feels wonderful. However, he is ignoring that his urge for life flows with the laws of the universe. Therefore, his intuitivism is in a constant state of flux, and his emotional high is only momentary. In a short while, he no longer admires that image or statue anymore, and at that point another death or stagnation takes place, which is his absorption by that statue without his conscious awareness. He then keeps jumping from one idol to another or from one image to another, always switching to different types of deaths. The reason that people throughout the pages of history jumped to make icons of and to idolize a multiplicity of gods, i.e., paganism, was not, as they claimed, because they were open minded to diversity, but because they experienced a death on a subconscious level that they completely ignored. They then camouflaged it by the expression, "It is better being in the known, rather than in a mystery." In fact, they were afraid to be in the mystery, because the mystery kept them flowing without image. The fact that there is no image is the fact of giving credit to the Absolute. However, since humans are selfish and scared to admit this reality and to admit their inadequacy, they always want to seize credit from the Absolute and then idolize it, and sometimes they call that science.

264

Q: Would you comment about the Medieval Age?

A: What about it?

Q: It is the age of renaissance, isn't it?

A: The Medieval Age was a period in history that lasted for roughly a millennium. It is commonly dated from the fall of the Roman Empire in the fifth century to the beginning of the early modern period in the 16th century. The influence of the Roman Empire on the Western Hemisphere was marked by three main phenomena that have absolutely nothing to do with Jesus' influence or with Christianity, but have to do with the influence that was inherited from Roman paganism. In addition, the whole structure of supposed Western civilization was built on the fabricated dogma of, "Don't worry; someone died for us," which, nonetheless, was spawned from paganism and which brought the whole Western Hemisphere into a hidden decay.

There were two phenomena on the domestic front of which we must be cognizant. The first was the iconization, idolization, and deification of Christ, which was then followed by the extermination of the fabricated god by crucifixion, which not only transmitted a one-time death, but transmitted an exponential death, which was death of the emotions. The second phenomenon was rampant nudism within their museums. On the international front, we had the beginning of those countries' overseas expansion, i.e., crusaders.

Q: It's a little foggy. By the way, you have been frequently repeating that things happened on a subconscious level. What do you mean by that?

A: A person individually, or a country collectively, can follow or do something. He may think what he is doing is his choice, but it may be the case that he is being victimized by previous conditioning or by some ancient doctrine that he previously learned and accepted. This prior conditioning or indoctrination may be affecting his present without him even realizing it.

Q: You referred to the fabricated dogma of, "Don't worry; someone died for us;" would you elaborate on that?

A: First of all, this fabricated dogma of, "Don't worry; someone died for us," is shifting the emphasis from self-based responsibility to someone else who is supposedly dead, which makes the situation even graver. The repercussions of this fabricated dogma on modern society shift the emphasis from self-based responsibility to institutional-based responsibility. It takes away any personal responsibility and replaces it with the deification of the institution, and it disempowers personal effort by having an intercessor as an intermediary between the theo-ethical and psycho-ethical dimensions, and this intercessor is supposedly dead.

Secondly, as was previously mentioned, there is a difference between intrinsic and extrinsic emotions. The good thing about extrinsic emotions is that they create a feeling of angst, i.e., death, and death is, in reality, a painful consciousness, rather than a state of unconsciousness, which is what most people consider it to be. Death is, in reality, being conscious of the pain of angst or inexistence. Those people who are influenced by the fabricated dogma of, "Don't worry; someone died for us," are not only forming superfluous emotions of death, but they are also creating a thick camouflage that serves as a buffer between the pain caused by those extrinsic emotions and the awareness those individuals need to overcome their current condition.

The reason why the Roman (so-called) civilization collapsed and

266

another one took over and continued was not because there was a renaissance. It was because they fabricated a dogma on a subconscious level, whether voluntarily or involuntarily, that affected the emotions in such a way as to allow them not to face reality. In other words, they suspended belief in the truth to maintain the functionality of their illusions.

Even though iconized and idolized emotions are superfluous with regard to the nucleus, they still create a standing jump—a refrain within the state of consciousness, because the victimized individual starts being conscious precisely because of that pain, and consciousness creates a moment of reflection, whether one is aware of the causes or not. However, the one who is living with the fabricated dogma of, "Don't worry; someone died for us," is not only carrying dead emotions, he doesn't feel the pain of the extrinsic emotions like the person in the former case does. He doesn't feel the pain because there is a buffer that deadens the shock or the pain and allows the fabricated dogma to loosen and to create a running jump. Therefore, what really builds those huge infrastructures is not a voluntary choice that bursts from the nucleus, but an involuntary recuperative process to compensate for what is lost within the psyches of the population.

Q: Could you comment on that with an example?

A: When a person commits a mistake, whether grave or minor, or when he is inadequate vis-à-vis a situation, but he nevertheless still engages himself in the mistake with pretence, this creates remorse. This remorse is not there for a bad reason; it is there to keep the person introspectively in touch with the self. You can picture it as air bubbles going to the surface of the water—I mean the state of consciousness. Now when there is a doctrine that is telling you not to worry and that you are fine despite the existence of these mistakes, in some ways this doctrine is a platform built in the back of your subconscious to not allow those air bubbles to reach your awareness. If you are aware of your mistake or inadequacy and deal with it, then in some ways you are allowing an externalization of something that you may call an explosion, not in terms of violence, but in terms of facing it. On the contrary, if you are victimized by the doctrine of "don't worry," what was going to be an external explosion becomes an internal implosion, and this is what is causing this entire psychological trauma.

In such a society, you find two phases in a person's age. Before the age of puberty, the child is unconsciously fed by expressions such as: "Don't worry; someone is in charge;" "Don't worry; someone is carrying our sins;" and "Don't worry; someone is our savior." By the time the child is on his own, you cannot imagine how overwhelmed he becomes. When you see a teenager in such a society with such a hectic preoccupation running and speaking about college, education, career, etc., you would think that this is enthusiasm, career orientation, motivation, etc. However, in fact, he is just overwhelmed with a fear about which he has no clue regarding its origin. Statistically speaking, the usage of tranquilizers and the suicidal rate in countries victimized by this dogma is the highest in the world.

Q: You spoke about nudism in their museums.

A: When you look at paintings of the Virgin Marry in any museum, the artists always symbolize her with a scarf on her head. They symbolize her with modesty, shyness, etc. Yet, next to paintings of her in those museums, there is extreme nakedness almost everywhere you look. These canvases and sculptures with their nudity clearly show that the cultural heritage being celebrated comes from Roman paganism with its perverted overexposure of their fabricated gods. Of note, shyness does not just pertain to women; it also concerns every aspect of life in the universe.

Now, let's get to the point. The whole existence of the universe is a mystery, and there is a treasure in that mystery that allows you to explore and navigate within its dimension with wonder and jolliness. There is a mystery in the sun, the moon, the stars, the galaxies, the mountains, the wind, the fire, the water, the seasons, etc., and all those mysteries from the macrocosm are recapitulated and miniaturized in a microcosm and stored in the shyness of women. Now, nakedness is the process of achieving a destination without a journey by the process of overexposure. In other words, it suspends your perception of the role of women as being the source of tranquility, the source of treasure, the source of compassion, the source of the recapitulation of the mystery of the universe, and the source of Paradise. Yet, all of that is narrowed down into the overexposure of a woman's physical body—there is no imagination left anymore.

Q: From where does the source of nudism come according to you?

A: From the iconization and the idolization of the emotions. It is like the way that the gods are incarcerated within time, space, and manner. It is in the same way that emotions flow within this labyrinthine wavelength. Therefore, the vacillation of emotions tightens and constricts the dimension of the heart. In return, this internal implosion spurs an individual to seek external expansion for the purpose of rushing to recuperate something, to compensate for something. That tightness does not allow a person to explore the mystery while slowly crossing distances. Instead, this tightness provokes a person to reach a destination rapidly without a journey; it is as if they were rapingnature.

In reality, rape is getting to the climax of orgasm without flirting; it is as if the obsession of reaching a destination consumes the journey. It is similar to the reason why they have this contradiction of putting a painting of a modest Virgin Mary next

269

to extreme nakedness.

Q: You said she is the source of Paradise. What did you mean by that?

A: When the Creator spoke to Adam, God told him to dwell in Paradise, although Adam was already in Paradise. However, the dialogue was very mysterious. Here is the text: "Oh! Adam dwell you and your complement in Paradise." Notice that God did not say, "...your wife;" He said, "...your complement." In other words, you need to complete yourself before you can dwell in Paradise. In other words, God was telling Adam that in order for him to enjoy Paradise, he had to dwell in the first paradise, which was his complement—Eve. This is what confirms our analysis about the chromosomal composition we spoke about earlier, how men include women.

Q: What did you mean by the expansion of countries overseas?

A: As previously noted, an internal implosion spurs a person to seek external expansion. This is what the severity of death does to a person. It mistakenly exterminates the external being in order to recuperate his internal death, which was what we saw with the two brothers, Cane and Abel.

Q: Who were the first victims of this extermination?

A: The first victims were the Unitarians and Moses' people.

Q: Who were or are the Unitarians?

A: These were and are a group within Christianity, at one time in the majority and currently in the minority. They are true believers who believe in One God, just as Moses' followers did, and that

Jesus was a messenger of God. That's why they were targeted for persecution. It was because they believed in the unseen.

Q: Getting back to my psyche…

A: Moses' epoch, which is Moses' frequency inside you, comprises the renunciation and the centering of yourself within your center of gravity, and this is done through humility. That epoch and this epoch, which is Jesus' frequency within you, are one. There is no before, and there is no after; there is no first phase, and there is no second phase. In one fraction of a second, you have renunciation with a state of humility, which is Moses' epoch, and then you have the receptiveness of the Observer. God is sort of like a laser that goes through your consciousness, which is Jesus' epoch.

Q: You said before, Moses was also exposed to the Sublimity; therefore, there is no difference between Moses' and Jesus' mission?

A: All God's prophets have the common ground of "There is no god except God," but there is a slight difference in their extended mission.

Each person will have extrinsic emotions; that's for sure; no one can possibly escape that. Those dead, superfluous emotions, even though they are dead, can still be resurrected by your humility and consciousness, and they can ultimately become intrinsic or alive, which combines Moses' and Jesus' missions.

It is for us to understand that we are entangled by the past and the future. When you have this allowance (the Oneness of God) within your consciousness, time won't have any effect on you; the duality disappears, and your singularity reappears?

271

Q: Is there any concrete example?

A: You have emotions; try to visualize them like air bubbles in the bottom of a container full of water. When you go through the process of retrieval, which is the process of recovering the encoded information from its storage in the back of the subconscious mind and of bringing it into consciousness, you are in some way shaking that water container and provoking those air bubbles to go to the surface of your conscious. Do you understand the allegory?

Q: Yes, I do.

A: Now those air bubbles are your emotions; they could represent any event from the past that you had accomplished mechanically as an automaton without your conscious awareness, or they could have been formed for the sake of another audience. Therefore, they are extrinsic; therefore, they are dead emotions; they don't represent you. Now when you go to the process of retrieval and bring those memories to the surface of your conscious, that leads us to Jesus' mission. Now do you remember when we spoke about the laser beyond time and space?

Q: Yes, I do.

A: You have those superfluous emotions that are like air bubbles, which you have provoked by the process of retrieval, that are going in an ascending dimension to the surface of the conscious. At the same time, you have your consciousness that is bringing the laser supposedly from outside. Once you have that wish, if you do it like this with consciousness, all this process animates and creates life from those dead emotions, i.e., the air bubbles. Now don't look at those emotions as being like air bubbles when they get to the surface of the water as air bubbles burst and disappear. However, the emotions with their memories never disappear. Rather, look at them like sugar in the water that dissolves and becomes a part of the water—I mean a part of your behavior, a part of the reality of the self.

Q: In terms of an individual self-resurrection, how about Jesus resurrecting other people outside or apart from the self?

A: Let's consider a small experiment. Imagine yourself under an apple tree; your right hand is grabbing an apple from a branch, putting it in the left hand, and then giving it to someone. Now try to do this so rapidly that the motion becomes as speedy as the electrical, neural circuit inside you transmits its current. As long as you are giving that apple to someone, the circuit keeps flowing. The first action is called a gravitational attraction; the following action is called a levitational repulsion.

Q: What are the factors of the gravitational attraction?

A: We are talking about consciousness, in other words, a volitional action, not just a physical action.

Q: I know that.

A: The factors of the gravitational force are how exposed you are to the Sublimity.

Q: What are the factors of the levitational repulsion?

A: The factors of the levitational force are your generosity toward your fellow creatures, how much you give, how much you care, how much you provide, etc.

Q: What is your understanding regarding the resurrecting of people?

A: This is in terms of expressing your emotions freely and unconditionally. Such emotions could include compassion, sympathy, generosity, etc. In such a situation, people are resurrecting each other by the intermediary of the Sublimity, not by the institutionalized gods.

Q: Repercussions?

A: Consider that the electrical circuit (from gravitational attraction to levitational repulsion) that is supposed to flow among people is interrupted. In such a case, a person receives an electro-shock. This is exactly what is happening when people claim the credit, don't humble themselves before God, and selfishly block the universal energy from flowing. Everything is in standstill; everything is clogged. Once the emotions are flowing severely among people with death, people live with fear, and from that fear they keep creating institutions. Then the rigidity of those institutions creates more deaths in people's lives, and then the wars come, supposedly to recuperate and compensate for what is lost spiritually.

Q: Regarding my psyche?

A: Your neglect of those extrinsic emotions causes a social leprosy in terms of your being alienated from people. You cannot stand them, and if they share the same extrinsic emotions as you, they won't be able to stand you either. Next, an organization is created that unites you with people who have the same mindset as you, and then people call this civilization. That's why you see a lot of organizations created, a lot of institutions created. If you count the number of those organizations, you will find them exactly equal to the number of extrinsic emotions. However, those dead organizations were already inside people, and now they have been extirpated.
Your neglect of those superfluous emotions can develop blindness in that you can't see or envision any alternative way in

274

life; you are blinded by simulation. Because those extrinsic emotions are like air bubbles flowing in your subconscious, even though you are deprived of them, anytime you want to behave in a certain way, you just simulate. Now bear in mind that one impulse of neglect within your psyche is a multiplicity outside you.

Q: What do you mean by that?

A: If you have one extrinsic emotion of supposed strength, it gives you a feeling of weakness. That feeling of weakness is one impulse that is manifested to the surface of your consciousness, and yet outside you it makes you feel that everybody is attacking you. You feel everybody is humiliating you. At that point, you simulate force to stop the pain of being down, to stop the pain of being oblivious, or to stop the pain of low self-esteem, as they call it in this modern society. This simulation then replicates another simulation, and it keeps going.

THE THIRD PHASE
OF HISTORY

CHAPTER 23

This is the end of history, where reality of the self, which is the "I" or the "Me," does not exist anymore, where mankind's life is posthumous in the sense of the death of the reality of the self and the birth of simulation. Then his reanimation goes into cryogenic storage and is ready for a subsequent death. Every human being's emotion becomes static and is as lifeless as some display in a museum. Humanity is living in the epicenter, far from existence, without realizing it. However, there is yet something that will protect an individual person in his center of gravity.

This period of history is close to the other world, the world of the Hereafter. In reality, there is no morning of history, no afternoon of history, and no sunset of history; they are, instead, all one segment of time. When he was by the sacred valley, Moses was instructed to remove his sandals when accomplishing any action. Jesus was instructed to breathe a soul into those actions. At this stage, we are going to see the projection of these actions into time and space, which is the metaphysical world.

The two worlds are established intuitively within the conscious state of the human and are engraved in his virgin nature. One of them is anterior in the sense of being meant for something else, and it is exterior in the sense of being behaviorally perceived with the naked eye in this terrestrial world. The other world is posterior in the sense of being the mirrored repercussions of the acts performed by a person in the previously mentioned world, and it is interior in the sense of being unperceived with the naked eye. The locations of these two worlds are not positioned one after another with frontiers between them, even though there is an

277

interspace of transference, i.e., a so-called death between the two. Instead, their location is one inside the other.

Actions are part of the terrestrial world, and the intentions behind those actions are part of the celestial world. In the terrestrial world, distances are crossed by foot or by any other form of transportation, but distances in the celestial world are crossed by will power that is gained from one's efforts and one's intentions in the world of labor. The terrestrial world is stagnant when it comes to the body, but the celestial world is in a constant metamorphosis in terms of the diversity of everyone's intentions and actions.

It was a night journey beyond time and space; Prophet Muhammad (may the peace and blessing of God be upon him) revealed those events to his people.

One of his greatest enemies and major persecutors was Abu Jahl, who was one of his paternal uncles. After hearing about Prophet Muhammad's night journey, Abu Jahl immediately went to see him. "Lift one foot off the ground," Abu Jahl said.

Prophet Muhammad complied. "Now lift the other," he continued. "I cannot," answered the Prophet.

"How can you, who cannot even lift your two feet off the ground, claim that you went to the highest heaven last night?" Abu Jahl demanded.

Muhammad replied politely by saying, "I did not say I went, but that I was taken."

It was a night journey, as previously noted. Muhammad left the region of the center of earth where God's house was located and went to Jerusalem. On his way to the Promised Land, he saw Moses praying in his grave with an indescribable dimension. In Jerusalem, he led all the prophets who came before him (from

Adam to Jesus, including Moses, may the peace and blessing of God be upon all of them) in prayer.

From Jerusalem, he went to the seventh heaven, met with different prophets on every one of the seven cosmoses, including Moses, who was on the sixth cosmos. (It is so strange that Moses was praying in his grave while simultaneously praying behind Muhammad in Jerusalem and being in the sixth cosmos!)

The night of Muhammad's ascension, he visited the seven heavens and had a dialogue with every prophet inhabiting each cosmos. He visited Paradise, visited Hell, and had discourse with the Creator. While traveling beyond time and space, he saw the beginning of the world and all the generations that preceded his epoch. Also while traveling beyond time and space, he saw the entirety of the future and all the generations that were to come after him, and he was given the obligation of prayer, which was the only adoration that was prescribed above the seventh cosmos.

When the prayer was mandated to the Prophet, the original command was to pray fifty times per day. However, on his way down through the seven heavens, Prophet Muhammad met Prophet Moses in the sixth cosmos and told him about the prescribed prayers. Moses suggested that Muhammad go back to his Almighty God and ask Him to reduce the number. Moses said, "I have tried with my own nation and noticed how neglectful people were, and I can see how it will be with your people." As such, Prophet Muhammad went back and forth between God and Moses. Each time, Moses advised Muhammad to return to God and ask for a reduction in the number of prayers per day, and each time God granted Muhammad his request. Probably nine different times (we don't know for sure) Muhammad went to God to obtain a reduction in the number of prescribed daily prayers.

Finally, the number was reduced to five prayers per day. Nonetheless, Moses still told Muhammad to go back and ask God to reduce it even more. At that point, Muhammad said, "I feel ashamed to ask God again to reduce the number."

Now after all that happened during that ascension, when Muhammad came back, his bed (actually he slept on the floor) was still warm. In other words, all that he did took a matter of seconds, maybe less.

The message that Muhammad carried from the Divinity was the same as that of his two brothers, i.e., Moses and Jesus, before him. "He has revealed to you the Book with the truth, confirming the scriptures that preceded it; for He has already revealed the Torah and the Gospel for the guidance of men, and the distinction between right and wrong."

Now, when we speak about the end of history, we're talking about either the end of collective life on Earth via some cataclysm, i.e., the end of the world, or the end of an individual's life, i.e., a person's death.

The next realm is the interspace, which is a human's temporary habitation between the two worlds. Here are the seven realms through which a person goes from the time of resurrection to his eternity: (1) the resurrection, (2) the book of actions, (3) the scale, (4) the path, (5) the heights, (6) the slaughter of death, and (7) the celebration or lamentation.

At the time of the resurrection, there is no external light. Everyone is resurrected with his own light, which is proportionate to his degree of faith. Sadly, some people will walk in darkness. As a result of the obscurantism they voluntarily accepted during their terrestrial life, they won't see anything. Others will walk with a light that flickers like a candle; sometimes it turns on and sometimes off, which reflects their alternating acceptance and refusal of the divine light. For some, their light will be brighter than the sun, but that doesn't mean that those who happen to walk beside them will benefit from their light.

It is a very weird and strange dimension. It is like a person who dreams and enjoys all sorts of pleasure within his dream, but a person who happens to be next to the dreamer doesn't enjoy the same pleasures. It is the same thing when it comes to experiencing misery. Everybody will experience his own state of consciousness, even while each individual is in the midst of that multitudinous crowd. Some people won't be able to stand; others will variously walk and fall; others will pass by like the speed of the light. All of this results from their prior terrestrial behavior.

Everyone will be naked, and no one will even be circumcised. Everybody will be totally preoccupied with his own fate. Some people will appear to be drunk and without any sense of equilibrium. Children's hair will become gray, not because they fear for themselves, for they are innocent, but because they fear for their parents. Similarly, the prophets won't fear for themselves, but they will fear for their nations.

Finally, the sun will come out. This is not the collective sun that we experienced in the previous life; instead, it's an individual sun. In other words, it does not come out to light up the scene, but it comes out with different effects on different people according to their predisposed nature, and their predisposed nature is according to their behavior.

With regard to a person's physiognomy on that day, each person will have either a deformation or beautification that will identify him according to his prior common sense and behavior. The image with which a person will stand that day will be a reflection of the logic or common sense that resulted from the platform in the back of his subconscious, the platform upon which he formerly relied and which in return directed the flow of his emotions.

The person who proudly identified with such platforms as wealth, beauty, knowledge, property, etc. will feel such humiliation and misery that he will wish he could extirpate that identification from himself, but he will not at that late date be able to do that. Those who possessed one or all of the above and yet sought prestige in servitude will have their lights dominate the sun.

A person may have claimed in the previous life that he belonged to such and such of God's prophets, but on that day he instead finds himself behind Nimrod, Pharaoh, Haman, or Korah. Why is that?

The personality that came spontaneously to the surface of the person's consciousness during times of idealism in his previous life in the material world is the personality behind which he will stand on that day. It is not a matter of choice on that day; it is a matter of a magnetic field and force that were already prepared by the person in his previous life. If it was the personality of Moses that came to his mind, then the person is Mosaic. As such, on that day, the magnetic field will place him behind Moses. If it was Jesus who came to his mind, then he is Jesus-like, and the magnetic field will place him behind Jesus.

With regard to Muhammad, he will not function on that day as an independent personality, because he was the encyclopedia and the recapitulation of all the prophets' personalities before him. The goodness that was done by the People of the Book (Jewish and Christians) before Muhammad will be rewarded twice that day if they also believed in the prophethood and message of Muhammad. Such people will stand with honor twice that day— initially behind the prophet that was sent to them and then behind Muhammad.

Prophet Muhammad revealed a number of different things to people upon his return from Heaven. For example, he saw people who were the size of ants, and there was a crowd stepping on them without seeing them. The tiny people screamed aloud to let people know about their presence, but nobody heard them. Muhammad was told that these people were the Pharaohs. These were the self-aggrandizing people who had humiliated others in their previous lives. This was their reality. This was the reality of the vain ego, and this was the reality of the "I" that never had a chance to be developed.

On the other hand, those who had been unperceived and humiliated in the material world had on that day an appearance that was shinier than the sun; people were amazed by their look and wonder. The proclamation came forth: "These are the patient ones who seemed to be weak and poor in their previous lives."

He saw people carrying burdens that they couldn't lift, but still they picked up more stuff and put it on their backs until it was heaped up like mountains. As they walked along, they suffered and screamed because of the painful fatigue that they were experiencing. Nonetheless, they carried more and more. He was told that these were people who carried their sins and the sins of other people who had been their victims.

On the other hand, some people, merely by throwing one seed or grain of wheat, found that the seed immediately gave an uncountable number of crops. He was told that those were people who had spent their money for God's sake. Just look how their investment was growing so very fast.

Someone was holding a sort of burning property. He tried to escape from it, but his property moved with him. He didn't know that the fire was inside his subconscious mind. This was the person who had thought he was smart by deceiving others in the courtroom while being aware of his own deceit. He had taken a share that was not really his, but he had taken it anyway. What he had taken were combustibles, so this was his reality. On the other hand, there were those whose shares had been taken from them; yet, they had kept quiet and patient for God's sake. What they had really lost were miniatures, but what they found over there were mountains of fortune.

He saw some people eating a stinking corpse while having clean, fresh meat next to them. Nonetheless, they continued to eat the decomposed corpse anyway. They suffered and wanted to vomit, but they couldn't. They tried unsuccessfully to escape. He was told that these were people who had left their legitimate wives and had engaged in illegitimate sex with others. This was their reality. On the other hand, those who had abstained from having illegitimate sex were rewarded with an indefinite beauty under the throne.

There were blind people screaming and saying, "Our Lord, why are we blind? We formerly saw with our eyes?" The answer came to them that these were the deviations they had created for themselves to escape reality; nobody else was making them blind. Just as they had blinded themselves to reality in their previous lives, they now blinded themselves again. On the other hand, for those who had been receptive to reality, their visions were not only visions with their naked eyes, but their visions also were contemplation and absorption of all kinds of joyous beauty.

Some people whose skin was black like charcoal, a sign of death, screamed, "Why?" The answer was that it was because they had chosen disbelief to please their masters after having previously chosen faith. Others of them had lied about God and had lied to God. On the other hand, other people's skins were reanimated and exponentially beautified, a sign of their prior flexibility while dealing with the metamorphosis of terrestrial life.

Some people were eating fire and screaming at the top of their lungs. They tried to stop their consumption of the fire, but they couldn't. These people were the ones who had illegitimately spent the money of orphans who were in their custody. They had been eating fire in the previous life, and they had not known it. Others were also eating fire, but their reason was different; they had formerly made money while lying about God. On the other hand, those who had only eaten from their legitimate labor were eating liver from the fish of Paradise, a truly incomparable taste.

Someone was biting his arms all the way up to the elbows. This was the regret of someone who had kept bad company with someone who had caused him misery.

Those whose love was for God's sake stood on a sort of tribune made of pearls and diamonds, and the whole of humanity was jealous of their shining light.

There was also someone swimming in a sea of blood. Whenever the swimmer came to the shore, another person put rocks in the swimmer's mouth and made him swallow them. Muhammad was told that this was a person who had dealt in usury and that what the swimmer was swallowing was the interest from his former usury. In contrast, those who had been vigilant about their financial expenses and means of income were walking on the water, and the water had an indescribable color, view, and odor.

If someone had asked the suffering people why they were in such a situation and under such domination, they would have said that they were driven by forces and that this was not their fault and was against their will. In reality, they had developed those forces themselves in their previous lives. They had thought that by using their stratagems they could get away with what they were doing, but they had ignored the fact that every action was recorded in their own world of the subconscious, a world in which they were now living.

The material world with its materialistic pleasures was then brought forth incarnated and miniaturized in the physiognomy of a very old woman with festering sores. She stunk worse than a decomposed animal body and was grotesque and ugly. Everybody encountered her approach except a few, but everyone was trying to distance himself from her. The people then heard the proclamation, "This is the material world that seemed to all of you to be a young and pretty woman. This is the world for which you lusted. This is the world that drove your greed and hatred for each other. This is the world for which you killed each other. This is the world of supposed eternity that Satan promised you and for which you lusted, but here you are, desperately trying to avoid it now."

The book of actions is the repertoire of all of a person's actions in the previous life. (It is called a book because it is archival, but that doesn't mean that it has the features of a book as we usually think of one). Every single detail is recorded within it, and each person reads the entire recapitulation of his acts. Every situation is exposed and projected in front of his eyes, as though he were in a movie theater, and yet he is living those actions again as if his life were being repeated. For some, their lives are lived within minutes or maybe less; for others, their lives are extended.

One person is given his book in his right hand, which is a sign of success, the cause of great joy, and a symbol of power. This person initially accepted and absorbed the divine Book, and then his good actions and transactions were absorbed by himself. Thereafter, he was not merely acting compassionately; he was compassionate. He was not merely acting gallantly; he was gallant. He was not merely acting politely; he was polite.

A second person is given the book in his left hand, which causes misery and desperation. This person is the hypocrite. He supposedly acted in a goodly manner, but he never really owned any of those good deeds; he just simulated goodness. He never absorbed them, and they became a burden to him. He acted as he did out of a very limited self-interest. As such, he merely carried those acts in his subconscious without absorbing them into his being.

A third person receives his book on his back. This is the one who didn't have any concern about existence, and he saw his existence as "just do whatever you please," a sort of nihilism. He put existence behind him, and the results of his former actions became astray.

The scale is the balance that weighs every single detail, whether good or bad. Every transaction and every word are externalized, materialized, and weighed—good and evil.

The path lies over Hell, and each person has to traverse it. It is thinner than a hair and sharper than a sword's edge. This path is the effort of the person who did his best to stick to loyalty and

287

common sense. The more he provided, the more his path became wider, shorter, and easier. It is an externalization of something internal within each person. What was already in the person's subconscious is projected in front of him. This is the special characteristic that distinguishes between right and wrong, between obligations and prohibitions, and so forth. In reality, each person is just walking along the path that was predetermined for him by his own subconscious.

The width of each person's path is proportionate to how much loyalty and common sense he provided. Some people spend longer crossing it than do others. For them, the path is hidden in an obscurity proportionate to the trickery and deceit they had toward others in the previous life. Some people cross this path while alternating between crawling and walking. At times, the sharpness of the path cuts their skin. Some travelers may encounter ferocious animals that attack and worry them from every angle. These animals represent the problems these people caused for humanity, and which they themselves created.

There is an exemption for some people during their critical journey along this path. An impetuous energizer facilitates their journey, because in their previous lives they once or periodically gave food while they themselves were hungry, gave money while they themselves were in need, or sacrificed their time for the sake of another when they were exhausted. These people experience a sudden speed coming from nowhere that helps them cross the perilous path.

There are others who cross this bridge with the speed of the wind in just a fraction of a second. They are totally unaware of crossing this hazardous bridge, just as they were previously unaware of themselves in their prior lives because of their preoccupation with doing good for humanity. They were gentle and flexible with people, and they did not make life hard for others.

The heights comprise the wall that is situated between the Garden and Hell. Its interior is supplied with mercy, which is a façade that leads toward the Garden; its exterior is supplied with chastisement, which is the side of Hell. This is the location of those people whose balance between their good and bad deeds was equal. While on that wall, they look at times on the Garden, where they see cities of silver, palaces of gold that are crowned with pearls, and colorful rivers. At those times, they pray to God to be among those in the Garden. They gaze on Hell at other times and see the fire blazing and all kinds of chastisements. At those times, they pray to God to keep them away from Hell. After being in this situation for a little while there will be a reason, which it's not our place to mention, that will cause their entrance to the Garden. They then finally prostrate their heads to God and enter the Garden.

Once everyone enters his world, John the Baptist (may the peace and blessing of God be upon him) comes with death incarnate in a male sheep. He carries a knife in his hand and stands between the Garden and Hell. Then there is a call to those in the Garden. The call is made with such a voice that everybody can hear it. "Do you know who this is?" The residents of the Garden reply that they know. Another call is made to those in Hell. Again, the call is made with such a voice that everybody can hear it. "Do you know who this is?" They also say that they know. Then John the Baptist slaughters the sheep, and death is no more. For the inhabitants of the Garden, they do not see the slaughter as blood; instead, they see a milky crystal being spilled from which they absorb life. In contrast, the inhabitants of Hell see the blood as dark and scary, and they absorb misery from it. It is one liquid, but how it is seen is different, depending on a person's predisposed nature.

Depending upon one's final circumstance, the celebration or lamentation then begins. For those in the Garden, there are screams of joy, and they celebrate an eternity in which they live forever at the same age as Jesus Christ, which is thirty-three. They remain this same age eternally, even if they were old when they left their previous lives. There is no person older than thirty-three in Paradise. This is also the golden age. Meanwhile, the people of Hell scream aloud in anxiety, sadness, and lamentation.

Regarding any sin, no matter how big it was, so long as it was between a person and his Creator, God is Merciful, will forget about it, and will wipe it out. However, killing, i.e., exterminating the life of an innocent someone, is what really fuels Hell.

Several dialogues take place in Hell. The first dialogue flows from the people of Hell to Satan. They tell him that it is because of him that they are in Hell. Then Satan says, "I did not force you. All I did was invite you, and then you answered my call. What God promised you was true; what I promised you was false. There is nothing I can do to save you, and there is nothing you can do to save me. Therefore, don't blame me but blame yourselves."

Then the dialogue shifts and is directed from the blind followers to the snobs who led them. "All we did was to follow you in the previous life. Are you going to lift some of the chastisements of the fire from us?"

The snobs who formerly led them then answer. "Did we really prevent you from the Absolute Truth after it was revealed to you? You chose to be criminals alongside us."

The blind followers then respond. "But you were controlling us, "teleguiding" us, and indoctrinating us night and day to disbelieve in God."

The residents of Hell next appeal to the guardian angel of Hell, whose name is Malik. The residents of Hell ask him to serve as a mediator to ask God to diminish some of the chastisement for them. The angel goes and then comes back after a very long time. When the angel eventually comes back, he says to them, "Didn't God send you messengers?"

They then answer in the affirmative. Immediately after which comes a proclamation: "You mocked them (the messengers); some of them you tortured; some of them you jailed; some of them you killed." Today is the day of loyalty.

In Paradise, every tiny motion and every thought is a pure pleasure. There is untold pleasure in the contemplation of beauty, and there is the pleasure of sound, pleasing odors, taste, etc. Every member or organ of the body has its own pleasure and enjoyment. As each wish crosses a person's mind and before he can even verbalize it, that wish is fulfilled in an even better way than he fashioned it in his mind, and he marvels at how this happens.

On the other hand, in Hell every movement is a chastisement. Each thought of fire, thirst, hunger, sadness, and fear that crosses a person's mind is immediately experienced by him. If only he could refrain from thinking about his fears, but he cannot. Each chastisement and agony spawns additional fears, which immediately inflict themselves upon his experiential self in an ever-escalating crescendo.

In the Garden, the interaction between people is full of politeness, smiles, laughing, joy, etc. On the other hand, in Hell the interactions between people are only curses and insults, and everybody is accusing the other.

It will take an eternity for this person to visit his own Paradise. Actually this is just a metaphor. The person in the Garden is not controlled by time or space; instead, he controls time and space. He can be anywhere in a fraction of a second. He keeps traveling and traveling through palaces of silver in cities of gold that are decorated with pearls and crystal and that are built on water that is whiter than milk and sweeter than honey. There are four main rivers in the Garden (honey, milk, crystal, and wine). They are all derived from the cascade of, "There is no god except God," and these four rivers are dispersed to an unlimited number of tastes, colors, and odors. They differ from one person to another. These rivers flow side by side with a beautiful and softly murmuring sound that brings music and joy to a person's heart.

It takes a riding cavalier one hundred years to cross the shade cast by the tree of Tuba, which is only one among others. Again this shows the vastness of space. The fruit from that tree, which again is just one among others, offers an exotic, exquisite, and delicious stimulation to a person's taste buds. Each time a person takes a bite of it, he discovers a new and rapturous taste that is never repeated. The fruit from that tree is immediately replenished as soon as it is picked. The various trees are not planted on the ground, but they are instead sheltering from above. Unfortunately, it's not in the capacity of our language to fully describe those dimensions.

A person's digestive excretion of food is nothing but perfumed sweat that comes out of the whole body, and the length of time of the pleasure of sex in Paradise and its manner cannot be put into words.

Consider that fluorescent lighting annuls the presence of a candle. A very powerful, high voltage light annuls the presence of a smaller one, and the sunrise annuls the presence of all the electrical lights of the earthy world. However, a dignified woman residing in Paradise annuls the presence of the sun— actually there is no sun over there; it is just a comparison. The light in Paradise is from the Merciful, and it is indescribable. Furthermore, it has been said that if this woman of Paradise were to spit into the sea of the terrestrial world, her salivation would transform the salty sea into sweetness.

The following statements concerning the seven days are not in reference to external days, since in Paradise time does not control the believer. It is, instead, the believer who controls time. Therefore, when the name of a day is stated, it is the person's choice what day that is. Everybody has his or her individual day, and yet it is also a collective day. It is a very strange metaphor.

On Saturday, children visit their parents, and parents visit their children on Sunday. On Monday, students visit their teachers, and teachers visit their students on Tuesday. On Wednesday, nations visit their prophets, and the prophets visit their nations on Thursday.

How can a person be in multiple places at the same time, and how can everybody enter his own Paradise while being collectively within other people's Paradises? There are a lot of beautiful mysteries that could have been mentioned, but they have been avoided because of weak minds. It is better to stop here.

On Friday, everyone in Paradise visits God. It is a visit that transpires without steps, without location, without dimension, without sound, and without time. The word "Friday" is with reference to man's time, not to God's, for God is above and beyond time, which is merely one of the creations of God. After this contemplation, people become speechless and intoxicated by the eternal beauty of a love that doesn't belong to the ego. It is, instead, the deep mystery that links creatures to the Creator. At this point, they forget about all the pleasure they had in the Garden, and they cannot find their way back to their initial palaces. They then receive help from the angels who take them back to their eternal palaces. When they look again at each other, each one is amazed by the new beauty that they absorbed from God and that is reflected in their faces. Everybody observes this

in the other, and this beauty increases each time they visit God.

__Introspective Exegesis__

Q: Would you elaborate on the answer that Muhammad gave when he said, "I was taken?"

A: Obviously, there was a cause and effect with which he dealt, but upon which he did not rely. The causality was from a self-determination that avoided claiming self-sufficiency. If the power of this navigation had not already been prepared by Muhammad, he wouldn't have been able to accomplish this night journey.

What is performed in the name of God in the previous life is a sign of absorption. It becomes a power of will, autonomous and autogenic, and a bootstrap that spurs a person to what and where he initially projected his view. In other words, a person navigates through the vastness of his own cosmos, which is and was in his own subconscious mind before it came into external being in time and space.

Q: Didn't he travel to Jerusalem with the companionship of Archangel Gabriel on a sort of flying animal similar to a horse that is called Bourak?

A: If it were the case, why didn't he mention that regarding this particular answer? Also we don't have a record that Bourak has risen above the biosphere regarding his ascension; we only have a record of it traveling to Jerusalem. Therefore, the ascension had another type of vehicle.

Q: Regarding Prophet Muhammad's answer, I don't know how to put my question into words. I personally, expect the Prophet or any saint, to teach during special circumstances, while preaching, and so forth, but here the Prophet simply gave an answer. Furthermore, it's an answer to a question from a person who happened to be his enemy.

A: Bear in mind that the presence of the Prophet is a part of the microcosm and the macrocosm, degree per degree, no more and no less. Every action, every motion, every word from the Prophet is part of the complete enigma of this universe. When we (regular people) speak by verbalizing words, we have this tendency to secure our insecurity with unnecessary words to complete our sentences. For example, we might say, "ehhhhhh...I mean...ehhhhhhh...you know...basically... ehhhhhh...I don't know... etc..." Now these gaps and this emptiness in our tongues were already gaps in our minds before we spoke, and before being in our minds they were in our existence in time and space.

Q: Is there any concrete example?

A: When you are flying on a plane, sometimes you feel this sudden drop in the air, which is a downward air current that causes an aircraft to lose its stable altitude; they call it an air pocket. It is the same thing regarding our emptiness in our existence.

Q: What do you call emptiness?

A: Our absence of consciousness during the struggle of collecting consciousness. When it comes to a prophet, particularly Muhammad, he doesn't have any interruption or emptiness in his existence—in his words. When it comes to dialoguing; he is very precise and articulate. When it comes to gestures, there is not a single motion from him that is a random motion. It is, instead, a part of the motion of the galaxies; it is meant considerably and

consciously to be that way. If a gesture is from right to left, that means the law of the universe is like that. When it comes to delivering a message, whether via words or silence, each word has meaning, and each silence from him has meaning and is not neglect or forgetfulness. There is an encyclopedia that he wants to deliver, and what you and I understand or grasp from this message is just a drop from its ocean.

Getting back to our event, when the Prophet answered his uncle, he was not merely dealing with his uncle; he was expressing an encyclopedia to all future humanity.

Q: Would you be able to comment again regarding that simple reduced answer?

A: In this life, we have our will versus external will, and we have external wills versus our will.

Q: What do you mean by external wills?

A: External wills are that which goes against our natural desires. It could be the company's policy; it could be a political philosophy from some nationalism under which we live, or it could be something else. From wherever it comes, after a forceful resistance against it on our part, we end up surrendering to it, to them, to her, to him, and so forth. In the beginning, we had our own will. However, once we were conditioned, we become merged and adapted to a different will than the one we had intuitively. In the beginning, there were two wills, i.e., our will and the external will, and afterwards these two wills become one will. Are you following me?

Q: Up to this point I am.

A: Do you remember when we spoke about attachment and detachment regarding Moses' cane when he was by the sacred valley, and how the world is in constant metamorphosis once we detach ourselves from it?

Q: It would be better if we get that text again.

A: The following was said: "Here comes the philosophy of the fourth dimension. Whether objects are properties of the material world or properties of our receptivity, we think about objects in terms of sensation via touch, perception with the eyes, and conception in the mind. However, all this analysis is spawned solely from our judgment, and our judgment is spawned from a very narrow, illusory slit. This slit is our conditioning about how to feel the world, how to see the world, and how to think about the world; in other words, it is our attachment to the world.

"If you attach yourself to the world, you will be conditioned by your agenda regarding how you want to see and deal with the world, even though the world is, in fact, in a constant metamorphosis. Therefore, your attachment is creating stagnation and decay in your state of consciousness, because your stagnation is contrary to the metamorphosis of the universe.

"On the other hand, if you detach yourself from the world, you will realize that the world is in a constant state of metamorphosis."

Now, all what was said before is about attachment and detachment. At this stage, we have to emphasize two very important definitions; the first one is the world of phenomena, i.e., the terrestrial world, and the second one is the world of noumena, i.e., the celestial world, or that which is apprehended by thought.

There is a logic that is derived from the world of phenomena, i.e., from the terrestrial world, the world of three dimensions and of external attachments. There is also a logic that is derived from the world of noumena, i.e., from the celestial world, the world that is beyond any conceptualization, the one that was revealed to us by the Divinity through the jurisprudence that is rejected by people most of the time.

Q: What do you mean by logic?

A: Logic is a science of concepts. There is an intuitive logic, which harmonizes you with both the material and the celestial worlds. There is also a logic to which we have been conditioned, which is a logic that satisfies special circumstances and special people only. Those circumstances are segments from the eternity; they function one day, and they make you miserable the following years.

The so-called logic regarding the world of phenomena, to which people have been accustomed, is a logic of routine; its vehicle and its energy are flowing within a limited segment from the eternity, and it is bellow the biosphere. In contrast, the logic regarding the world of noumena, which is a logic that most people reject, is a logic of metamorphose. That's why people reject it because it necessitates a duty of conscience all the time. Its bootstrap serves as an uninterrupted vehicle to the celestial world, and it is above the biosphere.

Q: We were talking about our will versus external will.

A: I didn't forget; I had to go through those steps in order to explain the following.
Under Divine jurisprudence, all man's acts are classified under five legal categories. Number (1) is what is considered absolute duty involving reward for acting or punishment for failing to act. Number (2) is what is considered forbidden actions involving reward for abstention or punishment for crossing those limits. Number (3) consists of reprehensible actions, which are disapproved of but not punishable; still you are rewarded if you abstain from crossing them. Number (4) includes commendable or meritorious actions involving a reward for doing them but no punishment for omitting them. Number (5) is the last one and consists of permissible actions.

When we look at the first two, which consist of obligations and prohibitions, we are considering categories of action where you must suspend your will and let God's will take over. Of course, this necessitates some struggle with the ego, because it's the celestial kingdom versus terrestrial gravity. Now when we say, "...take over," that means you become an astral gentleman on earth.

The third and the fourth categories consist of your choice between God's will and your will. Here you are flowing between terrestrial and celestial. As for the fifth category, which consists of permissible actions, there is an unknown world of specter

299

without image, without form, and without definition. You can gain a lot from it by just being a humble king who has the power to do anything he wants in his kingdom, but who nobly abstains from doing those things.

Q: How does all this relate to Prophet Muhammad's answer: "I was taken…?"

A: You have one force obliging you to do something. You resist it with your repulsive force, which is the effort you provide. You have a force prohibiting something that attracts you, you repel that attractive something with abstention.

Q: Is there any physical example?

A: When you resist the two forces (one time by an effort of repulsion, and another time by an effort of abstention), you are developing your muscles.

Getting back to will power, the logic that you gain from the Divinity through your respect of the jurisprudence that is God's will is the bootstrap to the metaphysical world. That is our explanation regarding what Prophet Muhammad meant in his answer to that question. In contrast, when a person submits to some other creature's will, a will that is antithetical to his own intuitive will, the will power that the person gained from being submissive to mere creatures is abolished. In such a case, the person is in a state of stagnation and decay; there is no vehicle that can raise him to the celestial world.

If someone wants to dive into the mystical world here is the mysterious treasure: "Praise be to God, the Originator of the

heavens and the earth, Who made the angels messengers with wings; two, and three, and four: He adds to creation as He pleases: for God has power over all things."

Keep in mind that the wings have nothing to do with physical wings with feathers etc., even though some people have ignorantly portrayed the angels as winged females in their temples. Instead, the wings are only a metaphor for the act of flying freely. Secondly, the angels are created from light (Nour), and this light is a potential energy that can be absorbed by a human through worship. A human has a tendency to become angelic, but he also has a tendency to become demonic.

Getting back to our analysis, the Creator spoke about the numbers two, three, and four regarding the wings. We have two wings that result from obligations and prohibitions that are against the person's will, and we have two wings that result from reprehensible and commendable behaviors about which a human has a choice. Then you have the permissible, which can extend your journey according to your respect for the four previous forces. Of note, in reality there is only the first wing or category. The second wing doesn't exist without the first one; the third one doesn't exist without the first one, and so forth. In other words, if there is no first wing, the second wing loses its rank. Likewise, if there is no first wing, the fourth wing loses its rank as well, and so forth. Therefore, understand that the wings are only an extension of, "There is no God except God."

Q: Would you comment a little bit on God's house on this planet?

A: The archetype of the Singularity, which is the humility that is concentric with the Sublimity and that supports the last point of the unperceived center of gravity on earth, was named Adam. The first house that he was instructed to build was quadrilateral. It was God's house on Earth; yet, it was also the heart of mankind. Primordially, this house was in the celestial world and

301

was circumambulated by Adam and the angels, and it was created seven thousand years before Adam.

The flood that occurred during the time of Prophet Noah, caused the disappearance of this house, and it was rebuilt after the flood by Prophet Abraham and his son, Prophet Ishmael. It was reconstructed with the same quadrilateral foundations previously made by Adam. This house still stands to this very moment, although it has been renovated upon occasion.

Q: What is behind the quadrilateral structure?

A: Each façade stands vertically from the foundation. Although it is a collective house in the center of Earth, everybody has his own unique house of stability in his heart (if he wishes to develop it) that synchronizes with that house and synchronizes with the Oneness of God.

With regard to this house, there is an unperceived center of gravity that is the last point on the descending vertical line in the heart or the nucleus of the believer and that consists of his confession, in which he says, "There is no god except God." Absent this confession, a person is living in a void—in the epicenter without a center of gravity. As to the four facades of this house that arise from its foundation, the first wall consists of prayers, the second of charity, the third of fasting, and the fourth of the pilgrimage. From this platform, a person can shelter his inner world. Of note, this is not to say that it is his eternal life or his salvation. These are merely pillars that secure his presence in the void, and further responsibilities do apply.

Q: Would you elaborate on that with regard to my psyche?

A: You have an unperceived center of gravity, which is your confession in which you say, "There is no god except God;" that is the unknown vertex. Now, when you add to your confession by saying, "And Muhammad is the messenger of God," that does not mean Muhammad with some particular ethnicity or any kind of polarization or sectarianism, as some people fanaticize the analogy. He includes all the spectra of all the prophets before him. Therefore, by him going to the Promised Land and praying with all the prophets, he was absorbing all their diasporic frequencies and unifying them into one. Thus, this center of gravity is your confession in which you say, "There is no god except God, and Muhammad is the messenger of God."

Q: What do those prophets represent in this existence?

A: Each prophet represents a puzzle or an enigma without which existence is incomplete. Those prophets' frequencies exist within everybody; however, this is not the place to discuss those details. As for Muhammad, he was and is the totality of the whole. This is the reason why we have a record of him finding every prophet on one or another cosmos, but we don't have a record of him inhabiting a cosmos. Why? It is because he includes them, but they don't include him; he is the macrocosm.

Q: Theo-ethically speaking?

A: Now this confession by you while being the mesocosm is, in reality, allowing the macrocosm and the microcosm to synchronize and exist within you—cosmic consciousness. After you close your eyes with such a confession, you have the whole vastness of the universe within you to be explored. That does not say that you have the pleasure of exploring it, but you do have the potential of actualizing what is in it by preparing yourself in the world of labor. With your sincere confession, there are no frontiers and no limits to your exploration.

Q: Would you describe the different categories of people?

303

A: When a disbeliever denies this confession, he is, in reality, denying the whole existence of the macrocosm within himself. As such, when he closes his eyes, he finds himself characterized in the dimension of his disbelief, which is only a labyrinthine aquarium. It is not made of glass, but it is sort of a circled magnetic field that nonetheless allows him to see the vastness beyond it; yet, he is incarcerated in and suffocated by his disbelief.

In contrast, let's consider the case of the believing philosopher, the believing scientist, etc., all of whom made science a condition of their belief. When such a person closes his eyes, he sees the vastness, as do the disbelievers, and he does have the possibility of navigating, but what is in his way is his science—the condition that he put on his belief in his previous life. It becomes an obstacle, and he no longer sees it as science, but he sees it as a paralysis. Whenever this person gets in such a situation, he finds his knowledge on which he was counting to be a misery, and he feels humiliation.

Now those who confess through fideism without the interference of their intellectual thoughts, those people have allowed the existence to remain intact; in other words, a human being is more in need of passivity then activity.

Q: How about the religious people?

A: The big danger is with the religious people. If a religious person is worshiping God while using the vehicle of religion without naming the vehicle except through submission and without glorifying the vehicle, this is a noble person. However, the person who is worshiping the vehicle or worshiping an ambiance gained from such worship is in great danger. Such a person, when he closes his eyes, finds himself skating in one place. As such, it is his own religion that causes his paralysis.

Q: What are the other four pillars?

A: The second pillar is prayer.

Q: Would you comment on that?

A: It is the vehicle of navigation. It is the only obligation that was prescribed above the seventh heaven; it consists of five daily prayers.

Q: Let me interrupt you here for a second. You said that prayer was made obligatory when Muhammad went to Heaven, and at the same time you said he prayed with the other prophets in Jerusalem before he went to Heaven. How is that?

A: Firstly, there was a prayer prescribed for each of the prophets in one form or another. Secondly, the prophets did not meet in Jerusalem for any other reason than to bring the whole universe and the eternity into the center of gravity, which is humility.

Now, God did not tell Muhammad to pray on the seventh heaven, he told him to do that on Earth. Again, why did Muhammad meet with Moses and not meet another prophet concerning the reduction of the prayers? This shows you that prayer starts from humility, which is Moses' frequency. Despite the fact that Muhammad saw Moses praying in his grave, he met him again in Jerusalem, and he met him again on the sixth heaven. This is how the freedom of the prophet is. Therefore, allegorically speaking, Muhammad's ascension to God, then his descent from God to Moses, and then his ascension from Moses to God conform to the movements of the prayer with its alternations among standing, bowing, and prostrating in a state of humility.

305

Q: Would you describe prayer's effect on a person during his daily activity?

A: These four pillars are connected with the time and space by which a person is characterized and conditioned. When the time of the prayer comes, it is as if a person withdraws from a tiny space and from a tiny segment of time into the vast expansion of the universe. Therefore, the praying person owns time and space. If a person doesn't accomplish that prayer, he is owned and conditioned by a tiny segment of time and space. That's why you find people suffering from all kinds of psychological distress, such as anxiety, depression, irritation, insomnia, etc. They think they need a psychologist, and they use all kinds of over-the-counter medications when, in fact, what they need to do is to absorb their time and their space, which are, in reality, the whole macrocosm that includes the seven heavens. This can be seen by reflecting on Muhammad's presence in heaven, which is actually a person's potential navigation and everybody's potential. Are you following me?

Now during your daily activity, there are events percolating in your mind, but they are still extrinsic. Those events, in reality, are captured as memories, and then they become emotions. Those emotions are, in reality, potential galaxies existing within you, either to be animated or to be cataclysmically destroyed with falling, dead meteorites within your psyche. When you withdraw yourself from this earthy preoccupation to your prayer with your Lord, you are gathering and seizing all that was rotating in your state of consciousness extrinsically, and then they become yours—intrinsic.

Q: Are you saying that those emotions are really planets?

A: Yes and no. Now let's get to something here and try to emphasize the word "potential." It's up to you; either you actualize them by animism, or you destroy them cataclysmically by

306

associating your volitional actions for the sake of otherness rather than the Oneness.

The primordial image of affection, to take just one example, is like water in that it doesn't have its own form and color. Its perceived form and color are derived from the water's container. Likewise, affection can only be developed by the intentions that lie behind one's physical actions in the terrestrial world. The performer of those actions is like the water's container; he gives image to the affection within himself according to his intention. Generosity also has its primordial image, which can only be developed through the intentions underlying one's generous gestures in the terrestrial world. Humbleness, sympathy, clemency, peace, and forgiveness also have their primordial images, but they can only be developed by the intentions behind one's transactions in the terrestrial world. Now those emotions are, in reality, galaxies that you either animate within yourself or ignore. If the latter is the case, then they become cataclysmic.

Q: How about the third pillar?

A: It is charity. It is to be given by the rich to the poor. We don't need to go through the details; this is not a book about jurisprudence. But there is something that we have to emphasize, and that is time. The time of maturity (i.e., the time at which charity is due) varies somewhat depending upon what is being considered. It is reached on one's economic surplus one year after reaching a certain amount of money, gold, and silver. On ownership of animals, it is reached when a certain number of animals (e.g., camels, cattle, and sheep) are owned. On grains and some dried fruits, charity is due at the time the crop is harvested. All such property has to be purged and purified by charity in order to secure not only the stability of the economy of the country, but to secure the equanimity of the emotions of the giver and to keep the flow of the universal energy unobstructed.

Q: What do you mean by the flow of the universal energy being unobstructed?

A: This is the flow of the emotions; if the emotions are obstructed by selfishness and greed, the whole repercussion will be on the weather, the ecosystem. Do you see all these natural disasters—earthquakes, hurricanes, tsunamis, etc. They are all in the epicenter of earth. In the same way, when a human being is voluted from the center, it causes a precarious and tumultuous position for him. Of course we have all kind of teachers; for every tiny science, we have researchers who deeply emphasize their research in their scientific discipline. However, we don't have mystical teachers because mysticism is not a school; it is spawned, instead, from worship.

Q: How about the fourth pillar?

A: Fasting is the fourth pillar. Here is the enthronement of the governor within the self; this is the *coup d'etat* within the self. Throughout the entire year, you have desires, addictions, etc. that become second nature. They control you; they condition you; they enslave you. When the month of fasting arrives, you either decide to get back your power—your kingdom, or you decide to continue to be a slave. With regard to fasting, before the dawn—your primordial age, it is as if you go back to the zone zero and begin your life again from scratch. When you give instructions through your intentions to your kingdom, your appetite and sexual desires, telling them, "No food, no drink, and no sex until the sunset," you are in some way in a process of ascension—lifting your level of existence from the world of phenomena to the world of noumena. Of course, there will be large demonstrations against you. If you follow the requirements of those demonstrators—your desires, you will be enslaved. If you stick to your decision, you will not only be the governor of this dusty world, but you will be the governor of your own galaxies. You see, people worry about the president or the governor, and they criticize and demonstrate; yet, the real kingdom is offered to them by God. However, many joyously wish to be slaves anyway?

Q: How about the galaxies?

A: When desire is manifested, it is always desire for this material world. When you abstain from following that desire, you are converting every desire from an earthy impulse to a planet within you. There are other beautiful things that could be said, but they are very deep and very heavy, and they are not mentioned here. If a person is open to that, he will surely find them.

Q: You are talking about how the person can benefit from fasting in his celestial world, are there any positive consequences regarding the person's daily life in his terrestrial world?

A: There is a big difference between feeding a habit and feeding the body; the whole of humanity is just feeding a habit but not their bodies. When it comes to nations, most supposedly dependent nations are, in fact, not in need of importation, but they are in need of exploration of what they have under their feet in their own backyard. However, before they realize what resources they have in their own backyard, they have to be aware of what faculties they have in their own psyches. Further, before they realize what they have in their own psyches, they have to be aware of what their physical body has. Still further, before they know what their physical body has, they have to go to zone zero.

Q: Zone zero?

A: Picture yourself as a small balloon; I didn't say in a small balloon, I said you are that balloon—a sphere. Now imagine another sphere much bigger than you outside of you, and imagine your center and the other center are concentric. Are you with me up to here?

Q: Yes, I am.

A: What is outside the big sphere is what is outside your existence. What is outside the big sphere could be your habits that you are feeding; it could be your segments of time that you are ignoring; it could be your intentions that you are neglecting. To summarize the whole: you are constantly an extrovert.

Now because of your position outside that sphere, which is another type of epicenter, you find yourself unsecured. You want more of everything. You want to store more food in your house because no matter what, you still feel hungry. You want another house because you feel unsheltered in the one in which you live. You want another means of transportation because you feel handicapped with the one you have. You are never satisfied with what you have. You are dissatisfied with the minimum, and you want the maximum, and once you have that maximum it becomes a miniature in your eyes. You want more and more, and you find every situation is boring you.

Getting back to the big sphere and what it contains; the differential volume between the big sphere and you, i.e., the small sphere, is full of entropic energy that you have stored and haven't been using. That could be calories, moments, personal intentions, etc. just to name a few. Now what is directing the flow of your emotions and your whole life is an extrinsic quantity, which is a burden to you, and which is not any energy in your possession, as you might think.

Now when you start fasting, your body starts using its own energy. It starts eating from the self. Your immune system starts exercising. You are in some way deflating the outside sphere, and it gets deflated differently from one person to another, depending on the physical and mental activities during the day. It is as if it gets socked and drained from the center, and once it reached your sphere, which is you, it bursts and gets inflated from the center toward the periphery, much like magma in the center of Earth.

Q: With regard to time?

A: Your twenty-four hours will be divided into three phases. You have a time of darkness, which is the time before the dawn, and then you have the daybreak up to the sunset, and then you have the time after sunset, which is the return to darkness again. The time before the dawn is your outside existence—outside the big sphere that was mentioned earlier. When sunrise begins, that is the time when your body starts using its own energy—you start dealing with the self. At sunset, the big sphere is almost or completely deflated, and you then touch the small sphere, which is you. In other words, you find the self; you find the reality of the "I". Then at sunset, what was originally night in the external world becomes sunrise in your internal world. In other words, there will be no darkness in your life.

Q: What about the fifth pillar?

A: It is the pilgrimage; this is your return to your primordial state in the pre-existence. In other words, in the pre-existence, you did not have an identity except for your confession to the Absolute. In the pre-existence, there was not even the expression, "There is no god except God," because this expression was confessed from the illusory state of a possible association with God. Therefore, it became necessary to confess it. However, in the primordial state, there was only the Absolute. Therefore, during the pilgrimage, you come without any uniform with which a person may want to be identified; you come with seamless clothes. This represents the effacement of one's habitual attributes, the erasure of errors from the visible self, and the return to the origin, which is nothingness— the recognition of the fragility of the self in front of the Sublimity that in turn subjectively spurs a person to develop his uniqueness.

When you are circumambulating the external house (i.e., the Kaaba), it is as if you were circumambulating the concentric house in the Garden that was made of light. Now internally within your own psyche, these are the extrinsic emotions that are pivoting in the epicenter. By glorifying God, you are in a state of involution—internalizing them into your nucleus. If you are glorifying God with your month while deeply inside yourself you are seeing your identity as being bigger than God, then you are externalizing your emotions from the nucleus to the epicenter.

Q: What is the length of time and the situation in the interspace between the two worlds that is called *barzakh* in another language?

A: It differs from one person to another. Consider the length of time a baby spends in the womb, which is nine months during its mother's pregnancy. That time was meant to complete the biological development of the baby. Once the development is finished, the woman delivers the baby, or you could say she pushes the baby out. You could also say the baby comes out by itself. Therefore, the biological development of the baby is not complete unless the period of nine months is spent, disregarding the premature exception. Now, do you see the difference in the length of time of: the physical encounter between the male and

312

the female, or I should say the length of time of the climax when the male's sperm enters the female's uterus; and the period of pregnancy, i.e., nine months? Do you see the difference?

Q: There is almost no comparison; the time of the physical encounter is very brief, and the time of pregnancy is very long.

A: When it comes to the length of time spent on the terrestrial world in comparison to the length of time of the development of the spiritual body in the interspace in the celestial world, it is like comparing the time of the climax, i.e., orgasm, which is a few seconds, to the time of the pregnancy, which is nine months. When it comes to the physical encounter, all that the couple does is put each other's seeds in a safe, protected place, i.e., the uterus, and then they wait for the crop, which is their replication in the future baby.

When it comes to interspace, time is different from one person to another. All man is doing in his brief life is putting seeds in his own consciousness, which is his metaphysical world. Then he waits for the time of the development of his future eternity. When the baby is biologically complete, the mother delivers him by pushing. On the other hand, when a human is metaphysically complete in the interspace, the earthly land delivers the human to the land of resurrection by externalization.

Q: If all humanity is in a process of development, then all of them are positive; therefore, there is no difference.

A: That's not what I meant. Someone is completing his positive development, while another is completing his negative development.

Q: Regarding will power, is this a one-time effort?

A: It all depends on the person. Time over there becomes space within a person's consciousness. Consider an effort of one minute in the terrestrial world. What can it give you in the celestial world? In the terrestrial world, you are in charge when it comes to creating your emotion. Consider this emotion to be like a ball, and this ball is inside you. Sometimes it's intrinsic, and sometimes it's extrinsic. As for the case when it is extrinsic, we won't talk about that because it's disintegration.

As for the case when it is intrinsic, this emotion is a secretion inside you; yet, you are inside it at the same time. This emotion is, in fact, a planet that you create. Its limited vastness has to do with your limited intention. Your effort of one minute can give you a planet through which you travel. Now, we don't say you travel between planets while having isthmuses or separations between them. No, those planets overlap each other. It is as if you were to say that you have emotions but that they are all merged in one mind; it is exactly like that. Now, when we talk about travel, we don't mean in terms of time and space; there is no time spent, and there is no space crossed. Everything is there in a micro-unit of time. You want it to be, and it is already.

Q: Would you elaborate on these extrinsic emotions and how they become linked to a person, one way or the other, after death?

A: After a person closes his eyes, each emotion that was formed for the sake of some audience other than the Oneness of God will be magnetically sucked by that audience, not in terms of it being externalized from the person, but in terms of its extrinsic existence with regard to the neural net or the nucleus.
Of note, both the believer and the disbeliever have a chance to see the same results of their actions but…

Q: Let me interrupt here. Since you already made a big

distinction between the two cases, what do you mean when you say that the believer and the disbeliever have a chance to see the same results of their actions?

A: The results of volitional actions in the celestial world transpire whether a person was a believer or a disbeliever. However, the believer with his intrinsic emotions joyously lives within those dimensions, while the disbeliever with his extrinsic emotions doesn't have any chance to even touch those dimensions or those pleasures, despite the fact that he sees them and even contemplates them. In the same way that they were extrinsic in the terrestrial world, they become distant from him metaphysically in the celestial world. He sees the pleasure that is almost at hand, but there is no way to touch it. This is what makes the difference between the two: everything depends on the predisposed nature of each individual. Bear in mind that the whole existence is the flow of, "There is no god except God." Therefore, anything that comes or forms for the sake of an audience other than God will be disintegrated. For the believer, pleasures increase exponentially from one realm to another, i.e., from the time he closes his eyes (death) through the land of resurrection and to his final habitation. For the disbeliever, those supposed pleasures that he sees but cannot even feel or touch decrease and disintegrate from one realm to another until he reaches his final habitation; it is as if you exposed a mummified body to the air. This is our explanation regarding real property and deprivation in time and space. As such, you can see the danger for those who are deifying and idolizing nature or humans.

Now, there is a big question mark concerning Neo-Platonism. The people behind this philosophy claim that they believe in the Absolute, even though they believe that humans are subject to the influence of the planets. We don't have the right to say those people are disbelievers, and we don't have the right to credit monotheism to those people either. If during their lives what pops up to the surface of their conscious is the power of the Absolute and not the influence of the planets, they could be on a safe side, but, as always, God knows best. However, if during their lives what pops up to the surface of their conscious is the power of the planets, these people are in big danger.

After these people's deaths, the superfluous emotions that have been formed from the absorption of the planets will be sucked by those planets, and those planets will nonetheless face cataclysm anyway. Why? It is because existence is synchronized with humans, and once humans disappear from this planet there will be a cataclysm, and what remains is only the animation of, "There is no god except God."

Q: Would you comment on the land of resurrection?

A: The land of resurrection is the first realm after the development of the interspace. This is not the earthy land; it is another land. It is flat and white, and there is nothing on it. There is no tree, no rock, and no mountain; there is nothing. This land both exists and doesn't exist at the same time. It was just named a land of resurrection, but in reality, everybody is standing in his own state of consciousness.

For some, this land is stable, not because of the land, but because of the stability of their consciousness, and the stability of their consciousness is the stability of their faith. Others cannot even stand or keep a dizzy equilibrium. This is not because there are earthquakes in that land, but because the disequilibrium is inside their minds. Others feel vertigo and a sense of free falling even though they are on land. Nonetheless, they still feel as if they were falling from the sky; this is the case with the hypocrites.

Finally, we need to emphasize that you don't hear even one

person on the Day of Judgment saying, "God, please give me." The only words being pronounced by people are: "God, please take me back to the terrestrial world so I can rectify my past misdeeds or do something good." Why? Because everybody sees his own crops resulting from the seeds he planted. There is such loyalty from the Creator that even those people in Hell thank God for His loyalty. They see how much goodness He provided to them and how much harm they were to themselves and to others!

His Almighty God said: I have prepared for my righteous servants what no eye has seen, what no ear has heard, and what no heart has perceived.

My Sweet Lord………
My Lord…..My Lord
I really want to see You
I really want to be with You………
I really want to go with you………

George Harrison